Lovernios

Heather Hearn

Lovernios
'The Lindow Man'

Heather Hearn

Copyright Page

First published in South Africa – October 2014

Contact: Heather Hearn
heather.hearn@gmail.com
25 Baker Estate
Baker Road
Edenglen 1609
Gauteng
South Africa
076 373 7173

Cover and Book Design by Clive Thompson
www.getclive.com cell: 083 761 0698

Dedication

This book is dedicated to
David,
the love of my life,
whose support and encouragement
of my writing has been unfailing.

Foreword

Iovernios, 'The Lindow Man'

In 1984, a 2000 year old, perfectly preserved body was discovered in a peatbog near Manchester. He became known as the *Lindow Man*. Extensive testing revealed much about his life, but also gave rise to many questions and assumptions about who he was, how he lived and how he died.

In Iovernios, the author has given the *Lindow Man* a life, a purpose and role to play in the history of the United Kingdom, during the Romano-British period of invasions, wars and tribalism. The story brings these very distant times to life, seamlessly mingling historic facts with dramatic fiction. Researched over a period of a year, the book is packed full of historic, cultural and religious facts of the time.

It charts the life of Iovernios, born a noble in the year 30 AD, through his early childhood, his life as a Druid, the Roman invasions, and ultimately his death as a supreme sacrifice in 61 AD.

It is a compelling story, that leaves the reader in no doubt about man's primal survival instinct and, at the same time, his ability to accept death as part of the journey.

Difficult to put down, hard to swallow in parts, this is a book that will not leave the reader untouched. It has the makings of an epic historical dramatic movie, albeit of the genre 'Fiction'.

Colleen Smith
September 2014
Johannesburg, South Africa

Acknowledgements

Anne Ross and Don Robins

I was inspired to write this book after reading "The Life and Death of a Druid Prince" written by Anne Ross and Don Robins, and I acknowledge their tireless work and faithful recording of events, which made this book possible.

My Family and Friends

To you who have always supported my writing, and have given me endless encouragement, I appreciate and thank you.

My Book Designer

Clive Thompson, thank you for your professional input and your outstanding cover and book design. You are so talented and obviously have a gift for this! Your patience is outstanding and you willingness to help is such a great asset to any author.

Review

Lovernios: The 'Lindow Man'

The purpose of this book is to educate – and it does just that, in story form, centered around one particular man. It is the story of a King and his family, particularly his first born son, starting from his tragic birth. The son's name later becomes known as Lovernios.

The story also revolves around the Druids and their close link to the King; their 20 year long training; their worship of many gods; sacred forests and very simple way of living. It is both interesting and informative, including some of their healing methods for injuries and illnesses. The Romans and their history come into the picture, showing their debased morals and how they try to take over Britain and how this affects the Kings and Queens of Britain, as well as the Celts and Druids, whom the Romans want to destroy. It is a well written book and recommended to anyone interested in history in that part of the world during the period AD 31 to AD 61.

A map of the area has been included in the book to make it easier to follow the travels of the various people, particularly the Druids and/or Lovernios. I hope it will help you to follow their journeys.

Contents

Early Map of England and surrounding areas

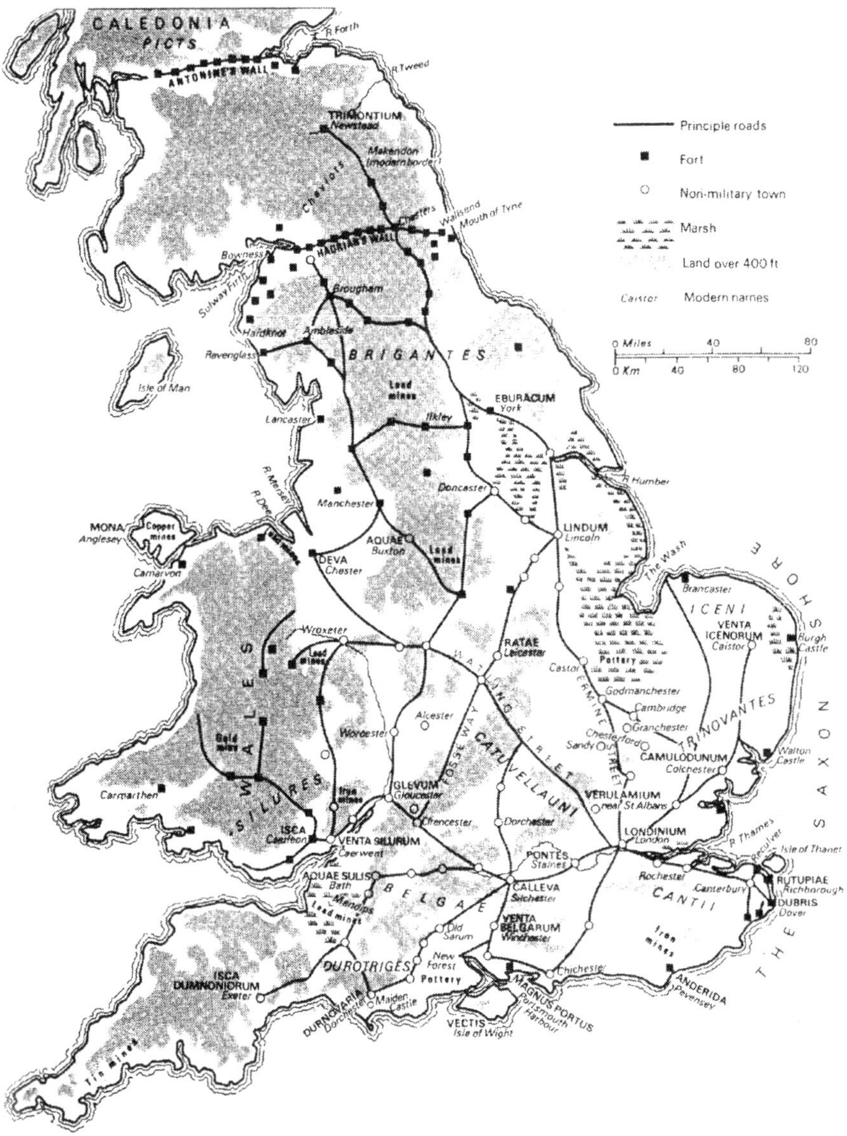

Part One

Chapter 1

AD 30
Autumn

HER piercing scream echoed throughout the castle. The midwife hurried to her side. It had been sixteen hours, and still the baby's head hadn't crowned.

The priest heard her repeated cries from the kitchen where he anxiously waited and hurried to the room. His eyes fell on the bloody pool of water that came from the woman's body, soaked the bedding and dripped onto the floor. One look at the colour of the sticky, fluid and the priest went pale. It appeared as if the muddy waters of the raging River Medway had spilled over its broken banks and flowed into the room.

"It's Teutates – the Supreme god," he muttered reverently to himself. He moved closer to the stricken woman and observed the wet, matted mess of her hair and the sweat on her brow. He stepped further forward out of the shadow of the fire burning in the fireplace, and the reflection of the flames flickered and danced in the shiny mirror of sweat on her chest. Her dark hair was tangled around her slender neck in the shape and form of a garrotte. In a frenzy, the priest repeatedly dipped his long tapered fingers into a cauldron of holy water, and sprinkled it over the listless form on the bed, in a desperate attempt to appease this second god.

"Esus," he whispered to himself, "the Lord and Master."

He turned to ask the midwife yet again the progress of the labour. At that moment the storm, which had been moving closer all night and was hovering in the skies directly above the castle, broke in a torrent of lashing rain. Sheets of lightning flashed through the window openings, and before the thunder sounded the priest fell prostrate to the floor. Taranis, the Thunder God had spoken. The priest lay trembling with arms spread, thinking furiously.

All three gods were present at the birth of this child. Surely no sign could be more compelling – it was already an auspicious day, but fast approaching midnight, and he knew the new day would be a most inauspicious one, he'd seen that in the moon as it set earlier on. He could not be mistaken, he had to appease the gods immediately. He rose swiftly, calling for his young assistant, who rushed to his side. The woman screamed again and the midwife peered desperately for some sign of the baby's head. Quite frantic now she groaned aloud, "this child will surely not survive."

Hearing her chilling words the priest sprang into action. He pulled his knife from its sheath, thrust it at the midwife and shouted in his desperation, "Take it, save the child." The midwife turned to him in horror. Take the life of her mistress to save an unborn child, never! Seeing her hesitation, the priest raised his voice even louder, "do it, or the gods will surely kill you – and us too." She looked at him in confusion.

"The gods have spoken," he continued more gently. "They are all three present. They've come to witness the birth of this special child. For the sake of us all take this knife and save it."

The priest's assistant nodded vigorously in agreement. The presence of the gods in the room was all she needed. The midwife raised the knife and in one swift motion slit the woman's belly from top to bottom. Already weakened from lack of blood, exhausted beyond belief from sixteen hard hours of labour, her young body wracked by pain she could not bear, she lost consciousness at the instant the knife pierced her skin. With great skill the midwife plucked the blue baby from the mother, slapping it vigorously as she swung it upside down by its tiny wrinkled feet, clearing its mouth with practised fingers. The child began to cry, a small piteous sound, but it was enough, it was alive. The priest strode from the room with just one quick glance at its sex.

As the blood that was flowing freely from her enormous wound, gushed onto the bed and ran down its side onto the floor, so life left the body of the young woman. Her death was swift.

Vitaicus was in the woods some ten miles away hunting boar when the storm broke. Knowing that his wife was in labour, he contemplated returning home, but after passing almost the entire day by her side, he dreaded the thought of more time spent watching her pain, helpless as they awaited the birth of their first child. He sheltered instead under a canopy of trees and waited for the rain to pass. He preferred hunting under the moonlight anyway, and his priest had already declared this a lucky day. If he didn't catch his boar before the night reached its peak and a new day began, he may never get it. He'd not yet caught a boar on an unlucky day.

He watched as the storm moved in the direction of his castle, and the skies above him cleared. One by one, stars began to twinkle brightly in the freshly cleaned sky above him. Before the last clouds shielding the moon passed on, millions of stars were visible, but this final cloud passed too and the full moon shone once again. Pleased with his decision, he continued on his hunt.

He'd been searching out a sleeping boar, more for the sport than for the food, although roast boar would be a wonderful feast with which to celebrate the birth of his child. His patience was rewarded. He spotted a full grown male under a tree and within his range. He gave quick thanks to Cernunnos, the Hunting God.

Vitaicus was quite oblivious to the desperate sounds of his manservant calling for him as he silently stalked his prey. Suddenly his horse, Iorrach, snorted at the sound of another horse. His prey bolted and it was with some irritation that he returned to where Iorrach stood restlessly waiting. Iorrach meant 'Peaceable' and he was just that – an excellent hunting horse, with a quiet and patient nature. Now however, he was clearly agitated.

Vitaicus looked in the direction of the hoof beats, and recognised Flauston by his hunched and earnest posture. Rushing forward eagerly to receive the good news that was sure to be the reason for Flauston's haste, Vitaicus failed to notice his servant's distraught face. Panting from the hard ride and choked with emotion, it was some moments before he'd recovered sufficiently to speak.

Vitaicus listened, first with elation to the news that he had a son, then with horror as he heard that his wife, his queen, had died during childbirth. Although his servant spared him the details, he was still shocked to his core as he mounted Iorrach to gallop for home.

Berating himself the entire way he felt certain that if he'd been there she wouldn't have succumbed to the Otherworld. Knowing she was going to that happy place to live eternally, awaiting his arrival, he was never the less grieved beyond belief. His beloved Hilfuth, so young and special, gone to the gods forever. His grief mounted with each mile he covered and by the time he reached home he was beside himself.

Leaving Iorrach in the care of the groom who'd been rudely awakened earlier by Flauston, Vitaicus stormed into his castle, striding swiftly through its many rooms. He reached his wife's chamber completely out of breath. Sobbing from heartbreak and his inability to breathe, he walked towards the bed where her sodden body lay.

The midwife heard the commotion of his return and hastily covered her ripped belly leaving only her once beautiful face visible. Vitaicus fell to his knees beside her and cried, as he'd not done since he was a child.

Eventually he got up and sat gently on the edge of the bed. He cradled her head in his arms, kissing her wet brow, her eyes, her delicate nose and cold lips. He moved down to her neck carefully lifting the covers and kissed her pale breasts. Then he saw the blood.

As he lifted the cover further his face registered his dismay at the sight of so much of it. Surely there shouldn't be blood this high up on her stomach. Flinging the sodden lambskin to the floor he recoiled in horror at the sight of her torn belly. Her insides were roughly pushed aside, protruding in part, and covered in blood. Everywhere there was blood except in her lifeless body, which lay pale and limp.

Vitaicus became aware of a strange noise, an inhuman wailing sound coming from deep within him. He lay on the floor where he'd fallen, covered in the blood of his beloved. Slowly the noise stopped as he faced reality. He got up and left the room stumbling like an old man.

The midwife was cowering in the hall. Not sure what to do when the king flung the cover from his wife's body, she fled. Afraid to leave her mistress untended for long, she stayed hiding in the shadows. Vitaicus saw her and was about to lash out at the instrument of his grief when the stern voice of the priest stayed his hand mid-air.

"It was necessary," he said simply. "Don't blame the woman, I commanded her to do it as the child was about to die. The gods were present, my Lord."

At the mention of the gods even from his own lips, the priest whispered. "All three at once. Teutates the Supreme God was there in the bloody waters that broke from her womb. Esus, The Lord and Master was in the flames reflected in the sweat on her body. The God of Thunder, Taranis, was in the storm that hovered and broke while the child was dying. We had no choice but to appease the gods. Your child has been chosen above all others on this auspicious day and I had no choice but to save him, to keep him alive for the gods who will demand his life back as a sacrifice at some time in the future. "

Without a word to the priest Vitaicus turned and fled to his own sanctuary, his hunting room where his trophies of many years surrounded and comforted him. He slumped in a hard wooden chair with his head on the table and his horror at seeing the ghastly death his beloved had suffered, overwhelmed him.

The room was dark and cold when the priest knocked on the door some time later and entered without waiting to be asked.

"Master," he quietly addressed his king. "I've good news for you. I've been meditating and seeking the will of the gods for the prince, and they've been kind. The time for his sacrifice will not be yet, maybe not for a long while. I've seen through my meditation the number 'thirty,' a number favoured by the gods. I've counted the number of hairs on his head and they confirm what I've seen. The child has just thirty hairs. It may be that he'll be allowed to live thirty hours or thirty days, perhaps even weeks. The gods may even give him a long span of time, they may leave him until the age that they prefer – thirty years." He mused. "Then again, it may be that they mean to come for him when there are thirty birds, horses or thirty chariots present."

"What do you mean, thirty birds, horses, chariots, how can you be so sure of the number thirty and then have no idea what it means?" raged Vitaicus.

"The gods are often wily, they don't always show us things clearly. They like to tantalize us lest we change the course of events that they've ordained. They have simply said thirty. In my vision I saw bees – they will be significant in his life. It may even be thirty bees that sting him. But I also saw his body as healthy and strong, in perfect form and condition."

"At what age was he when you saw him thus?" Vitaicus interrupted the priest.

"In a vision one sees apparitions my Lord, it was but a blurred impression of a healthy strong body, there was no sense of age, of time. We must watch and wait. Be diligent in keeping the child healthy, feed him well and keep him strong. Don't allow anything to harm or scar him so that he'll be perfect when the gods call, and be watchful for thirty. Be grateful that the gods require him as a Supreme Sacrifice, an honour seldom bestowed."

Having said these words, Obetach the priest, left the room as quietly as he had entered it.

'An honour indeed,' thought Vitaicus bitterly, 'isn't it enough that they've taken my wife, now they require my only child of me. There's no honour in that unless they've chosen to give him the full thirty years then at least he'd be at a special age, befitting a Supreme Sacrifice. Surely that's the gods' intention.'

"Oh let it be so, Esus, our Lord and Master, I plead with you Teutates, our most Supreme God. I will ever be respectful to you Taranis, mighty God of Thunder, if you'd give me thirty years with my son. Leave him in my care and I will ensure he is fit and strong to be a Supreme Sacrifice for you, worthy of you, not a helpless babe as he is now. Allow me to mould him into a worthy sacrifice," Vitaicus whispered as he fought to control the new and awful emotions that washed over him in waves of anger and despair that made him feel ill with their strength, yet followed by surges of hope.

He paced the room, feeling a new confidence pulsing in his veins at the thought of the gods granting him his desire. 'Thirty years, why that's a lifetime,' he thought as he rubbed his throbbing temple, 'an entire lifetime to spend with my son, to make up for the loss of my wife, your mother. Time to teach him to hunt and fight. Thirty years, may the gods be thanked for their generosity, may the gods be blessed.' He rose with fresh energy, already believing that his pleas had been answered and went in search of his child.

Sebilus, the midwife, worked feverishly sewing up the queen's body, stripping the room of coverings that were soaked and stained with blood, sending them directly to the fires that burned in the kitchen. She woke the slaves and they scrubbed the floors, removing every trace of blood. The queen's body was bound and taken to Wrucald, the man the most learned in the preparation of bodies, imminently suitable to prepare the queen's earthly body for its final journey. Her spiritual departure would be left to the Druids.

Wrucald was seldom called on in the middle of the night, normally a body would be left until morning, but with the queen, four servants were sent out in the damp cold of the night in search of Wrucald. He lived deep in the woods and was almost impossible to locate even in daylight, and their task proved difficult. The sun was about to rise by the time Wrucald was found although he lived just four miles from the hamlets surrounding the castle of the King.

The queen's room was cold and bare, the fire too had died as if in sympathy with her death. The door was closed and Vitaicus didn't enter. He knew he'd never go in that room again. Instead he made his way to the chamber that he and Hilfuth had set aside for their first child. It was a small room, but had a fireplace of its own and a large opening for the sun to shine in through when the weather was pleasant. On this cold and wet night it was securely boarded up. A slave who herself had recently given birth was already feeding his son. His tiny fingers still weak from his ordeal, clutched loosely at the soft leather cloak she wore over her simple short robe.

Vitaicus lifted the baby from her arms and by the light of the fire, counted the hairs on its head. Aware of the great honour bestowed on the child, the honour of one day being a Supreme Sacrifice to the gods, Vitaicus held his breath as he examined the tiny head. Praying silently that his trusted priest had been wrong when he spoke of his vision, he willed himself to believe that the gods intended him to see a strong, healthy man of thirty years. He hoped against hope that Obetach's own vision had been clouded.

Vitaicus held his breath, then very carefully so as not to miss any or add any twice, he counted again. Thirty hairs, thirty shiny golden hairs, an auspicious and significant number with an unknown meaning. He had to be content with that and his fast growing belief that it would not be thirty hours or days, or some other un-definable thing. He was beginning to feel grateful too that his child had been chosen, that his passage into the Otherworld would bring pleasure to the gods and they would surely bring good harvests to the land because of it. He prayed that all people would prosper and be happy in love due to the birth of his special child.

Vitaicus' respect for the gods was almost as strong as the respect that the Druids held for their many gods. He thought fondly of Obetach, the highest priest of the Order in his kingdom, the land of Canti. Under Obetach was a strong band of priests. The Bards were the singers and poets, the Vates were the interpreters and philosophers who divined the will of the gods, and there were those who were trained first as Bards, then Vates and then went on further, becoming senior Druids. They studied natural sciences and moral philosophy and knew the gods intimately, understanding their many desires. Collectively these men and women were the priests and priestesses of the country, they were the Druids.

Obetach had studied for twenty years and his entire life had been devoted to the gods and the people of Canti. For the past eight years he'd been the king's personal priest. The harshness of the years during which he'd lived in forests, travelling the country extensively, showed in his fine features, which were lined far beyond his age. His hands and feet were calloused and he suffered severe arthritis from the hours he spent each day doing ritual dances. Obetach's appointment to Vitaicus literally saved his life as his health had been failing him. Now he no longer lived in the forest, and although his home was still relatively cold and damp, his health improved quickly and within the first year he felt a new person.

His tall stooped frame began to straighten somewhat, his girth broadened with each new moon as he ate at the king's table and shared his ale. His sense of humour increased and as his personal wealth doubled, so did his lease on life. Obetach had never felt so at peace with the world, the gods and himself. He fulfilled his duties with the dedication that comes from satisfaction at doing what he loved, and his priests and priestesses, the king, and the people of Canti, all respected him.

Vitaicus thought fondly of the twinkle in Obetach's eye whenever he acquired new wealth, or his predictions proved correct and especially when he beat the king at their favourite board game. As Vitaicus held his newborn son he was satisfied that the child would grow up under the care and protection of a wise priest. He gazed at the baby in wonder, a bond of love more powerful than he could have imagined already beginning to soothe his aching heart.

Chapter 2

WITH the start of the new day news of the death of the queen spread like a fire in dry bush, and mourning began throughout the kingdom. The grieving was two-fold, as the birth of a child here meant the death of someone in the Otherworld.

Obetach and his Druids began preparations for the funeral while the king turned with a heavy heart to the task of gathering his wife's most treasured possessions to take with her on her journey into the Otherworld.

Vitaicus spent hours in her chamber going through her belongings. He finally chose the golden torc that he'd given her on the day they'd married. It had been made especially for her delicate neck from fine threads of gold and silver intertwined into three strong bands plaited together inset with precious stones. It was a magnificent work of art and had taken Mananius, the goldsmith, six full moons to complete to the satisfaction of the king.

Alongside the torc Vitaicus laid out her wedding gown, an exquisite garment of silk woven into a soft flowing robe using the seven colours worn by royalty.

It was the first time that Hilfuth had been allowed to wear seven colours, she'd previously worn five as all lords and ladies did. Only graduate Druids were allowed more colours than aristocrats and they could wear six colours in their robes. Governors were permitted to wear four colours, while young gentlemen were allowed three.

Warriors were above common people and privileged to wear two colours, as opposed to the single colour allowed to common people. This was Hilfuth's first royal robe and with its seven coloured stripes she'd looked magnificent.

Vitaicus' heart constricted at the thought of her on that

memorable day. She was barefoot, but had wild flowers woven into thread and twined around her feet. Her shapely legs were exposed under her short garment and she wore a golden band draped over her right shoulder. Flowers adorned a headdress across her forehead and were plaited into her long dark hair.

She looked like an ethereal creature from the land across the sea, the Otherworld. Unreal and untouchable, Vitaicus had held his breath and forbidden his eyes to blink at the first sight of her, afraid that she may be an apparition and disappear. But she was real enough then and his grief threatened to overwhelm him now at the thought of her. He picked up the robe and fingered the fine lace that edged it, purchased from a merchant from Belgic Gaul at great cost, but nothing had been too much for his Hilfuth.

Vitaicus finally decided on one last item to place with her body – the golden goblet that he'd given her to celebrate the impending birth of their child. The goblet had also been made for him by Mananius who'd painstakingly engraved over every inch of it. It had miniature pictures depicting their meeting, marriage celebration and birth of the expected child in the wild and imaginative way that was common to the Celts.

Each picture was bound together with spirals and tendrils, every character floated and changed into something else in an ambiguous and imaginative circle of events that had neither beginning nor end. Perhaps that was what had angered the gods, Vitaicus thought suddenly. Perhaps depicting something that hadn't yet taken place was presumptuous and arrogant of him and had made him seem superior. He resolved to appease them immediately for his disrespect. He picked up the goblet, robe and torc and left the room in search of Obetach.

Although each king had his own Druid at his disposal, Vitaicus couldn't imagine any Druid in the country being as good to him as Obetach, and he wondered what he would have done these past hours without the priest. Not only was Obetach a constant source of wisdom and knowledge, an advisor on spiritual and economic affairs, he'd become a confidant and friend. The nature of Hilfuth's death indirectly at the hand of Obetach hadn't damaged that relationship, but had strengthened it and drawn them together with a bond that could surely never be broken, either in this world, or the one to come.

Although ten years older than Vitaicus, Obetach seemed his

equal and they enjoyed hunting together, talking round a fire at night, or drinking heartily of the mead they both loved.

Despite having consumed far more mead than he intended to and although his head felt thick and fuzzy, Vitaicus was well aware of the hours that had passed since those first awful moments when his servant had fetched him from hunting. Thirty hours were fast approaching and he made his way unsteadily to the room where his son lay sleeping.

Not daring to go too close in case he woke him, afraid to see him lest he fall deeper in love only to have the child snatched away, Vitaicus sat on the cold stone floor at the foot of the baby's wooden basin, propped himself against the hard wall where sharp stones dug into his back, and pleaded with the gods through the passing of the first thirty hours of his son's life.

He wasn't entirely aware when the thirtieth hour began nor when it ended, but he knew that he'd done all in his power to keep his child alive. Without checking to see if the gods had heeded his pleas, he left the room, stiff and numbed through from the cold and the intensity of his grief.

Vitaicus watched the setting sun with dread. It was the third day since the death of the queen and time to set her mortal body free. He thought sadly of the last royal funerals he'd attended, one after his father's death eight years earlier, the other his mother's.

Vitaicus was just twenty-five years old at the time and the last thing he'd expected was to become king at such a young age. His father, Morenta, and his Druid Klavius, had been on a winter hunting trip. They'd travelled far from home towards the mountains in the west, and during a blizzard had become separated from their party. Without food or shelter, their horses lame from hours of tramping through the snow, the men tried in vain to reach a hut on what they believed was a familiar mountain.

They were close to the summit as night was falling, the darkened sky allowing slivers of light and shadow to fall upon the ground causing weird shapes and illusions to dance before their snow burnt eyes. Certain he'd seen the hut, Morenta dashed forward only to find the shadow was the edge of a precipice. He plunged silently to his death. It took Klavius a split second to make the decision to follow his king into the Otherworld and he threw himself off the mountain into the dark crevice below.

It was four days before news reached Vitaicus of his father's disappearance and only in the spring that the bodies were recovered. By the time a proper funeral was arranged for Morenta and Klavius, Vitaicus had been king for three months, the youngest king in the history of his land. Mourning for his father had lasted for weeks and before it ended, the queen succumbed to pneumonia.

Vitaicus' first task had been to appoint a Druid to his already full household, to assist him in the awesome duty that lay ahead. Obetach had been an obvious choice and Vitaicus had never regretted the decision.

Obetach and his priests were assembled in the large central courtyard of the castle. Flauston was in charge of the servants and slaves and they too were waiting for the king, standing silently, shivering under their thin cloaks with their bare legs exposed. They wore simple leather thong sandals and their feet ached with the cold but they knew the procession would begin soon.

Gamenta, Obetach's assistant, began lighting torches from his own already flaming one. With the disappearance of the sun below the horizon, darkness came quickly. Heavy clouds obliterated the moon and the courtyard began to glow eerily with the light of many torches. Vitaicus entered the courtyard with a sigh. At Gamenta's signal, the procession moved off down the wood paved entranceway and onto the rough sand and stone cobbled roadway, where the people waited. Commoners and aristocrats joined in and walked slowly behind the procession.

It wasn't long before the castle and surrounding hamlets of the king were left behind, and more people came out of their humble homes to join them as they passed by. Some were crude wooden huts, others built of stone, and among the very poor there were homes that were just hollowed out rooms, burrowed cave-like into the hillside.

One and all joined the solemn file. Mile after mile they walked, leaving behind farmlands, hamlets and open barren areas, until they reached the heavily wooded outskirts of Vitaicus' kingdom. The king was unaware of the size of the following behind him, had he known he would have been moved to tears. Young, old, able and unable, moved slowly behind the Druids, on horseback, in carts, or walking through the cold night.

The Bards chanted softly and as more Druids joined them along the way, the chanting grew louder. As they entered the woods their voices seemed to bounce back off the trees and echo round them filling the night. It was an eerie, wailing chant and had Vitaicus not already been so deep in grief the sound of it would surely have driven him deeper.

After many hours, they reached the well-concealed sacred grove of the Druids, the place where Obetach himself had trained and studied for twenty years before being chosen by Vitaicus. The Druids separated from the crowds and grouped at the foot of a hillock. The king and his entourage stood to one side, while everyone else fell back, leaning against trees, or sitting in exhaustion on the damp earth, spread out over a large area, many too far away to see or hear what was taking place, but happy to be there with their king.

The Druids stood solemnly in their long robes, the only ones present with some covering for their legs. Although they kept their hair short, their beards were long and bushy and gave them a little warmth but their robes and beards were small comfort to the Druids who lived in forests and groves and didn't have the warmth or protection of homes that the rest of the gathered people would return to after midnight on that sad evening. The Druids had on white surplice over their ceremonial dress, the more senior standing out from among the others because of golden threads woven through the robes as a sign of authority.

The chanting came to an end, the funeral pyre waited to be lit. The novices had gathered wood throughout the morning and they'd done their task well. This would be an enormous pyre, the flames would leap high into the sky, and would be seen throughout the king's domain.

Obetach stepped forward and in a booming voice called for the gods to be present. He pleaded with them to welcome into the Otherworld this most treasured possession of the people, their queen. As the chant ended the body of the queen was carried forward on a stretcher woven of reeds and covered in a white silk cloth. Six Bards, three on each side, held the stretcher above their heads and walked slowly and solemnly past the king, singing softly, before coming to a standstill in front of Obetach. They lowered the lifeless form to the ground, with

Hilfuth's beautiful face pointing northwards. She was dressed in a magnificent lace robe threaded with gold and pearls. The garment had been ordered and paid for by Obetach and a seamstress had been busy day and night since the queen died in order to finish in time.

Obetach chose four Druids by touching them briefly on their left shoulder with his wooden staff, and then called on the gods to bless the fire they were to light. The Druids walked slowly round the pyre moving from east to west completing three full circles, while the Bards played their lyres and chanted in the background. At Obetach's signal they thrust their torches deep into the bottom of the wooden heap. The base of the pyre had been prepared with dry moss and at the first touch the fire ignited, tentatively at first, but gaining its grip with each gust of wind. The assembled crowds held their breath. If the fire failed it would be a bad omen and the gods would punish them all.

The Bards chanted louder, the novices trembled. Obetach felt sweat running down his cold neck. The king watched in fascination as the tiny sparks that set the fire going gained in strength and greedy tongues of flame, small and searching at first became stronger, leaping gleefully from branch to branch, devouring twigs and leaves, searching for larger prey. Within moments the pyre was afire, and as the smoke rose the chant of praise for the life of the fire changed to one of mournful sorrow at the final death of the body of the queen.

Obetach called his senior Druids, and the eight men walked slowly towards the body of Hilfuth, arms outstretched, as the Bards sang.

"We come to you, oh queen to send you on your journey.
We come to gather your mortal body to preserve you for eternity.
We send you on your way with your possessions.
We send you to the gods with all our blessings.
Pray for us oh queen, as we pray for you.
May the gods favour you all the days of your new life."

As the last words rang out, the Druids lifted the body of Hilfuth. There was absolute silence, only the roaring of the strengthening fire was heard.

Obetach ran his right hand lightly up and down the length of the body as he chanted under his breath. Three times he did this then in a voice that carried to everyone assembled in the grove he shouted, “It is done, the gods are pleased.” At those words the eight men, flung their lifeless charge high into the air towards the top of the enormous pyre.

Once again the assembly held their breath, for with a pyre of such height it would be quite possible for the body to roll down, another dreadful omen. But the aim and strength of the Druids was good and the body settled neatly into a hollow at the very top that had been prepared with coverings of lambs skin and wool. It nestled there in a foetal position as the flames leapt towards it.

It was time for the king to give her the possessions he'd chosen for her journey. He held out the torc first and waited for Obetach to bless it. Obetach asked the gods to accept the meagre gifts and allow them to be placed beside their Supreme Offering, the queen. Once thrown towards her body, if they didn't land and stay, Vitaicus would know that the gods weren't pleased with the gifts.

He couldn't bear to watch as a Vate took the torc from him. He swung it back and forth three times before releasing it. It flew so high that the intake of breath from those closest was audible above the noise of the raging fire. Still Vitaicus didn't look, until he heard the soft moan of pleasure from his people as the torc landed perfectly at the foot of his beloved's body. He passed the robe to the same Vate who again swung it three times and the draft that it made stung fresh cool air onto his hot face. The fire made those closest to it perspire in the otherwise icy night.

The robe floated and took an eternity to reach its destination before wafting down, covering the legs of the queen. Lastly the goblet of gold was passed to the Vate and once again his aim was true for he had spent years training in preparation for occasions such as these. The goblet landed in front of the torc, dangerously near the edge of the pyre, but the gods were obviously pleased as it wobbled momentarily, then settled.

The crowd cheered and chanting began afresh with the assembly joining in, only the king couldn't find his voice. He watched the flames reaching closer to his lost love and found his desire to join her overwhelming. He stepped forward in a trance, ready to climb the pyre and lie beside his beloved, to join her on the journey she was about to take to the Otherworld in the west, passing through caves and lakes before reaching her final destination where they could be happy together for eternity.

Sensing his king's emotion Obetach placed his arm in front of him and quietly but persuasively reminded him of his newborn son, and of his people and the great responsibility he had towards them. He led Vitaicus away from the extreme heat of the pyre, and helped him to sit against a tree where he finally gave way to his grief.

With the sound of the fire raging as it bit into new wood, reaching towards its final quest, it was impossible to hear anything else, and Vitaicus was unaware of the shuffle of feet on the cold earth. He never heard the farewell chant of his people as they made their way out of the grove respectfully leaving him to his tears, as they shed their own. This was a sad night for them although it may be a triumphant and happy one for the gods, as they said farewell to a queen for the second time in a few years.

Tragedy was a way of life for the Celts as weather and war took their toll and one seldom gave it much thought, but on a night like tonight, Vitaicus felt he'd been through enough personal grief and wished the gods would turn their attention elsewhere.

As he sat huddled against the tree allowing himself to grieve for those he'd lost, only the Druids remained to watch over him and ensure that every remnant of the queen's mortal body burned in the great fire that could be seen for miles.

Chapter 3

KING Vitaicus sat lost in thought, unable to stand company yet lonely through and through. He pondered the future of his son without a mother in this harsh Celtic world where a father's duty was to fight for survival, nothing more? His train of thought was broken as his priest entered the room.

"Obetach," he said. "My trusted priest and friend, my heart is troubled over the future of my son. How am I to bring him up when I need to see to my kingdom, to travel, and provide for him? I can't feed him while he's so tiny and I don't want a slave feeding him. He's been at the breast of a wet-nurse for many days and I can't bring myself to touch him in her presence. It doesn't seem fitting to have the son of a king – a future king himself and chosen by the gods – in the arms of a slave girl."

"You've spoken wisely my Lord," answered Obetach, "but you've no need to worry. While we speak Gamenta is out searching for a substitute mother for the little prince. I 'll have news for you shortly." The words 'substitute mother' stabbed at his heart but Vitaicus swallowed hard.

"You are wise and full of forethought Obetach. Come, let's go and drink some ale and play a game of Chelta. My heart is too heavy to work and too laden with dark thoughts to sit alone."

Not long before the end of yet another short day, for the weak and watery sun set early in the autumn months, Gamenta returned with news of a suitable wet-nurse for the prince. Obetach left the hamlet at once to follow his young protégé. It took an hour on horseback to reach the circular mud hut of Midamail and his wife Trasand. Their humble dwelling was alongside six similar huts made of the branches of wattle trees, with mud daubed walls and straw roofs.

The men of this little hamlet jointly owned a small tract of land, which they farmed.

Due to the power of the Druids and the awe in which the people held them, they were welcomed into the hut without question. Obetach had no need to introduce himself, he was known throughout the kingdom, however Gamenta was not and although the identities of Trasand and Midamail were of no consequence, Obetach took the time to make introductions. He'd spent the morning consulting with the Vates and divining the will of the gods, and knew that when a suitable woman was found, the husband would be sacrificed but not her child.

Midamail and Trasand had little doubt of the nature of the visit and felt neither fear nor dismay. They'd been part of the funeral procession for the queen and were aware that she'd died giving birth to a son. They knew that sooner or later Obetach would begin the search for a wet-nurse for the baby. Having given birth to a son of her own on the same night as the queen, Trasand realised she may well be the chosen one.

As for Midamail, he was reconciled to his fate before it had even befallen him. He knew if his wife were chosen he'd be sacrificed to the gods. He was the right age having just seen his thirtieth summer – and was aware this would count in favour of Trasand being chosen. His only concern was for his son, Pren. While he had no doubt of his own fate he had no idea what the gods would decree with regard to Pren. Having completed the introductions, Obetach refused the offer of a meal.

"You've both been chosen for a high honour." He said simply. "Midamail, you will be sacrificed to the gods under the next clear night sky in return for the birth of the prince. I'll send for you later. Trasand, you'll be taken to nurse the queen's child. Gather your clothing but leave the rest of your possessions, you'll have no need of them. Bring your child. Come." And he turned and left knowing his orders would be carried out unquestioningly.

Without a word Trasand put a few items for herself and her child in a basket she'd woven with grasses from their own fields and glanced briefly and lovingly at her husband one last time before leaving the hut.

Midamail squeezed his eyes tightly shut to stop the tears as his wife left with his only son. He hoped it wouldn't be long before the next clear night and his journey to the Otherworld, or too unbearable a wait for Trasand and Pren to join him in that happy place.

Trasand's arrival at the castle went unnoticed, as she wasn't taken to the king, but straight to his son. The slave was dismissed without a word of thanks or the opportunity to hold the baby one last time. Her work was done and she was required to leave the royal household immediately.

Trasand's first sight of the little prince brought a smile to her thin, pinched face. She'd been unwell during her pregnancy, drained since the birth. She was stressed and emotional at the death of the queen and the anticipation of being wrenched from her husband whom she loved. But the beautiful baby with his chubby round face and golden strands of hair sticking straight up from his perfectly shaped head, staring up at her with large brown eyes, immediately melted her heart and lifted her spirits.

She looked at her own son snuggled in her arm, so different in every way from the prince. She reached into the wooden basin and lifted the baby and holding both tightly to her breast, vowed to love them equally for as long as she was required to nurse the prince.

The sacrifice of Midamail took place two nights later at midnight. Trasand knew Midamail was going to a wonderful place where she'd join him before long, perhaps in just a few winters when her use as a wet-nurse was over. She neither grieved his death nor the possibility of her own at a young age, as that was simply the way of life. Ones life in this world could be short and hard, while life in the Otherworld would be eternal and happy.

The ceremony took place on a relatively mild night but even so Trasand was happy that she wasn't permitted to attend. Her place was at the side of the prince, her husband was hers no more and his earthly body held no significance to her. The ceremony was for the benefit of the gods.

Trasand could picture in her mind exactly what would take place having just witnessed the same for the queen, only this pyre would be smaller, the possessions sent along with Midamail meagre and simple. He and Gamenta chose his work tools and stool, for there were no torcs among the commoners, no wealth with which to purchase fine materials. Their life had been frugal but ample, simple but happy.

Chapter 4

IN the first weeks following the loss of his wife and birth of his son, King Vitaicus was too busy and distraught to spend any time with the child. He left all matters concerning the baby and his wet-nurse to Obetach. The priest had served him faithfully for many years, perhaps nine winters, Vitacus thought idly as he waited for two of his subjects to be brought before him. He was seated in his audience chamber, one of the larger rooms in the castle built of solid stone. It was warmed by two fireplaces in winter and had few window openings to let in the cold breezes and mist that blew in from the coast, ten miles to the south. Some of the rooms that had been added to the castle were built of timber and were pleasant enough in summer, but were boarded up and avoided during winter.

Vitaicus waited impatiently for the men so this latest matter could be resolved. He was seldom called to arbitrate an argument as this was normally the task of the Druids, but this particular disagreement had remained unresolved for too long and needed to be settled.

The men in question were farmers and important in his kingdom, owning large tracts of land, employing many people who supported large families and clans. Both men served well in his army and held the highest rank that a commoner could, with many warriors serving under them. Vitaicus had no desire to alienate either of them.

Manede, the elder of the two, claimed that his neighbour had stolen fifty head of cattle from him, while Eskerns blamed the theft on the raiding tribesmen of Goidel, an area near Tara in Ireland. Obetach had been consulted and a court case held. Each man brought along twelve witnesses to testify to their word, thereby cancelling out the statements made by the other. The Druids were forced to believe them both and therefore punish neither. The feud raged on, with Manede stealing seventy head of cattle from Eskerns in compensation. Eskerns in turn torched Manede's barn in the middle of the night, burning the feed stored for winter. As Manede threatened to torch Eskerns entire farm, the feud threatened the livelihood of hundreds of people. Vitaicus had to intervene.

Before meeting with Manede and Eskerns, Vitaicus met with Obetach and the Bards and Vates under him. The party of priests assembled in the courtyard early in the morning and the Bards chanted quietly, while the Vates followed the course of the birds in the sky, discussing animatedly the signs they read in their flight. Obetach strode forward and asked their verdict.

"In the path of flight the birds have taken we have indeed seen the raiding tribe of Goidel and the fifty cows." Gamenta began.

Vitaicus was so relieved to hear the number was fifty, not thirty, that he lost the thread of the pronouncement. He knew however that a band of warriors frequently came over from Ireland to plunder the land and had moved further into their country, being so bold as to set up several homesteads where they kept and farmed the cattle stolen from the Celts.

The band grew and was now a force of warriors strong enough to wreck havoc wherever they chose to strike. Every few months the Goidels would send home a portion of their newly gotten wealth before setting out on another raid. As soon as he realised that Gamenta was referring to one of his greatest foes Vitaicus brought his mind back to sharp attention.

"In the number of wings," Gamenta was saying, "we counted the cost of recompense. In the strength of the bird leading the flock we have seen Manede, and in the timidness of the one following some distance behind we've divined the presence of Eskerns."

Through a long and flowing speech to which Vitaicus paid little attention, Gamenta reported that Manede should return to Eskerns the seventy head of cattle he'd stolen, and that Eskerns should give to Manede one half of the fodder stored in his barn. Furthermore the feud should be called off immediately and as a sign of good faith and renewed friendship, each should give to the other their most prized bull. They should gather their clans and celebrate with a feast after which they were to call together every warrior in the region to take up arms and fight against the tribe of Goidel once and for all.

Obetach thanked Gamenta and his priests and dismissed them. Vitaicus retired to his audience chamber to wait for the men and was startled out of his reverie when he heard their footsteps on the wooden floor outside the heavy oak door. Without any preamble Vitaicus repeated what Gamenta had said and on hearing the king's declaration, they left the room with their heads together, eagerly making plans for the feast and the fighting that was to follow. It was hard to say which they anticipated with more glee.

Each planned to outdo the other with the size of the bull he would deliver that evening. Each planned to bring the most meat to roast, the finest vegetables for the women to cook, the strongest mead with which to celebrate their renewed friendship. They looked forward to taking out their weapons and polishing them until they gleamed, sharpening them so they could slice an ant in half. This was a fine day and they were delighted with their king's verdict. He was indeed a wise ruler.

The king didn't feel very wise, he was actually feeling utterly foolish. He'd spent hours staring out of the window onto the open plain at the back of his castle, into the distance where the hills changed colour with each hour of the day. He'd stood in the courtyard at night, searching the sky, the moon, the stars, looking for the elusive, and always found himself counting instead of finding that which he searched for. Always counting, hoping that he'd never stumble across the number thirty. He wandered far from home, on horseback and on foot, looking for that which eluded him – an appropriate name for his son.

After many days and nights of searching, he'd come up with nothing. Embarrassed, he'd not even visited his son during that time and barely seen him since the night he was born, save for the first thirty hours when he'd sat on the floor of the child's room and pleaded with the gods for his life. Now it was time to name his son and he had no name to give.

He called for his servant Flauston to fetch Obetach. They needed to set aside a day for a naming ceremony before the child turned thirty days but after the fight against the Goidels. Obetach wouldn't go to battle but would remain behind to see to his king's household. He could spend that time planning and preparing for the ceremony.

Chapter 5

THE night Vitaicus and his warriors left for battle an ice-cold wind blew in across the plains, mist swirled around the legs of the assembled warriors, and their breath came out in wispy white clouds. They stood in the courtyard stamping their feet and rubbing frozen hands together under a starless sky. Heavy clouds obscured the moon. The only sound came from their horses as they snorted restlessly.

The king walked to the front of his men, his standard bearer at his side proudly holding their emblem – the sacred red fox. The king did a quick count of the chariots lined up in the roadway outside the castle. There were thirty-five and he let out a sigh of relief before signalling for the horn to be blown and crying, "To battle."

"To battle," roared his men as they moved forward, on horseback, in chariots and on foot. The mood changed in an instant from one of despair and mourning to one of anticipation. The Celts were a people of sharp contrasts, either up or down in spirit, seldom anything in-between, and there was nothing a Celt loved more than to fight.

Although a large number of his army was already gathered, many more would fall in along the way. The men were assembled in groups at each farmstead they passed as they marched to the northwest. They'd cross the hills during the early hours of the morning, and turn westwards as the sun rose, surprising their foe before midday. It had been just two days since the king had pronounced his verdict to Eskerns and Manede, and in that time riders had crossed the length and breadth of the kingdom calling men to arms. Always ready for a good battle, they'd dropped their farming implements and picked up their arms, anticipating the fury of the fight and the celebrations afterwards.

All along the way Druids stood by the side of the road, the Vates praying, while the Bards chanted to Modron, the God of War.

"Our king goes out to battle,
To conquer and defeat.
His warriors follow him and fight for him,
Their illustrious king.
He'll lead them into victory,
As in battles fought before.
He'll conquer every foe,
For he's a victorious king."

Their attack was a surprise and the cold weather played greatly in their favour. Under normal circumstances no-one would have ventured out on such a cold, dark night, and even the light of morning brought little relief. The sky was grey and a heavy fog cut visibility to a few feet. Even the sound of a large army marching, was muffled by the heavy mist. Their enemy was caught sleeping.

After a victory of their own in a battle against the Atrebates, they'd celebrated for two nights, drinking excessive amounts of mead and ale, satiating themselves with rich food and other spoils of war. The victorious army lay sleeping off their headaches, before moving on to their next raid. Their camp was a wreck with litter everywhere. Temporary shelters were falling down on the men as they slept. Fires had been left untended and gone out, but the Goidels were too drunk to notice the numbing cold. Arrogant in their victory they'd only posted lookouts on the first night, now the sentries too lay drunk and asleep.

Vitaicus' rode among them in his magnificent war chariot followed by his chieftains holding their javelins and chanting in deep harsh voices, proclaiming their valour in battle and that of their ancestors too. As their foe woke, the chanting changed to screeches and shrieks as they slashed at everything that moved, stabbing and thrusting at their victims as they violently roused the enemy from their drunken slumber. As the horsemen moved through the camp taunting the men, the warriors on foot followed slashing off arms and legs, stabbing through hearts, challenging men to single combat and decapitating the defeated foe, until only a handful of men and their leader, the fearsome Fer Niall remained.

Vitaicus stepped down from his chariot and arrogantly challenged Fer Niall to a duel. Vitaicus warriors' fell back, relieved to have a break. Breathing hard, their bodies aching, they stood beside their exhausted horses and watched. Fer Niall's men fell back too, looking in stunned silence at the death and destruction around them, realising how heavily outnumbered they were as so many of their men lay dead. Knowing their fate should their leader fall in the duel, they watched incredulously, all fight gone from them.

Vitaicus walked towards Fer Niall. When he was ten paces from the villain, he stopped.

"How do you choose to duel?" he asked. Fer Niall didn't answer but simply pulled a knife from its sheath.

The king stood ready, his own knife in his hand, waiting for the enemy to move first. Stooping low Fer Niall came at Vitaicus with a blood-curdling scream, thrashing at the air with his weapon, aiming for the king's throat. Vitaicus watched him with amusement.

In the eight paces he took to move towards the king, Fer Niall had shown his intention so clearly that Vitaicus felt a sense of disappointment, this was going to be too easy. He stood ready to counter the swiftly moving knife as Fer Niall lunged the last two paces towards his throat. Vitaicus knocked the weapon clean out of the warrior's hand, slicing two fingers off as his own sharp blade was brought down with all his weight onto the outstretched hand. Fer Niall didn't seem to feel the pain, but looked down at his useless right hand momentarily, before pulling out a longer knife from a concealed pocket behind his back. However, his left hand was unpractised and blood was pumping out of the gaping holes where his fingers once were, as he made his second move towards the king.

Vitaicus let him get in close, watching the quivering blade intently, and once he judged that Fer Niall was committed, he stepped lithely aside and watched his quarry stumble and fall to the ground, where he lay amongst his fallen men, his blood mingling with theirs.

Vitaicus hesitated long enough to see if the remaining Goidels were still watching before stepping over the stricken man, pulling his head off the ground by his long and filthy hair, and slitting his throat from ear to ear, while watching the eyes of the man glaze over.

It took just a few moments for Vitaicus' men to raise themselves. They bound the terrified survivors, threw them across their own horses and then gathered loot to take home with them.

Trasand watched the returning victors with mixed feelings. Their singing and shouts of victory alerted each homestead they passed and people came running to the roadway to cheer them. Hanging from the neck of every horse was the head of an enemy, proudly fastened to the bridle as a trophy for each warrior. It was a massive victory and a proud day for the Canti and King Vitaicus.

They'd annihilated a tribe that had troubled them for months and retrieved the cows stolen from Manede. They had sacks full of loot, gold as yet unset, torcs to give to their king, vases and cauldrons, and bridles inlaid with precious stones – all stolen from the Celts during the season's raids.

Horses and cattle were herded by slaves at a much slower pace, and arrived at the king's hamlet the following day. Those belonging to Manede were returned to him, the remainder were rested, watered and fed in readiness for the victory celebrations that would take place under the next full moon.

As Vitaicus rode into the courtyard with his own trophy displayed on the side of his horse, the head of Fer Niall himself, Trasand moved back out of sight. This head would be preserved in cedar oil and forever remain a proud souvenir for the king, given a place of honour in his trophy room.

Trasand was dismayed, not at the horrid sight of the lifeless head, she was accustomed to that, but at the behaviour of the king. His son was over three weeks old, and he'd hardly seen the baby in that time. She'd respected his mourning, but here he was back from battle, no longer the bereaved widow but a triumphant victor, shouting and gleeful, his dead wife forgotten as his foe's head dangled from his horse, its eyes bulging gruesomely out of their sockets.

Trasand had been in the household for many days and had yet to meet the king. Perhaps he had no intention of meeting with her, she thought, perhaps she'd be asked to leave if he came to see the child, but surely he'd come!

The king left his horse in the care of a stable hand and asked Flauston to take care of the head of Fer Niall. He flung a sack over his shoulder containing some of the trophies his warriors had given to him. The rest would arrive over the following days as men chose to bring them to him personally and thank him for leading them into victory. He knew the finest reward would come from Eskerns and Manede.

Vitaicus went directly to his trophy room and tipped the contents of the sack onto his working table. He called loudly for Obetach who had been hovering close by anticipating the need of his king. They sat together, kings in their own right, but basic men in the sight of such treasure, fondling each ornament, marvelling at the workmanship, debating the value, exulting in their acquisitions.

Finally Vitaicus sighed and turned to gaze into the fire. The flames leaped and danced merrily, but once again the king's heart was heavy. He was home again and there were issues to face.

"What is it that makes the king so low in the presence of such trophies?" Obetach asked solicitously, waving his arm over the table.

"Ah," replied Vitaicus, "it's the matter of the child. He's nearing his first month and I've barely laid eyes on him since that first best-forgotten night. I can't bring myself to see him."

"I don't understand Sire. Is it your grief at your loss that stays you, or the sight of the wet-nurse? I can have her removed before you enter?"

"Nay, my good friend, it's my own embarrassment that I should have a precious son, a fine prince for whom I've not yet found a suitable name. I can't bear to see him, to pick him up, and have no name with which to address him. I find myself obsessed with counting, looking for thirty in everything I see, and I've been distracted and unable to find a name."

Obetach fought the impulse to laugh at the king who was not only deadly serious but would not take kindly to being mocked, even by Obetach.

"Have you arranged the naming ceremony yet?" the king asked, but the Druid appeared not to hear him.

Obetach looked into the fire and began to meditate, watching the flames without blinking until he was in a trance. He called on the gods to speak to him. He thought back to the night of the baby's birth and suddenly sat bolt upright, eyes wide, startling the king out of his own reverie.

"You shall call him Dylan, in honour of Dylan the reat, the Son of the Sea, and in keeping with the nature of his birth," he announced. During the Great Flood many generations earlier, only a single ship on all the earth had prevailed.

It was the ship of Dylan, Son of the Sea, and he alone with his family survived the drowning of the entire world, Obetach explained, saying that the survival of the king's son during the great storm on the night of his birth, surrounded by the bloody waters of his mother, was symbolic of that great event which surely saved the world for further procreation. Dylan would be a fitting name for one who survived such a bloody birth on such a wet and dramatic night. Well satisfied, the king agreed, Dylan it would be.

Vitaicus was desperate to see his son again and his heart all but burst at the sight of him. The hollow ache he'd been feeling for so long left him as he lifted the little figure out of its basin, all wrapped in lambs wool, snuggled up and warm. He held him close to his heart and gently kissed his soft round face, covering it with his own large lips, feeling love so immense it frightened him.

"Dylan," he whispered, "Dylan the Great. That is what you shall be, the greatest son a man could ever have. The greatest prince a king could wish for. You shall be my Dylan."

At last he returned the baby to its basin and turned to leave the room. A movement close by startled him and he stopped and stared. There before him in the fading sunlight shining through the beams covering the window openings stood the most beautiful woman he'd ever seen.

He stood absolutely still, mesmerised, and admired her lovely face, her hazel hair glistening in the sun, her tall slender form and penetrating green eyes, even her perfectly formed fingers caught his attention in the brief time that he stared at her, until he felt a sharp stab of guilt as it was all so soon after bidding his own beloved farewell. Vitaicus was embarrassed and unable to speak.

Shy and unsure how to behave before the king, Trasand bowed her head and looked at the floor, remaining silent. After an interminably long pause, Vitaicus brushed past her, muttering a quick apology for touching against her arm, leaving Trasand flustered and confused. She'd seen the grief of the king at the funeral of the queen, but she'd also seen how he'd looked at her now, his eyes said much, and she sensed his embarrassment. Uncertain of what to do next she was saved by the cry of her new charge, but determined to speak to Obetach at the first opportunity on how to behave in the presence of the king.

The celebration for the victory over the Goidels was a simple affair. It took place in the forest where priests and priestesses had been gathering since the warriors returned. Two huge pyres were built and one by one the captured animals were driven between them and then sacrificed to Modron, the God of War. The blackened sky could be seen throughout the kingdom and the stench of burning flesh and hair could be smelt for miles.

The Goddess of Victory, Andraste, required human sacrifice, and the remaining Goidels were brought forward late on the second day. The pyres were built up with fresh wood and the Goidels were offered to Andraste, to the victorious chant of the Druids and the people of Canti. Taranis, the God of Thunder, also enjoyed human sacrifices and loved to see them burnt alive.

Once the last of the prisoners was flung into the flames, the feasting began. Choice stock taken from the royal cattle pens had been roasting on nearby fires since dawn. As the portions were divided up, the people settled themselves on the skins of wolves, warming themselves around the huge pyre. The children served the food to the warriors, and the bravest warrior got the finest portion of meat, the thigh. On this night it was deemed to be Vitaicus himself, for having ridden into battle up front, screaming and slashing at the enemy with ferocity his men seldom saw. That and his duel with Fer Niall were talked about for weeks. A child was chosen through the drawing of straws and he walked towards the king with pride, bearing the specially prepared portion on a silver platter.

Silence descended when the third portion was presented, raised high above the heads of the servers. The head of the boar, gleaming with oils, adorned with fruit and with a glazed cherry red apple between its bare gums, fat dripping off the edge of the platter onto the shoulders of the bearers, this was for the charioteer who'd led the king into victory.

As the serving was placed before the man, the people burst into spontaneous applause, and ribald comments were flung at the proud warrior. Platter after platter of meat was brought to serve to the rest of the warriors and when the Bards came later on to entertain the satiated people with their poetry, laughter and singing accompanied their efforts.

By the time the celebrations were over, the gods appeased, and the people returned home to once again take up farming implements, the blood had drained from the heads of the enemy. Each head would be hung from the doorpost of the warrior's home, and no one would dare to remove it. For those men who'd not been able to go to battle, some sick, others wounded, a head could be bought at great cost, but cheaper than the certain death for stealing one. The heads remained on the doorposts for many weeks as a constant reminder to the people of their great victory.

Vitaicus looked at the moon and was surprised to see that it was almost full once again. The naming ceremony would take place under a full moon, despite the fact that it would be after the child turned thirty days old. Although everything had been planned and prepared, Vitaicus knew something was bothering his priest and so invited Obetach to join him on a hunt. Although a number of sheep and cows were already in the royal kitchens roasting, Vitaicus wished to catch a boar himself to celebrate the naming of his son. They'd stalked their quarry for an hour when it finally stopped to rest.

Vitaicus lay flat on the cold earth with his bow drawn, his aim accurate as always, his arrow flew straight. The boar died instantly as the steel pierced his heart. Satisfied, Vitaicus sat up and motioned to Obetach to sit beside him.

"What troubles you Obetach?" he asked. "You've something on your mind. I've seen you about to speak many times of late, but you hesitate."

Obetach was surprised and uncomfortable. "It's the delicate matter of the wet-nurse Sire." Obetach responded finally. "She's uncertain of her role in the royal household other than that of nurse. Does she have a role? How should she act in your presence? What does her future hold, and that of her child, and uppermost in my mind, what of the ceremony tonight, should she be present? This is a most unusual situation, I've decisions to make and I'm somewhat at a loss. I've even hesitated to consult the gods. I feel as your chief councillor, your priest, I should make these decisions for you, or at least have some recommendations to bring to you, that's why I've been so hesitant to approach you, and now the night is here. This is all so unprecedented," he sighed.

Once he'd begun, Obetach felt the words flood over and he spoke his mind. The king too sighed deeply and lay back on the cold earth.

"I don't know the answer to these things Obetach," he said almost sadly. "It's in the hands of the gods," and with that the subject was closed.

The day before the baby was named marked the beginning of the thirtieth day of its life and Vitaicus woke with a constriction in his chest. This may be the day the gods require their Supreme Sacrifice, this may be the last time I see my son, he thought miserably, as he flung his bedcovers clear across the room with all the pent up fury and frustration of the past month. His earlier certainty that the gods would give him thirty years had deserted him, and he was weary of watching for that magical number. His head ached with counting and his heart hurt at the thought of more loss.

With a robe carelessly thrown about him he stormed off in search of Obetach. The entire household was wakened and in an uproar before Obetach was located, but once found the priest was either unable or unwilling to do the king's bidding.

"But don't you see," begged Vitaicus like a child wishing to get his own way, "if we spend the day beside the child praying to the gods, if we make a special sacrifice and plead with them, they'll surely spare him beyond today."

"My Lord, I warned you on the night he was born," Obetach began patiently, "we can't change the course the gods have set. If they require him today, they'll take him today. I've much to do for the ceremony tonight, I can't spend the day with you watching his every breath, but, if it will give you any comfort, I'll leave Gamenta with you. It'll do no harm to spend time together praising the gods for the life of the child, but I warn you against pleading with them. He'll be the Supreme Sacrifice in their good time. Don't anger them, I beseech you." He ended sternly.

"Why Gamenta, Obetach, why not you? Can't he complete the arrangements for tonight? I need you today." Vitaicus felt panic stricken.

"You do me great honour my Lord, but this is about the child, not you. If it makes you feel any better, I've seen nothing in my meditations this morning that disturbed me, so go in peace, and I'll send Gamenta to you."

Vitaicus was angry that he never seemed to get his own way. He was the king after all! He hardly knew Gamenta and was disturbed at the thought of spending a day with him, but this was a spiritual decision and out of his hands, he had to accept it.

Vitaicus and the Druid spent the entire day in the room of the prince, with Vitaicus sitting quietly beside the priest as he chanted and prayed, praising the gods. By the time the moon rose, Vitaicus felt a great sense of peace and was ready to give up his son to the gods. He left the room and the restful presence of the young man reluctantly and with a new respect.

Obetach and the gods had chosen wisely when they chose Gamenta to be a priest.

Chapter 6

ALTHOUGH part of the naming ceremony would be held under the full moon, the baby wouldn't be present until the first sign of the new day. Despite the cold, the Druids were assembled in a sacred grove in their bare feet, waiting for the moon to reach its zenith. Chanting together the priests and priestesses set off to fetch holy water from a spring a mile away, with novices carrying a large cauldron for the water.

As they approached the lake that the spring fed, they fell silent. The icy ground numbed their feet, but they couldn't approach this holy place with shoes on. They walked along the side of the lake a short way, the water frozen to ice and treacherous under foot. Obetach motioned for the party to stop as they neared the rocks under which the spring flowed. Only senior Druids would be allowed to go closer and they too stopped short of the largest rock, its wet surface gleaming in the moonlight.

Obetach stood with his arms stretched towards the heavens, calling on the gods to bless the water they were about to draw. He chanted for a full five minutes while the rest of the assembly waited, so disciplined that even the cruel cold and their numb feet would not make them move, they wouldn't risk offending the gods at this important juncture. Satisfied that he'd asked every possible blessing on the water, Obetach held his hands out for the cauldron and a snow-white cloth that had never been used before.

He reached into a cleft between two large rocks and felt the ice-cold water gush against the bare flesh of his arms. It gurgled into the cauldron and only when he judged by its weight that it was full, did he stretch his stiff back and stand upright.

They returned to the grove with the precious holy water held safely in the magnificently carved cauldron and wrapped in the cloth. After the priests and priestesses had rubbed their frozen feet vigorously and brought them back to life, they wrapped them in wool, bound them with cloth and put on their sandals. They drank berry ale from a large shared cup and then began their journey to the king's residence.

They arrived before the first glimmer of dawn lightened the horizon and waited silently and patiently in the courtyard. The king stood ready holding his son. He hadn't thought further on Obetach's dilemma regarding the wet-nurse. Although he'd tiptoed into the baby's room earlier, his heavy shoes made a noise on the wooden floor, but he needn't have worried about waking his son. The prince was already dressed in several layers of soft silky material and overlaid in a robe that hung below his tiny legs. On his head was a soft cap filled with duck down, and Trasand had him tightly wrapped in his warmest sheepskin covering, ready for the cold morning air. He'd been fed and was lying contentedly in Trasand's arms when Vitaicus entered.

"My Lord," she whispered as she rose.

"My lady," he responded, which took Trasand off guard. She didn't expect to be addressed in any form by him, let alone as a lady.

"May I?" Vitaicus reached out and gently pried his child from her arms. She was aware of the strength and width of them, muscled through years of fighting. He was aware of the fragrance of her body as he reached close to retrieve his son. Before the silence grew uncomfortable and without more than a moment's thought, Vitaicus placed his free arm through hers and invited her to join the ceremony in the courtyard.

They emerged from the castle linked together and looking as natural as any parents about to attend such a joyous occasion. Obetach bowed briefly to the king, out of respect rather than duty then inclined his head towards Trasand and greeted her by name.

The cauldron of holy water was placed in the centre of the courtyard, which had been decorated the previous evening by the housemaids. Garlands of laurel leaves interwoven with snowdrops hung from each of the torch stands. Vitaicus was relieved to complete his count and find twenty not thirty of them. The cobbled floor was strewn with petals from flowers picked in the forest. Carnations and roses from the royal gardens were placed in earthen pots around the perimeter.

Their fragrance was overwhelming in the fresh morning air and as the first rays of sun lit the sky with gentle shades of mauve and pink, the mist began to swirl higher around the yard and the scene took on an ethereal appearance. A small fire beside the holy water flickered weakly, its flames barely lighting a few feet round it, its meagre warmth not reaching even those standing closest. Everyone was silent as they waited for the light to grow and strengthen.

Vitaicus stood near the back of the yard and as soon as the first ray of sunlight struck the forehead of the baby the ceremony began. The Bards began a cheerful chant singing of the future well being of the prince. The Vates dipped miniature cauldrons into the larger one filled with precious holy water and walked too and fro sprinkling the ground where the child would tread, the walls that encompassed his home, the gatepost that would guard him and the people that would nurture him.

Wyndem, a senior Vate, drew his own cauldron and came and stood directly in front of Trasand who was beside the king. He sprinkled her liberally while the Bards begged the gods to give her wisdom in bringing up the child.

Trasand shivered at the responsibility made real by their words.

"Keeper of the royal son,
We call blessings upon you and
ask of the gods, wisdom and strength,
to raise the prince to be a worthy king.
We order you to discipline and care for him
until he is placed into our keeping, eight winters from this day.
We call curses upon you should you fail.
You were separated out from among many,
and honoured above all others.
Do not fail your king, do not fail the prince.
Do not fail the gods,
for then you will never see the Otherworld,
but will remain for all eternity in a place without rest.
Keeper of the royal son, heed our word.
and obey the gods
Keeper of the royal son,
Guard him well."

Even Vitaicus was taken aback at the words that were chanted over the wet-nurse. Surely he was responsible for his son and held accountable for the child's upbringing and future. He stood stunned, not only at the high responsibility placed on the young woman but also at the pronouncement that his son would be taken into the care of the Druids when he was eight winters old. That meant so little time, so little of the thirty years he prayed he'd be given.

Vitaicus felt devastated afresh and his despair at his losses one on top of the other began to overcome him once again.

Wyndem finished sprinkling water over Trasand and a second cauldron of water was drawn, this one for the king. The Bards began to chant once more, this time their words were addressed to Vitaicus.

"Oh great king of Canti, we call blessings upon you.
We command that all sadness be removed from you from this moment forth.
We place in your care and responsibility the life of your trusted servant Trasand.
We command you to honour her, protect her and keep her.
We call upon the gods to witness the charge we give you.
We call curses upon you should you fail.
Keeper of the royal nurse, heed our words,
and, obey your gods
Keeper of the royal nurse,
Guard her well.

Vitaicus trembled and could feel Trasand swaying beside him, and reached out his arm to steady her. Trasand didn't even know her name and now he was responsible for her in a way that made his knees weak. And she, she was responsible for his son in an even greater way than he. His head spun and he wished he could be alone to think these momentous things through, but the ceremony continued.

He was aware of the baby being taken from his arms, he heard in the background the sweet singing of the Bards. He felt and smelled the presence of the beautiful woman beside him, as if in a dream. This should have been Hilfuth, yet he wasn't displeased with Obetach's choice. The sight of her charmed him although he'd only seen her twice and so briefly. His mind was a whirl of confusion.

The baby's clothing was stripped from his body and he came awake with a start. He was immersed in the cauldron and his little lungs issued forth one loud screech after the other as the cold water turned his body blue and his skin rose with goose flesh. A warm covering was wrapped round him, but it wasn't over yet. The screaming brought Vitaicus back to full consciousness and he watched alertly as the Vates began to walk three times round the fire. Obetach held the baby close, stilling his sobs, as the story of his name unfolded.

Trasand stifled a sob as she watched the frozen child, her protective instincts crying out to take him, dress and nurse him. Vitaicus looked at her with respect as he leaned across and wiped away the tears that flowed freely down her cheeks with the palm of his battle-scarred hand.

"He'll be alright," he whispered, "don't worry yourself, he'll soon be back safe with you."

Trasand listened to the story of the great flood with interest. She'd heard it many times before as a child, but today she realised it held a new significance. The audience comprised the entire household of the king, his family, slaves and staff and they listened attentively as it reached its climax. The orator grew passionate as he told of the great waters that drowned the earth many generations ago, leaving only one boat and one man with his family to survive. That man was the famed Dylan.

Obetach took up the thread of the story and in detail described the difficult birth of the baby in his arms. He told how the three gods had been present, watching, waiting for their charge. He told in a low lamenting voice of the death of their beloved queen at the birth of this special child, and then pronounced the name chosen for the baby.

"The gods who were present at his birth saw fit that he be named in honour of the great flood. Teutates, the Supreme God, Esus, the Lord and Master, and Taranis, the God of Thunder, each of these three mighty gods witnessed the water and the blood, even the sky rained down on the auspicious occasion. The copious amount of water held the most significance and so it is in honour of Taranis who brought about so much water from the belly of the mother and from the sky, that this child will be named Dylan."

At the announcement the gathering sighed with pleasure. Obetach uncovered Dylan and sprinkled water over his frozen body.

"I name you Dylan, from this day forth until you earn your own name," he repeated three times, before returning the sobbing baby to Trasand. She fled for the warmth of the fire that blazed in the baby's room.

The remaining holy water was thrown over the fire, which signalled time for a feast to begin with much drinking and eating of meat and other delicacies. Everyone in the courtyard was invited into the castle to take part in the celebration which would last for as many days as there was food to eat, mead to drink and citizens to partake.

On the first night Trasand joined the celebration briefly, sitting on the floor before the long row of tables set out in the huge eating room. She sat barefooted beside the king, on his right hand side, in the highest place of honour, but an arms length away to give him room to use his weapon should he need to. Obetach was in the second highest place of honour on the king's left.

The men and women who were chosen to feast at the castle were afforded the highest distinction, and assembled each day were aristocrats and noblemen, warriors and Druids. Slaves brought in the meals, a seemingly endless supply of fresh meat and vegetables from the royal gardens, and gifts of foods delivered to the royal kitchens by his people. The finest piece of meat was served first to the king on a wooden platter, and each night it seemed bigger and better than the previous one.

Trasand was served the second portion, the haunch, which was brought in to her on a beautifully crafted silver platter. It was a meal on its own larger than a month's worth of eating in her previous life.

The feasting continued until no one could eat or drink another morsel, and after a full week of celebration of the highest order, Dylan was officially named as the king's heir to the throne.

Chapter 7

AD 31
Winter

ROMANS, Romans, the Romans, was the whispered talk in the passages and chambers of the king's residence. Everywhere he went he was aware of his slaves and staff whispering, until he couldn't stand it any longer.

"Flauston!" he bellowed, "Bring Obetach to me at once."

Obetach was in the forest in consultation with other senior Druids and although unhappy to be disturbed by the arrival of Gamenta, he left immediately to the bidding of his king. When he walked into the king's audience chamber he was hungry, frozen and caked with mud but he bowed before Vitaicus.

"What is it my Lord requires?" he asked patiently.

"There's much whispering in my castle," Vitaicus sounded perplexed, "and I hear the word 'Romans' repeatedly. What is it that I don't know?" he demanded.

"My lord, allow me to freshen up and eat before I answer you. I've just returned from a meeting with Druids from across the land and have a report for you."

Vitaicus waved him away, knowing he was showing disrespect, but his lack of knowledge was gnawing at him. It seemed the entire land knew what was going on while he, the king, knew nothing.

Perhaps he'd been spending too much time with his sons, he mused Sons, did he really think of them both as his. This revelation startled him. It was true the boys fascinated him, so different from each other it was astonishing. At the age of four months they were becoming interesting, and Vitaicus had to admit this wouldn't have been so had there not been two to compare against each other. Even if he'd ignored his own pride at being the father of Dylan and been totally impartial, it was plain to see that Dylan was the stronger and quicker of the babies. He'd smiled first, found his shrill voice and noticed his own hands first.

He began to catch one with the other before Pren had been aware even of the large hands of Vitaicus. The king spent many fascinated hours watching the boys awake and at sleep. He'd come to love seeing them feed, listening to their hungry guzzling at the warm breast of Trasand, and even then Dylan had sucked longer and harder than Pren. He was taller and sturdier with a ruddy complexion, while Pren was a little slip of a thing with the same pale unblemished skin as his mother.

Vitaicus longed for the day the boys could walk and talk and he could get down on all fours and play with them. He was so enjoying this time of peace and quiet in the land that the very word 'Roman' disturbed him immensely.

The Celts were a nation that loved to fight and were always ready to take up arms at an instant's notice and Vitaicus was no exception. Under normal circumstances he would have been delighted to hear news of Rome and an impending battle, but now, with these little lives happily growing in a room down the passageway, he neither wanted to leave them, nor risk losing his own life in battle.

'I'm getting soft he thought, not a good trait for a king. What I need is a good fight to get my mind off women and babies. Women, now where did that thought come from' he mused 'the only woman in my life is Trasand, but what a woman! Were it not for memories of my Hilfuth, I'd have taken Trasand to my bed already.'

Having brought a deeply subconscious thought to the fore, Vitaicus was stunned, but now it was there, he had to admit it. The reason he spent as much time watching the boys as he did, was his growing fondness, admiration, and yes, lust, for the charming person that had been chosen as mother for his child. She was a soft, warm and loving woman who adored the boys, making absolutely no distinction between them. He would have to do something about Trasand shortly, he decided, just as Obetach re-entered the room and interrupted this new and pleasant train of thought.

Obetach was in no mood to hurry and Vitaicus knew from experience that he'd have to wait for the Druid. He took his time to pour them both a goblet of ale, then pulled a large comfortably padded chair closer to the fire. Before sitting, he knelt before the burning logs and gazed intently at the flames, divining some future course of action. The king sat patiently.

Finally Obetach lifted his large frame off the floor and made himself comfortable in the chair. Exhaustion showed clearly on his weathered face. He and the party of Druids he'd recently left had spent forty-eight hours in prayer and meditation as they sought the gods and the best course of action for the future. Now at last they were ready to share with their kings, the fate of the nation as a whole.

"My Lord, there is grave trouble in Gaul." he began. "The Romans have once again vowed to wipe out the Druids entirely, but having failed so dismally in Britain before, they've set their eyes on Europe. Emperor Tiberius has declared that not a single Druid shall remain on the face of the earth and has troops in Gaul ready and waiting. The Romans have massacred thousands of our numbers, and those that remain alive are in hiding."

He paused to take a long drink of ale before continuing. The king remained silent.

"It's been agreed that we should travel to Gaul immediately to help call on the gods to stave off the Romans. The Druids of Gaul need us."

At this, Vitaicus choked on his ale, spilling a good amount down his chin. The frothy drink bubbled among the ginger hairs of his thick bushy moustache and it took some time to wipe himself down and regain his composure.

"Obetach, while I don't question your judgement, I cannot see that this is a sensible course of action. Surely the arch Druid does not expect every senior Druid in this country to travel to Gaul, to leave us unprotected against our enemies and all the evil gods. What if the Romans should find you and your priests while you are there, then we'd be left with nothing but novices and no one to teach them, no one to teach our children. This is surely far too risky a venture. You can't take such a chance. No, I don't believe I should allow you to go!"

As his argument gained weight, Vitaicus became more forceful, until he was almost shouting. Obetach remained unmoved having fully expected the reaction of the king.

"My Lord, with all respect, we'll not leave the land unprotected. You'll be in the care and protection of the Supreme Druid, and the many druids under him who are too old to travel. There are thousands of novices in their final years of training, and under them thousands of younger novices. These priests and priestesses will be entrusted with the care of the land and will sit night and day in prayer and meditation. They'll ward off evil and divine the intention of the gods at all times."

He paused, looking thoughtfully into the fire. "Those of us that travel to Gaul will be quite safe, you needn't fear. You know too, that you have no right to forbid me to go, lest you anger the gods. It is they who have decreed that we should go."

Once the gods had spoken the subject was closed and Vitaicus knew it.

"Tell me what has taken place in Gaul," he asked.

Obetach sighed deeply and told the king how the Romans were determined to wipe out all trace of the Druids, the manner in which they destroyed their sacred groves just as Caesar had done, and tore down their temples, profaned the gods, and killed every priest and priestess they found.

When he finally finished, he asked the king's permission to leave. He'd spend the next two nights and days in the forest with the priests and priestesses praying to the gods. Already exhausted, he had a formidable task ahead of him and couldn't afford to waste any further time in idle conversation with the king.

It was with a heavy heart that Vitaicus said farewell to his priest and keeper of the well being of his household.

He went in search of Trasand in order to cheer himself.

Chapter 8

IT was the very heart of winter, the weather extremely cold and the roadways treacherous, making the going tough. By the time Obetach and the fifty-three Druids accompanying him reached the coast, they were numbed with cold, pain and exhaustion, but no one complained or asked for rest. No one stopped to wrap an injury, or rub life back into a frozen foot. They marched until they reached the beach and only after they'd clambered aboard their boats, did they collapse.

They were so deeply asleep after the past days of preparation and lack of sleep, that few of them were affected with seasickness. Their passage was relatively smooth and quick and they reached the shores of Gaul far quicker than anticipated, but once there they were shocked to see how few Gaulish Druids remained alive. They were overwhelmed at the welcome they received, as the Gauls saw them as their salvation.

After a nervous day and night of non-stop praying, begging the gods to forgive them for not offering a burnt sacrifice, as they dared not light a fire, the Druids feared that the gods had deserted them.

The first day of the Festival of Imbolc was two days away, and the excitement of the people was tangible. This was the festival marking the 'Return of Light' when the first stirrings of life were noticeable in the ground, and farmers could begin to plough their fields. It was a wonderful time after the hardship and uncertainty of winter, a time of Renewal and Purification, dedicated to the Goddess Brigid.

Vitaicus called for Gamenta early in the morning. He'd not slept the entire night and knew he would accomplish little that day unless he spoke to the Druid. Gamenta, unaccustomed to being summoned by the king, rushed into the chamber with his hair awry. His clothes were thrown on roughly and his gown was askew while his feet were bare on the cold stone floor.

'My Lord, you called for me?" he panted. Vitaicus smiled at the sight of the young priest, but he didn't doubt the youth's earnestness or wisdom. Obetach wouldn't have chosen him as his assistant or left the king's household in his charge unless he was the most promising of novices. He surely had some gift, some connection with the gods that Obetach sensed.

"I wish," the king began hesitantly, "at the Festival of Imbolc, during the Renewal and Purification ceremony, to renew and purify my life. I wish to make a new start now that my wife Hilfuth lives in the Otherworld. I need you to seek the Goddess Brigid, who'll surely be the goddess most present at this festival, and implore her on my behalf for her blessing, that I may marry the wet-nurse Trasand."

'There, I've said it,' he thought. 'Now let the gods decide. I can't think on this any longer. I've a country to run, wars to fight, let the goddess Brigid decide.'

Gamenta took the news as easily as if he'd been asked to pour a goblet of ale. He bowed and left the king, who stood bewildered, thinking that Gamenta would at least have passed a comment. He knew that Obetach would have and realised in that instant how much he missed the counsel of his trusted friend.

Since the departure of the Druids, strange things had taken place in the land. At first it was as if the people had decided to hold off all quarrels, stave off all wars and keep their peace until the priests returned. However, after the first few nights the natural tendency of the people who'd grown up with fighting, whose way of life was to exchange farming implements for arms at the slightest provocation, found the peaceful way of life was not to their liking. In what seemed a deliberate attempt to provoke a fight, a farmer crept into the homestead of a neighbour in the still of night and kidnapped his wife from the man's own bed.

Deep in sleep after a day of feasting and drinking with the same neighbour who now stole his wife, he never heard a sound. Knowing the strength of the man and his temper once crossed, the wife allowed herself to be taken, and spent the remainder of that night in her kidnapper's bed, having surprisingly enjoyable wild sex, which would be labelled rape in the morning. Four priests were called to settle the ensuing dispute and spent the entire day reading the signs of the gods.

They watched flocks of birds, studied branches of trees and even stabbed the belly of a dog, observing its convulsions as it bled to death, but they couldn't agree on what the gods were saying. The land of Iceni waited with bated breath, and when it seemed that the Druids couldn't resolve the conflict, they took up arms. Without prior arrangement the people split in half, some supporting the aggrieved husband, Mulafatin, others supporting the boasting neighbour Slutain, who still held the not so unwilling wife Gerdia, as hostage. The battle that followed was bloody and swift.

Slutain and his band quickly wiped out his neighbours, killing Mulafatin first, then attacking and wiping out most of the members of his clan. Those who could flee in time joined Slutain's warriors, strengthening his force. Within the day Mulafatin's farmstead was ransacked, his cattle stolen and taken to the farm of Slutain, where it was divided up amongst the warriors. All other spoils were for Slutain and his family and they were carried away with glee.

Finding herself without a husband, Gerdia happily settled into her new home and into the bed of Slutain. Her wealth doubled, the size of her farm trebled and her new homestead was better built and contained more than she'd ever owned before.

Once word spread of the outcome of that incident, trouble broke out across Britain. A vicious battle took place among the Silures, in the southern mountains on the west coast. A feud that had brewed on and off for years was finally resolved, with the loss of one hundred and fifty lives, and the burning of fourteen farms.

The Cornovii who lived further north and were continually being raided by the Ordovices, recognised this as the momentum they needed to strike back. They sent a raiding party in the still of night to lay hold of the most valued person in the kingdom, their aging king. The shock of seeing warriors attired in nothing but blue paint standing at his bedside in the gloom before daybreak proved too much for the old man, and his heart failed him. He died before he could utter a word.

Once word spread that the Cornovii had slain their king without laying a hand on his body, the Ordovices were filled with fear and vowed never to set foot in the kingdom of the Cornovii again.

The Durotriges marched right through the land of the Belgae and raided their neighbours, the Dumnonii, and although the outcome of the battle was unsure, the fighting lasted two days. Many lives were lost and both sides returned home with heads hanging from their horses' brightly decorated bridles.

Life remained somewhat quieter among the Trinovantes on the east coast, with household fights taking place. A few rapes were reported and some stock theft, but on the whole they weren't as affected by the return to normality after the first few days of unearthly peace and quiet.

The biggest reversal of peaceful living to normal fighting took place among the Brigantes. They lived in the largest and most northerly area of Britain. For years skirmishes had taken place between them and the Forthri tribes of Scotland, and after a relatively quiet few months the blood of the warriors was boiling, they were spoiling for a fight. When news first arrived of the outcome of the dispute over the kidnapped wife in the land of Iceni, they were elated.

A good battle had been fought, the strongest man had won and they were stirred up by it. Within hours men and women left their farming implements and took up arms. They were going to attack the Forthri and stamp out their plundering and thievery. Queen Boudica was furious when she heard their plans. Her interests lay more in the Romans and their doings in Gaul.

She knew they were determined to seize Britain, especially after Caesar had tried and failed twice. They wouldn't be deterred forever, she reasoned. She kept abreast of all that took place in Rome and Gaul and made it her business to find out as much as possible about each new ruler. From her information it appeared that the current Emperor of Rome, Tiberius, seemed the right man to brave crossing the sea. In her opinion it was a particularly unwise time to be going into battle with the Forthri, while the Druids of Gaul were being wiped out and the Romans were gaining a stronghold in Europe.

Boudica attempted to put a stop to the battle, but she was too late. A band of warriors some five thousand strong had already crossed the border and were marching on the Forthri at a suicidal pace. Fuelled by talk of battles over the past few days they were in a bloodthirsty mood and struck the first small tribe of raiders with such force and ferocity that not one man remained alive within the first hour.

Now they were truly fired up and they advanced, a band of shrieking, raging men and women covered in the blood of their spoils. They set about killing everything that moved, man and beast alike. By the first nightfall their estimated kill was three thousand men, and one thousand livestock. That night they slept the deep and glorious sleep of the victorious.

Day two saw them braver and bloodthirstier than ever and they slaughtered a further four thousand men without loss to their own number. They suffered many injuries, some severe, but no deaths, and were made braver for their valiant effort and became careless the second night. The night watch tended the wounded, the warriors drank themselves into a deep stupor on hot ale brewed for them during the day by their women.

Once the news spread to other tribes in Scotland, neighbouring groups of Forthri banded together and marched at speed from further up country. Each time word reached them of the massacre of their people, they became more enraged.

They arrived at the camp of the slumbering Brigantes as the sun was rising on the third day of battle, and with blood curdling screams tore through the sleeping victors, wiping every last breath out of the five thousand men and woman. They took back the decapitated heads of their fallen brothers, and left the torn and bloody bodies of their foe lying in the fields, easy pickings for the wolves and vultures who would have their own fight over the bounty.

Queen Boudica was furious when she received the news. Although young, she was no fool, but she felt her people were. They'd lost five thousand able-bodied citizens who were not only warriors, but also farmers. Now they would have years of hardship while farms were short handed or unmanned, crops unplanted, harvests unpicked. And all the while the Romans were knocking at their back door.

Boudica had two young daughters to look after, and her

protective instincts were fierce. Beside her daughters, her husband, King Prasutagus, was a wealthy man and was accumulating more wealth with each year that passed. As a shrewd business woman and ruler she was not about to see her future jeopardised. Had her warriors not all perished, she would have had them punished.

She sent urgent word to Gaul recalling her personal Druid, Pantra, to Britain.

Chapter 9

THINGS were not going any better in Gaul and the Druids from Britain hadn't been able to make any difference whatsoever. The gods in Europe would not heed their entreaties.

They hadn't been able to move inland from the forest where they hid as they were constantly driven back by word of soldiers approaching the coast. They moved across the land with speed and agility, driving deeper into the few remaining forests those Druids that they didn't meet and kill. Many fled into neighbouring countries, but most agreed to seek the sanctity of Britain, to re-group in Mona, and it was apparent that if they didn't move swiftly, even that route would be closed to them.

The Druids of Britain had drawn aside from the Gaulish Druids to confer. They agreed their trip had been fruitless and they should return home, but knew that once boats started to leave, the Romans would get word and would fall upon the beach and slaughter them. They were discussing the best way to get so many priests spirited across the water unnoticed when a young messenger came rushing into the glade, breathless and ruddy in the face.

He fell at the feet of Pantra. "I'm Nobud, from the land of the Brigantes. I've been sent by Queen Boudica to address you my Lord Pantra."

"Speak!" was all Pantra said.

"There's great need for you to return to the queen," he began. "There's been much trouble in the land since you left and five thousand of the queen's warriors are dead. The Festival of Imbolc takes places in seven night's time and there are few labourers alive to plough the fields, or sow new seed. The queen needs you to implore the gods to be merciful, for without a good harvest we will surely not survive a further winter."

There was no need to say more, Pantra understood the gravity of the situation, and would hear the details many times over in the coming days from Nobud and others as soon as he crossed back into Britain. He knew the queen wouldn't have sent for him unless she had real fear. In many ways, it seemed to be the working of their gods, finally come to Gaul to assist them. They had no choice but to leave immediately, before the Gaulish Druids, whose fate was in the hands of the gods who seem to have deserted them.

The messenger Nobud travelled back with Obetach and the priests in his boat, and told them in great detail of the battle with the Forthri, as well as other incidents that had taken place in the time that the Druids had been gone, and they were aghast.

This time the crossing over the channel was not easy. A storm whipped the sea into a frenzy, the sky grew dark and menacing and rain poured into the boats, forcing the Druids to assist their slaves and bail water. Each wave seemed to grow higher and stronger than the next and the priests were seasick and terrified, barely able to chant or pray.

One of their normally robust boats, rendered flimsy with the might of the storm, took a huge wave. The sound of the sea smashing against its hull was like a lightning crack, followed by a noise not unlike thunder as the wooden craft broke in half, spilling its human cargo into the sea. Fifteen Druids made their way to the Otherworld through the cold watery grave of the treacherous channel between Britain and Gaul. There was silence on the remaining boats as the priests prayed and asked the gods to accept the sacrifice and to save Britain from the Romans in return for those lives lost.

When they finally reached land they were a shocked and drenched group. Too sick to move, they huddled under bushes and slept sitting upright until the sun rose and warmed them, and cheered their dampened spirits.

Gamenta and Vitaicus were preparing to leave the castle and make their way to the Festival of Imbolc when Obetach strode through the courtyard. Vitaicus couldn't contain himself and rushed to his priest, arms open wide in an unusual show of affection. Emotionally charged after his ordeal in Gaul, Obetach returned the embrace.

"Obetach, what a surprise, you've made it in time. We are on our way to the festival now."

Too tired to respond, Obetach fell in step with them as they walked out of the courtyard towards a group of waiting priests and priestesses.

Once again Vitaicus' mind was filled with conflicting thoughts. Since speaking to Gamenta about marrying Trasand, he hadn't seen the priest again until this morning. He had no idea what the Goddess Brigid had decreed, and as was the way of the Druids, knew he would only find out in their good time. He was finding it difficult to be patient. Since his admission he'd felt uncomfortable when seeing Trasand and avoided going to the babies. He knew she'd be at the festival, but didn't know if he'd see her. He wondered if she would bring the boys, it was a mild evening and pleasant for them to be out in the fresh air, even though it would get cooler before the long night was over.

They finally reached the clearing where a large bonfire had been set up. For the past week preparations for Imbolc had taken place and the scene around him was spectacular.

All morning his people had been arriving, bearing their gifts. There were offerings of seed, the remainder of the winter's flowers and food, and the sheep and cattle they trusted would produce offspring in the summer. The sounds and smells that surrounded the king brought back happy childhood memories of festivals past.

The first day of the celebration was an introduction and Gamenta spent time explaining to the crowd the reason for the festival. Although they could all have recited his words back to him, having heard them faithfully presented each year, they listened with interest and respect. Once he'd finished speaking, the Bards began chanting songs of jubilation and thanksgiving. Happy songs that the people could sing, to the accompaniment of lyre and harp, as more arrived to join in the festivities.

By midday the entire kingdom was present and their gifts were brought in order of standing in the community, with the commoners going first. Many were only able to bring a meagre offering, a head of corn, a handful of seeds or a bunch of wild flowers, but each gift was laid before the priests who gave thanks to the giver and blessed the offering.

As the wealthy and eminent people came forward the gifts had to be carried by slaves, large cauldrons of food and drink, cattle, sheep were placed in the circle and blessed by the priests.

Last in the proceedings came the turn of the king by which time it was growing dark. Exhausted after a long day, everyone settled down to eat whatever food they'd brought with them, then they lay where they were with each family huddling closely together for additional warmth. They covered themselves with their cloaks and slept.

At first light the people began to stir. They rubbed their cold feet and stiff bodies and washed their faces in the icy water of a nearby stream.

As soon as they were re-assembled, the novices lit the fire. They took their task seriously and although nervous they worked together and made sure that the fire was burning strongly before making way for their seniors. Pleased with their young charges, the Druids faced the assembly and Gamenta introduced the second day's proceedings. This would be the day of renewal and purification, as signified by the earth renewing itself after a long dark winter. The offerings showed the gratitude of the people for this renewal, after which they were given the opportunity to renew and purify themselves.

Once again, each member of the community came forward and asked the priests to bless them, their crops and livestock. It was an emotional time with wailing from the people and equally loud chanting from the Bards. By midday all but the king's household had been blessed and purified.

Gamenta held up his hands for silence, and it was eerie after so many hours of chaotic noise.

"Before the royal household comes to be blessed, we'll sleep for an hour and refresh our bodies."

The assembly nodded gratefully and immediately lay down where they were. No one had taken food or drink as yet, and they were hungry and emotionally drained. The slept happily, dreaming of the prosperous year ahead that this festival would ensure them. Gamenta alone remained awake, watching the course of the sun, and once he judged an hour had passed he woke them.

The Royal household was assembled, slaves, servants and

family members spread over a large area. Trasand stood at the opposite end of the brightly burning pyre to the king. The novices fed the fire constantly throughout the morning, and her cheeks were flushed pink from the heat. She was dressed in a simple gown of white decorated with gold and a vibrant blue. Gamenta and his assistants blessed the royal household one at a time, starting with the slaves and working up in order of rank, until only the king and Trasand remained.

Gamenta guided her to the centre of the holy circle to stand beside Vitaicus. He invited the king and the wet-nurse to join hands. The crowd who'd been watching respectfully fell silent. This hadn't been done with other families during the morning. The Bards who'd been chanting loudly fell silent too.

Gamenta raised his hands to the sky and called on the blessing of the Goddess Brigid over the king and Trasand as they renewed and purified their lives. He turned to the two in front of him and took their hands in his, looking at them fondly before announcing to the assembled people that they were now husband and wife. The crowd was delighted, the king stunned.

Vitaicus looked at Gamenta with amazement. The lean and stringy priest with his unruly red hair, freckled and pimpled face, smiled at him showing large teeth that protruded too far out of his upper jaw, a jaw which seemed to move perpetually and gave him the appearance of a hare munching on a tasty meal. But his unusual features had become less startling and strange to the king the more time he spent in the young man's company, and he began to realise that Gamenta was extremely wise, despite his reticent nature which could easily lead one to believe that he was dim witted. His greatest strength, thought Vitaicus on reflection, was his unflappable and determined nature, nothing seemed to throw him, least of all Vitaicus' strange request regarding Trasand.

Vitaicus felt secure in the certain knowledge that the gods had blessed this union – he had absolute assurance that Gamenta had received a favourable reply from the Goddess Brigid. He smiled contentedly back at Gamenta.

Trasand also smiled at him but for very different reasons. This was undoubtedly the happiest day of her life because it assured her future and that of her son. Gods permitting, they both faced a safe and secure life with this powerful man who stood beside her – her new husband, the king.

Gamenta announced to the assembly that the feasting could begin. They again roared with pleasure, as novices led forward a large boar that had been kept for last.

A long and extremely sharp knife was handed to the novice chosen for the task of slaying the beast. He took a nervous breath and aimed at the chest of the boar, and then squeezed his eyes shut as he lunged the knife deep into the animal's body.

Having closed his eyes for those final and crucial split seconds, he missed his mark and instead of dying instantly, the beast reared up in pain as the knife went in, before collapsing in a heap before the frantic priest. Blood spurted from its wound and sprayed across Trasand's wedding gown. The boar thrashed around making a hideous groaning sound accompanied by the hiss of its punctured lung and the gurgle of blood frothing at its mouth.

Its convulsions went on and on as the stunned crowd watched silently, the priests prayed frantically and the Vates divined the signs seen in its movements. Trasand clamped her hand over her mouth to stop herself from gagging. Finally the awful sounds and thrashing of the boar ceased and the stricken beast died at the feet of the novice.

Obetach addresses the shocked crowd. "The signs are of a good omen," he cried, "the king and queen will be blessed."

The crowd sighed with relief and for the remainder of the day sounds of merriment and celebration filled the air, and the smells of roasting meat and vegetables being cooked over hundreds of small fires. The people ate and drank well into the night.

The last day of the Festival of Imbolc was the day of closure, and after the Druids had spent time with the gods, they came before the people and retold stories of the past, of festivals such as this one, and of the goodness of the gods.

The Celts loved the story telling and settled down to listen with the patience of people who knew and understood the hardships of life and appreciated a day of rest. They knew the gods would smile upon them for their faithful offerings and so they sat and listened and enjoyed themselves. Tomorrow would be time enough to face life once again.

Chapter 10

AD 31
Summer

VITAICUS and Trasand sat in a field of wild flowers, watching the boys. Dylan had grown tired of crawling and was desperately trying to walk. He went from tree to tree where he'd hoist himself up against its trunk onto his wobbly legs, stagger forward a few steps before falling down and crawling off to the next tree. Pren watched with bright eyes, clapping his hands each time Dylan walked, laughing gaily when he fell.

Although Pren could crawl, he preferred to sit still and watch what went on around him. He'd shown no inclination yet to stand or walk. He appeared to his parents to be a thinker, unlike his brother who was always busy doing. However, Trasand reasoned, nine months was very young for a boy to be walking, Pren will follow soon enough.

She was quite sure there was nothing wrong with her own son but knew without doubt that Dylan was special. She watched his strong little legs as he gained confidence and progressed a few more steps.

She smiled and looked across at Vitaicus but he'd not noticed, the furrow of his brow showing his concern at something.

"What troubles you so on such a glorious summer's day. You should be enjoying our sons, not troubled by thoughts so dark they've taken the sparkle out of your eyes and set a straight line along your lips."

Vitaicus was startled by her perception. "Ah my love, it's the Romans again." He lay back against the trunk of a tree and looked up at the cloudless sky. "I hear talk that Tiberius is mounting a campaign against us. He feels he can accomplish what Caesar couldn't."

Trasand's life before she married the king had been a simple one, working hard each day in order to survive. Planting, harvesting, sewing, cooking and preparing for the next winter. These were the only things she knew about until she met Vitaicus. Only then did she begin to learn of the greater world around her, of merchants, wealth and wars. Her father had often gone out to fight, just as all farmers had, that had been a way of life, Celt fighting Celt and was in no way related to the recent talk of Gaul, of Rome, and of Britain being taken by foreign peoples.

"Tell me about Caesar," she asked, and knowing that she was really interested, he did, fetching the boys to sit and listen too, even though they were too small to understand.

"When my father was the age of Dylan and Pren, the Romans first came, seventy-seven winters ago. Julius Caesar, their Emperor was a wily character, a warrior to be feared. In the years before he attempted to annex Britain he'd won many victories in other countries. He wanted to rule the whole of Gaul. Then he set his sights on us, saying he wished to explore Britain as he'd a keen interest in customs. But in truth he was aware of the trade between Gaul and Britain and knew we had great wealth. He wanted to enrich his war chest and earn a tribute back in Rome."

"Anyway, to get to us they had to cross the channel and the Romans had little experience of these treacherous seas. They put together a major force with two legions and eighty ships but they left too late in the season, which was ultimately their undoing. One morning, just about dawn, Caesars ships were spotted nearing the cliffs of Dover, but he realised he couldn't land there, so he went further up the coast and as he sailed our people ran along the cliffs, keeping pace with his force, gathering in number as they went. By the afternoon he'd found an open beach at Rutu Piae, here in the land of Canti, where he could land, but we were waiting when they tried to disembark. His legions were seasick and weary, we were on our own soil, and we're born warriors, so we had an advantage?"

He looked at her with affection. "Although they did manage to get off their ships, Caesar spent a lot of time and energy beating off attacks on his camp, but he managed to stave them off while he waited for his cavalry to arrive. When they came it was a great shock, they were Caesar's strongest and most famous legion, the one known as the Tenth, of whom all Britain had heard. But they too were sick and afraid to disembark, so their Standard Bearer stood up and yelled at the soldiers. 'Jump, unless you wish to lose your Eagle – Follow Me'. The honour of their standard was high, and just as my warriors follow my standard, so they followed him. They jumped off the ships into the sea and followed him ashore. My great grandfather said he'd never seen a more disciplined army with such great numbers of foot soldiers, and they all had body armour, which is something we'd never used. They used javelins and short swords, which were more effective than our longer weapons, but we used our chariots and fought from our hillforts."

We learnt a lot from them," he reflected. "We attacked them as they tried to move inland, and as we had greater numbers than they, and we knew the land, we had many a small victory. I think though that we were most vulnerable because we were both farmers and warriors. When we fight against each other tribe for tribe, we respect our land, but we couldn't let the Romans near our farms, so we had to draw them away to fight."

"In Caesar's first attack he didn't progress far managing to march ten miles only. We fought hard and they suffered losses, even their victories weren't great ones, but what really defeated them was the weather. Caesar never counted on that. Our Druids called on all the gods who sent great gales to save us. Taranis, the God of Thunder came to our aid and their galleys suffered enormous damage. When Caesar saw how strong our resistance was and how even the seas obeyed our gods, he knew it was over. He was running out of food as well and so he tried to make treaties with us, the people of Canti. Some of our forefathers came to terms with him, but not many because he only stayed four days for fear of his ships breaking up, and his soldiers starving. After four days of hard fighting, little food and a battered fleet, well he was no fool, he knew it was best to leave, and so we were victorious."

"Of course, our people were fools to enter into any treaty with him. They should have known he'd be back. Caesar was not one to just give up and walk away. He wanted his trophy badly, so he went back to Rome and he built flat-bottomed boats which would stand up better to the seas."

Vitaicus sat up and rubbed his back where the tree had been digging into it.

"Go on," Trasand begged, fascinated. The boys had become restless and were off playing once again.

"I believe Caesar wanted to come back early the following year, but fighting in the south of Europe kept him there until later in the season than he planned. He finally joined his legions and his fleet at Portus Itius, near Boulogne, midway through the year."

Vitaicus drew a map in the sand with his finger. "Many merchants and adventurers voyaged with him, and he had five legions too, a much larger force than the previous year. Our people weren't ready and because some of them had treaties with him, and refused to fight, Caesar landed unopposed. With his larger force he marched right through our kingdom on the night he landed. According to my great grandfather they marched until they reached the Thames, winning a great victory on the way. But news soon reached him of another great storm raging on the coast where his galleys were. Our gods were still protecting us." He chuckled.

"When various tribal chiefs asked for peace, he agreed to some treaties but knew he had to leave quickly and get back to his fleet. He spent time re-beaching and entrenching his galleys, the ones that had survived, then marched on. At the River Stour in the land of the Trinovantes, Caesar first encountered real resistance from the formidable King Cassivellaunus. The Catuvellauni had many chariots but were no match for the Roman soldiers and Caesar defeated Cassivellanunus, capturing his main fortress at Wheathampstead."

Vitaicus shook his head in disbelief. "That left the way clear for Caesar to cross the Thames valley. The Trinovantes didn't even wait for him to reach them, they just submitted, but the rest of Britain held strong and fought off the legions bravely. It should never have been allowed, and wouldn't have happened in my time!"

He was indignant now. "Our warriors would never have allowed the Romans to land unopposed," he snorted, and then laughed as Dylan came crashing down after a particularly long wobbly walk, landing on Pren who howled in displeasure.

"Well," he continued, "they took over Cassivellaunus' entire kingdom. Our people finally woke up and launched an attack, and the fight began to get difficult for both sides. Our warriors put up a stout fight against Caesar, even though our style of undisciplined fighting was a little useless against their legions. They fought in an ordered line Trasand, can you imagine that! But I remember my great grandfather telling me how our athletic warriors in their scythed chariots clattered across the battlefields and were heroes! They fought so fiercely that they frightened the legions of Rome. They were veteran soldiers who'd fought in many campaigns in many countries but we scared them! Eventually Caesar stopped fighting and reached an agreement with Cassivellaunus, so he didn't win, but neither did he lose. When they came to a settlement, hostages and tributes were promised by the local rulers to Rome, and many were rewarded by being installed as client rulers. I believe Caesar wanted to spend the winter in Britain but the situation in Gaul was deteriorating, and so he gladly accepted the offer of hostages and tributes and left, fully intending to come back I'm sure."

He rubbed his neck and continued. "Our payment of tribute to him soon stopped and that is why I believe the Romans haven't given up on us yet. They'll be back for our wealth."

Vitaicus sighed deeply at this disturbing thought. "During his campaign in Gaul Caesar felled an entire sacred forest near Marseilles. It was tragic. Skilled Druids had spent many years sculpturing tree trunks to represent their gods Belenos and Ogmios. It was the most holy and sacred of places and Caesar simply came in and desecrated it, wiped it out. You can imagine what that meant to the Druids and how it must have angered the gods. After that there was much trouble in Gaul and an entire Roman legion was wiped out. People rebelled everywhere. Anyway, after the rebellion, there was a year of civil war in Rome. Do you know what happened next?"

Trasand shook her head, spellbound by the tale.

"We are told that Caesar was killed by his own men, those he trusted the most. Brutus and Cassius were their names. They killed him on a day the Romans now call the Ides of March, ten years after he first tried to conquer us. So the gods were avenged for the desecration of their temples," he mused.

"So that is why when I hear talk of the Romans, I'm dark in spirit. We can't allow them to come here and take hold of us. It's enough that we still have some subjects loyal to Rome. And even though Caesar is long dead, someday some Emperor will want to finish off what he started. We've too much wealth for them to ignore us. We need to keep watchful against Rome."

Despite the pleasure of hearing Vitaicus talk, his tale depressed her and although it would still be some time before sunset, Trasand was happy to gather up the children and make their way home.

Trasand's life before she married the king had been a simple one, working hard each day in order to survive. Planting, harvesting, sewing, cooking and preparing for the next winter. These were the only things she knew about until she met Vitaicus. Only then did she begin to learn of the greater world around her, of merchants, wealth and wars. Her father had often gone out to fight, just as all farmers had, that had been a way of life, Celt fighting Celt and was in no way related to the recent talk of Gaul, of Rome, and of Britain being taken by foreign peoples.

"Tell me about Caesar," she asked, and knowing that she was really interested, he did, fetching the boys to sit and listen too, even though they were too small to understand.

"When my father was the age of Dylan and Pren, the Romans first came, seventy-seven winters ago. Julius Caesar, their Emperor was a wily character, a warrior to be feared. In the years before he attempted to annex Britain he'd won many victories in other countries. He wanted to rule the whole of Gaul. Then he set his sights on us, saying he wished to explore Britain as he'd a keen interest in customs. But in truth he was aware of the trade between Gaul and Britain and knew we had great wealth. He wanted to enrich his war chest and earn a tribute back in Rome.

Anyway, to get to us they had to cross the channel and the Romans had little experience of these treacherous seas. They put together a major force with two legions and eighty ships but they left too late in the season, which was ultimately their undoing. One morning, just about dawn, Caesars ships were spotted nearing the cliffs of Dover, but he realised he couldn't land there, so he went further up the coast and as he sailed our people ran along the cliffs, keeping pace with his force, gathering in number as they went. By the afternoon he'd found an open beach at Rutu

Piae, here in the land of Canti, where he could land, but we were waiting when they tried to disembark. His legions were seasick and weary, we were on our own soil, and we're born warriors, so we had an advantage?" He looked at her with affection.

"Although they did manage to get off their ships, Caesar spent a lot of time and energy beating off attacks on his camp, but he managed to stave them off while he waited for his cavalry to arrive. When they came it was a great shock, they were Caesar's strongest and most famous legion, the one known as the Tenth, of whom all Britain had heard. But they too were sick and afraid to disembark, so their Standard Bearer stood up and yelled at the soldiers. 'Jump, unless you wish to lose your Eagle – Follow Me'. The honour of their standard was high, and just as my warriors follow my standard, so they followed him. They jumped off the ships into the sea and followed him ashore. My great grandfather said he'd never seen a more disciplined army with such great numbers of foot soldiers, and they all had body armour, which is something we'd never used. They used javelins and short swords, which were more effective than our longer weapons, but we used our chariots and fought from our hillforts. We learnt a lot from them," he reflected. "We attacked them as they tried to move inland, and as we had greater numbers than they, and we knew the land, we had many a small victory. I think though that we were most vulnerable because we were both farmers and warriors. When we fight against each other tribe for tribe, we respect our land, but we couldn't let the Romans near our farms, so we had draw them away to fight."

"In Caesar's first attack he didn't progress far managing to march ten miles only. We fought hard and they suffered losses, even their victories weren't great ones, but what really defeated them was the weather. Caesar never counted on that. Our Druids called on all the gods who sent great gales to save us. Taranis, the God of Thunder came to our aid and their galleys suffered enormous damage. When Caesar saw how strong our resistance was and how even the seas obeyed our gods, he knew it was over. He was running out of food as well and so he tried to make treaties with us, the people of Canti. Some of our forefathers came to terms with him, but not many because he only stayed four days for fear of his ships breaking up, and his soldiers starving. After four days of hard fighting, little food and a battered fleet, well he was no fool, he knew it was best to leave, and so we were victorious."

"Of course, our people were fools to enter into any treaty with him. They should have known he'd be back. Caesar was not one to just give up and walk away. He wanted his trophy badly, so he went back to Rome and he built flat-bottomed boats which would stand up better to the seas." Vitaicus sat up and rubbed his back where the tree had been digging into it.

"Go on," Trasand begged, fascinated. The boys had become restless and were off playing once again.

"I believe Caesar wanted to come back early the following year, but fighting in the south of Europe kept him there until later in the season than he planned. He finally joined his legions and his fleet at Portus Itius, near Boulogne, midway through the year." Vitaicus drew a map in the sand with his finger. "Many merchants and adventurers voyaged with him, and he had five legions too, a much larger force than the previous year. Our people weren't ready and because some of them had treaties with him, and refused to fight, Caesar landed unopposed. With his larger force he marched right through our kingdom on the night he landed. According to my great grandfather they marched until they reached the Thames, winning a great victory on the way. But news soon reached him of another great storm raging on the coast where his galleys were. Our gods were still protecting us." He chuckled. "When various tribal chiefs asked for peace, he agreed to some treaties but knew he had to leave quickly and get back to his fleet. He spent time re-beaching and entrenching his galleys, the ones that had survived, then marched on. At the River Stour in the land of the Trinovantes, Caesar first encountered real resistance from the formidable King Cassivellaunus. The Catuvellauni had many chariots but were no match for the Roman soldiers and Caesar defeated Cassivellanunus, capturing his main fortress at Wheathampstead." Vitaicus shook his head in disbelief. "That left the way clear for Caesar to cross the Thames valley. The Trinovantes didn't even wait for him to reach them, they just submitted, but the rest of Britain held strong and fought off the legions bravely. It should never have been allowed, and wouldn't have happened in my time!" He was indignant now. "Our warriors would never have allowed the Romans to land unopposed," he snorted, and then laughed as Dylan came crashing down after a particularly long wobbly walk, landing on Pren who howled in displeasure.

"Well," he continued, "they took over Cassivellaunus' entire kingdom. Our people finally woke up and launched an attack, and the fight began to get difficult for both sides. Our warriors put up a stout fight against Caesar, even though our style of undisciplined fighting was a little useless against their legions. They fought in an ordered line Trasand, can you imagine that! But I remember my great grandfather telling me how our athletic warriors in their scythed chariots clattered across the battlefields and were heroes! They fought so fiercely that they frightened the legions of Rome. They were veteran soldiers who'd fought in many campaigns in many countries but we scared them! Eventually Caesar stopped fighting and reached an agreement with Cassivellaunus, so he didn't win, but neither did he lose. When they came to a settlement, hostages and tributes were promised by the local rulers to Rome, and many were rewarded by being installed as client rulers. I believe Caesar wanted to spend the winter in Britain but the situation in Gaul was deteriorating, and so he gladly accepted the offer of hostages and tributes and left, fully intending to come back I'm sure." He rubbed his neck and continued. "Our payment of tribute to him soon stopped and that is why I believe the Romans haven't given up on us yet. They'll be back for our wealth." Vitaicus sighed deeply at this disturbing thought. "During his campaign in Gaul Caesar felled an entire sacred forest near Marseilles. It was tragic. Skilled Druids had spent many years sculpturing tree trunks to represent their gods Belenos and Ogmios. It was the most holy and sacred of places and Caesar simply came in and desecrated it, wiped it out. You can imagine what that meant to the Druids and how it must have angered the gods. After that there was much trouble in Gaul and an entire Roman legion was wiped out. People rebelled everywhere. Anyway, after the rebellion, there was a year of civil war in Rome. Do you know what happened next?" Trasand shook her head, spellbound by the tale. "We are told that Caesar was killed by his own men, those he trusted the most. Brutus and Cassius were their names. They killed him on a day the Romans now call the Ides of March, ten years after he first tried to conquer us. So the gods were avenged for the desecration of their temples," he mused. "So that is why when I hear talk of the Romans, I'm dark in spirit. We can't allow them to come here and take hold of us. It's enough that we still have some subjects loyal to Rome. And even though Caesar is long dead, someday some Emperor will want to finish off what he started. We've too much wealth for them to ignore us. We need to keep watchful against Rome."

Despite the pleasure of hearing Vitaicus talk, his tale depressed her and although it would still be some time before sunset, Trasand was happy to gather up the children and make their way home.

Chapter 11

A messenger arrived at the castle early one morning to announce that the Supreme Druid, who lived on the island of Mona, was desperately ill. The senior Druids of the land were summoned to his side.

The journey to Mona was a long and dangerous one, and the Druids faced much hardship as they marched across the land, coping with the weather and passing through kingdoms where there was continual fighting between the tribes.

Most of the senior priests were elderly and some still weakened from a strange disease they seemed to have picked up when in Gaul just before Imbolc. The older priests had been more susceptible and had coughed continually and grown weaker daily since leaving the shores of the continent. Obetach knew in his heart that many would not return from Mona.

Obetach's group travelled north, crossing the River Thames into the land of the Trinovantes, where more priests joined them. They continued marching as Druids joined them from the Iceni and the Catuvellauni. They'd just reached the land of the Cortiani when they were required to settle an argument between two women.

They came upon the pair at the edge of a raging river. The elder of the two, Nylluwa, had spent the morning collecting woad with which to paint her warrior husband who was preparing to go to battle along with his neighbours. A raiding party had stolen some of their livestock and Nylluwa's husband was determined to catch them, retrieve his livestock and wipe out the thieves. He refused to leave though until he and his men were painted blue from head to toe as was traditionally done in summer, when warriors preferred to fight naked but for the blue paint. Nylluwa had been sent to collect the woad.

Her neighbour, Parmeld, was determined to stop Nylluwa from taking the woad back to the warriors. Her own husband, the champion warrior in the region, was suffering from a strange ailment. His body had broken out in boils and lesions that seeped pus continually. While he was covered in his daily clothing, he'd been able to keep his condition from his neighbours, but covered in a coat of thin paint, they would spot his condition and taunt him, perhaps even forbid him to fight.

Parmeld felt certain that if her husband didn't go to battle, he would lose his position of champion to their closest neighbour and archrival, the husband of Nylluwa. The thought of seeing her enemy afforded the best portion of boar at the celebratory feast was enough to make her devious.

In order to save his honour by refusing to go to battle in a coating of woad, Parmeld decided to prevent any of them wearing the paint by getting rid of any woad found in the area.

The Druids arrived as Parmeld was about to push Nylluwa into the raging water, with her armload of the precious blue plant. Stifling a laugh, Obetach ordered Wyndem to see to the feud.

At the sight of the priests the woman had no choice but to leave their argument and sit at the feet of the learned men. After a lengthy prayer invoking the gods, two priests seated themselves directly in front of the women. Wyndem asked the reason for their fight. Each woman began to speak loudly, pointing and poking at the other, until they tumbled over in a heap, pulling hair and scratching faces. Wyndem forbid either of them to speak.

They waited a full hour in silence while the Bards chanted, waiting on the gods, until a plover who'd been pecking around in the long grass moved closer. Curious at the sound of the chanting, it hopped around, stopping on the left side of Parmeld. Seeing that as a sign from the gods, Wyndem gave her permission to speak first. Once she'd told her story with a minimum of interruptions and restraining, Nylluwa was permitted to speak.

The priests nodded, shook their heads, muttered and murmured throughout the tales. Wyndem instructed the women to sit with their backs to each other, one facing east, the other west while the Druids again awaited word from the gods.

Men of patience they would sit all day, all night, as many days and nights as the gods needed. Fortunately for the women, who were growing cold and anxious about their men, the gods were swift to answer and it was a mere half hour before a crow flew past, circled above the curious scene, spotted a leftover morsel of food from the priests midday meal, and landed. The position in which it landed was vital. The prayers and incantations of the Druids had been that the gods would reveal which woman was the wisest, and the gods had sent this crow to land beside her.

Although many of the priests had been eating while they'd waited, and there were crumbs and other remnants of food spread all over, the crow had no hesitation in landing at the feet of Nylluwa. It was therefore decreed that the warriors would go to war painted in blue with no other covering, and the fate of Parmeld's husband rested entirely with the gods.

The woman wouldn't dare question the Druids and after having heard their fate they helped each other up, took an armful of woad each and started on their way back to their men folk, chatting happily together.

Having wasted a large portion of the day, the Druids prepared to spend the night at the side of the river. They still had five days march ahead of them before they'd reach the coast in the land of the Degeangli where they would make their crossing by boat to Mona. They prayed they'd arrive before the Supreme Druid passed on to the Otherworld.

A messenger found them shortly after they'd risen the following morning. They were cold, stiff and hungry but delighted to hear that the Supreme Druid was better and no longer required them. Without so much as a sigh, the priests who were so accustomed to hardship and obeying the gods and their leaders, turned and began marching towards Vernemeton, where they would offer sacrifices and give thank-offerings for the improved health of the Supreme Druid.

Their march took them the remainder of that day and once there they rested and waited for the arrival of those priests who'd already reached Mona and were now returning. Their prayers and sacrifices at such a holy place pleased the gods immensely, and they stayed there, united in spirit, praying and sacrificing for three nights before making their weary way back to their own lands.

The news that the priests were returning was greeted with delight, as it was time to prepare for the Festival of Lughnasa, choice festival of the God Lugos, to celebrate and thank the gods for the harvest. Now the senior priests would be able to prepare for the ceremony and continue in their endless task of teaching the novices.

Chapter 12

AD 31
Autumn

AS Obetach approached the outskirts of Vitaicus' kingdom on his return from Vernemeton, the gods delivered into his hands a gift of great value to give to Prince Dylan. He'd decided to make his report to the king before returning to the forest where he'd hear from Gamenta and the other priests whom he'd left in charge.

He'd just crossed the field of an affluent farmer, whose wealth was evident in the huge herd of cattle grazing in the pastures, and was nearing the roadway leading towards the king's outer hamlets when the barking of a dog startled the exhausted priest.

Obetach strode in the direction of the sound, gingerly clambering through the thorns, following the yelping, which grew louder as he approached. The dog had evidently heard or sensed his presence, and Obetach realised that the bark was one of either a really weak or young dog. He judged the animal to be close when a squeal made him reel back in surprise. He'd trodden on its foot as it was partially hidden under a nettle bush, where it had become entangled. Obetach considered his options.

There seemed none other than to cut the animal free and suffer the consequences of the nettles! No sooner had he reached into the bush, than his hands began to swell and sting, but having lived his life with the hardships of the elements, he neither flinched nor stopped, but patiently cut the dog free.

Once it was safely in his arms he sat down to examine the little creature. It was a puppy of just a month or two in age, soft and fluffy with a luxurious coat the colour of gold, although it was presently coated with mud and stank of some putrefying odour. Despite this Obetach was enchanted and as the puppy licked his face the priest's heart melted. He would have sat there all day enjoying this love and affection, something so rare in his life, but the pain and swelling in his hands and arms forced him to his feet. It only took a moment to decide what to do with the puppy.

Dogs were highly esteemed animals among the Celts, along with the wolf and the fox, and this puppy would be a most suitable early birth anniversary gift for Dylan and Pren, one that they could share and which would enable the boys to grow up respecting and loving nature in a way that would make their own training as Druids easier to bear, when they were taken from home to live in the forest. Elated with his gift, Obetach continued on his way to see the king.

The puppy was so filthy when it was presented to Dylan that Trasand immediately ordered slaves to wash the smelly creature. After three separate baths, his previously matted coat was soft and shiny, and his odour that of lavender.

The soap that was used time and again to scrub him had been made for the queen's use, and crushed lavender was boiled into each bar before it was left to cool and set. The puppy was immediately named Sopa, the Celtic word for the soap that transformed him into the handsome animal that lay contentedly curled up in the little lap of Dylan who himself was fast asleep.

It was a week since Obetach rescued the puppy and his hands and arms were no better, if anything they were worse and the priest was unable to perform the most simple of tasks without the help of Gamenta.

His priests had administered different poultices and medications, and many prayers, chants and sacrifices had been offered to the gods, but there was no improvement in his condition and he became weaker by the day. The poison from the nettles seemed to have affected his entire body, he was unable to eat or sleep and his usually sharp brain became woolly and stupid.

In desperation Gamenta sought other learned priests and priestesses, some so old they were said to be as ancient and wise as the oak tree. They agreed they needed to gather fresh mistletoe, and make a significant sacrifice to the gods. This could only be done on the night of the sixth day after the full moon when it reached considerable influence. Fortunately for the stricken priest the moon had been full just three nights previously.

Once the Druids were gathered in the king's courtyard, they began marching towards the woods, chanting as they went and calling the people to join them. As more people joined the column, the chant grew louder and louder,

"Aidhe, doire luchd – doire luchd,
Aidhe doire Leigh, doire Leigh".

"Hey to the woods people! To the woods people!
Hey to the woods for healing, to the woods for healing."

For this ceremony the Druids wore thick hooded cloaks made of the softest wool and dyed in many colours and they looked quite unlike they did at any other official ceremony. The king's people who were only too pleased to give their best to sacrifice to the gods offered white oxen to the Druids.

Those who chose to attend the ceremony were led by the Druids into the mysterious world of the sacred forests, deeper than they'd ever been before, to a place without sky as the trees entwined to form a thick canopy overhead. The Bards chanted as they walked where even the Druids had never been before, but they marched unerringly, knowing instinctively where they would find the mistletoe.

After several hours when the people were many miles from their homes, the Druids stopped. They'd found the sacred tree and there was a hushed, expectant air all round. The crowd was afraid, as they knew they'd never find their way home again without the priests, and amazed that the Druids were able to find this sacred tree so deep in the forest.

High in this one tree's twisted branches grew a bunch of bright green leaves, the single tree that the gods had chosen to bless. Each year the Druids would lead the people to whichever tree had been honoured, and although never in the same place, they'd always find it, the only tree where this strange and sacred plant with its enormous healing powers, could grow. A plant with no roots in the ground but which had green leaves symbolising life coming out of death, it would be used to bring life back to Obetach.

The exhausted people sat on the hard ground while the Druids prepared a banquet for them. Slaves carted huge quantities of food, animals to slaughter and roast, vegetables to cook and fruit and mead to finish off the banquet. Novices prepared fires and made preparations for the sacrifice. Once the banquet was ready, four novices led two white bulls with their horns bound together, to the fireside. The bulls stood by quietly while the feasting took place, even they seemed to realise the solemnity of the occasion.

Once satiated, the people watched in reverent silence as the priests and priestesses removed their sandals. A cauldron of holy water was brought into the centre of the gathering and one by one the Druids washed each other's feet, drying them with their robes. Once they were purified, a simple offering of grain and wine was made to the gods.

This was the signal for the people to form a circle and begin to walk slowly round the tree following the course of the sun. Gamenta, in a sparkling new white robe with his golden sickle in his hand, began to climb the sacred tree.

With few footholds and his long robe catching his feet, it was a difficult climb but the thought of Obetach's suffering served to spur him on, and he stretched his arms and legs until with the tips of his fingers, he touched the precious green leaves. Far below him a white cloak was spread on the ground.

Gamenta stretched his arm to its limit and gathered up the entire plant, then with a quick prayer of thanks to the gods, he cut it with his sickle and threw it into the safety of the cloak. Most of the mysterious plant would be used to heal the poisoning that had taken place in the body of Obetach. The remainder would be made into a potion and fed to all barren animals in the kingdom.

There would be a bounty of new livestock the following spring.

Chapter 13

OBETACH came in search of the king the night before the celebration of the first anniversary of Dylan's birth. They discussed many trivialities over a goblet of wine, before Obetach finally came to the reason for his visit.

"My Lord," he began somewhat haltingly for a man usually confident in the presence of the king. "Tomorrow is an important day in the life of the prince."

Vitaicus nodded and waited. "It's imperative that he be told of his birth and his future, of the requirements of the gods."

He paused while Vitaicus absorbed this news. The king had lived through the traumatic first thirty hours, thirty days, thirty weeks. He'd counted chariots, warriors, flocks of geese, and even bees on one auspicious occasion when a commotion had shattered the tranquillity of a peaceful summer's day.

Vitaicus had been consulting with a wealthy merchant when much shouting and hysteria from the nearby courtyard had interrupted their business. Vitaicus tried to ignore the noise, but could see the agitation on the face of his visitor and eventually they'd both rushed outside to witness an astonishing sight.

In the middle of the yard were three of the kitchen hands, pretty young girls who'd just finished scrubbing out the large earthen pots used for the previous evenings meal. They'd chosen to rinse them in the pond at the centre of the courtyard rather than going through the tedious routine of rinsing them in the water reservoir at the bottom of the yard set aside for kitchen use.

The honeysuckle that grew up the oak tree beside the pool had attracted a swarm of bees. The most amazing aspect of the strange scene before the king was not that the young maidens were screaming, they were calm and quiet, but the stable hands that were on their way to the kitchen for their morning tea were the ones who were hysterical and responsible for disturbing the king.

Before Vitaicus could react, Gamenta rushed into the courtyard and began an incantation, which sent the sacred creatures on their way. Vitaicus managed a quick count of the bees and once well past the number thirty sighed with relief and guided his guest back indoors.

He was tired of waiting on the gods to take his son but immediately regretted the thought and wondered if they could read his wayward and rebellious mind. He shook his head as he remembered the incident and with an effort brought his mind back to the present. He didn't want to be reminded that on some unexpected day his son was required to be sacrificed but he listened to the wise man before him without comment.

"There is another issue that needs to be addressed." Once again Obetach waited while the king drank from his goblet, giving him time to adjust to anything that the priest had to say.

"The prince needs his own Druid, one who will guide and teach him and prepare him for his years of training. It's time that the appropriate priest be set aside, and it's also fitting for that priest to relate to the prince the circumstances surrounding his birth."

Vitaicus nodded thoughtfully.

"It will be a requirement of the priest appointed to the prince to relate the story to him every year on the anniversary of his birth. He must never forget his special standing with the gods and must always be ready for the day of his calling, his sacrificial death."

Vitaicus shivered with the chill of a man sick to his bones, but nodded once again. It did seem a wise decision. He knew that Obetach wouldn't have approached such a subject without already having set aside the priest who'd take over the enormous responsibility of raising his first born son, the task of teaching him all things spiritual and otherwise. He waited, barely daring to breathe, to hear the name that would alter his future dealings with his child.

From this day forward Dylan would become more the responsibility of this unknown person, and less that of his father, the king.

"I have spent much time in meditation and consultation with the gods, and it has become apparent that there is only one Druid worthy of this high honour, only one priest to whom I'd trust the future upbringing of the prince."

Vitaicus waited, looking at Obetach, willing him to say the name without delay, but Obetach was staring into the fire seemingly oblivious of his king's impatience.

"Gamenta," was all he finally said.

Vitaicus sat stunned, then slowly felt relief flood through him. He'd expected the chosen priest to be a stranger, a learned man from another land even, not someone from his own household, someone whom Dylan knew and even loved. The more he pondered on this news the more amenable he became.

Why, Gamenta was a fine man, and although perhaps younger than the king would himself have chosen, he'd already proved himself to be responsible and well learned. He would be most suitable.

The following morning, Obetach asked for Dylan to be sent to him. Mystified, the king himself took the boys to the audience chamber where Obetach and Gamenta waited for them. Gamenta sat on a wooden stool beside his senior. Obetach smiled at the boys, and told them to sit on the floor in front of him.

"I have a story to tell you, a most important tale, and one which you'll hear often in your life."

The boys were delighted and settled down to wait even though they didn't understand the words. They'd spent many hours in their first year listening to their parents and attendants relating the history of their clan, the land, and the Druids. Poems, chants, songs and war cries were sung, and they delighted in this time that adults spent with them.

Vitaicus settled into a large chair, intrigued, and waited too to hear the tale. Like all Celts he loved stories and as there was no written word, their entire history was learned and recited from generation to generation.

"On a stormy night just one winter ago, the gods desired the life of a gentle and kind person, someone to keep them company in the Otherworld. She had to be a very special woman, and so they chose your mother, the great Queen Hilfuth, may her soul live forever with the gods."

Dylan smiled as he gathered he was being spoken about. "The

gods chose to give to your father our exalted king, a special gift. They sent you, Prince Dylan, to replace the life of your mother."

Dylan grinned again, while the king shifted uncomfortably in his chair. He'd hoped all that was behind him and he'd no intention of raising it with Dylan at any stage, but it was too late, Obetach was continuing with the tale. Gamenta listened intently.

"I was present when it took place and I saw the great Gods Taranis, Esus and Teutates." He paused.

"They took your mother and told me that you could remain here with your father for a while. Your life is to have great significance, as they require you, Prince Dylan, to be a Supreme Sacrifice to them at their decreed time. This is an honour above all others, and only a truly blessed and special person could ever become a Supreme Sacrifice. The gods require divine and perfect offerings such as princes and kings. Remember this well, and keep yourself perfect until they require you. Don't allow your body to be harmed in any way, keep it unblemished, undefiled and perfect. You are to join the order of the Druids on the eighth passing of your birth anniversary, to learn the ways of the gods and to serve them until the appointed time."

He looked across at Vitaicus who'd gone pale, but nodded at Obetach in reluctant consent.

"It will be the duty of Gamenta to remind you of this each year on the anniversary of your birth."

Vitaicus knew he had no choice but to agree to this new situation. Obetach continued telling the boys of the choosing of Dylan's name given to him by Taranis, the Great God of Thunder, and although they grew restless and understood none of what the priest said, they sat through the long tale, until eventually Vitaicus was able to pick them up and carry them off to play.

In the weeks prior to the first birth anniversary of Dylan and Pren, all around his kingdom Vitaicus' subjects were preparing presents for the boys. It was accepted that Pren was equal to the royal prince in every aspect but blood, and so duplicate gifts were made. Carpenters carved elaborate toys for them, miniature horses and carriages, wooden warriors and weapons. Seamstresses sewed clothing of the silkiest cloth. The goldsmith, Mananius fashioned two tiny torcs of the finest strands of gold he could weave together, creating a neck-dress light enough to be worn around their small necks.

When the celebration began the first order was for Gamenta to be installed as Dylan's personal Druid. As the true prince only Dylan was being given a priest, Pren remained in the background throughout the ritual.

Obetach had recovered sufficiently to officiate in the simple ceremony, naming Gamenta as Dylan's guardian and priest and reciting his many responsibilities in the life, education, safety and well being of the future king.

Chapter 14

AD 32

Autumn

A messenger arrived at the castle just as the sun was setting on the third day after the Festival of Samain. It was apparent that he'd ridden hard. Dylan and Pren were playing in the courtyard under the watchful eye of Trasand when the man came rushing in, hair awry, face flushed, and too breathless to speak. The boys ran over to greet him, talking animatedly, their vocabulary growing as fast as their two-year-old bodies. Their constant shadow, Sopa, bounded after them.

Trasand led the messenger inside where he could take a drink and catch his breath, while the excited boys prodded him with endless, unanswered questions. When he'd recovered sufficiently he asked to speak to Obetach.

Trasand was taken aback as she'd assumed he was carrying a message for the king, but sent the boys scurrying away to find the Druid, while she herself went in search of Vitaicus.

The news was devastating and would bring about turmoil throughout the land. The Supreme Druid was dead. All senior Druids were required to make their way with the greatest of speed to Mona where a new Supreme Druid would be chosen. The priest who excelled in dignity above all others would succeed the dead Druid and be required to remain on the sacred island, overseeing the Druidship of Britain.

This was a time of great trial for all priests and tensions ran high among them and their kings and queens as they faced the possibility that their Druid would be chosen and their kingdoms disrupted. No king was more anxious than Vitaicus, as Obetach was highly respected, more senior than most, and had the natural ability required for that high position.

After a quick meal the messenger left on a fresh horse to continue spreading the word. Eight nights later the entire country had heard the news, the Supreme Druid was indeed dead and immense sadness and despair took hold of all priests and priestesses across Britain. For as many years as most of them could remember, this wise old man had led the country in spiritual affairs. Now that he was with the gods in the Otherworld, they wondered if they'd ever find one as wise to replace him. What if the gods were angry with the people, what if they now faced disaster, famine, even war from across the sea? The threat of a Roman invasion was ever present in their minds.

The chants of the Druids could be heard from deep within forests everywhere, while the wailing and mourning of the people brought farming and fighting to a standstill.

The Druids assembled at various points, ready to make their second journey to Mona in a short time. For Obetach it would be a long and weary way as he wasn't entirely well and he said a sad farewell to his priests, not sure if he would see them again in this world.

Almost beside himself, Vitaicus couldn't bear to see Obetach leave, and sent his greetings with Trasand. She hugged the priest gently and begged all the gods to be with him as he made his dispirited way out of the castle.

No sooner had the Druids clambered aboard boats for Mona, than word reached Vitaicus that Emperor Tiberius and his legions were on their way. Having carried out ongoing skirmishes and battles in Gaul, the Romans were determined to conquer the Celts on the island over the sea, and Vitaicus and others feared for their kingdoms. Word was sent out calling together an assembly of kings, queens and noblemen and women.

Without senior Druids at hand, the priests in training who were left in charge of the spiritual affairs of the people hurriedly agreed that the assembly would take place in the land of Iceni. This meant that Vitaicus had to travel far from home to attend.

He went in search of Trasand to tell her the news and found her singing to the boys, who were snuggled up in their bed, covered with a soft lamb's wool blanket, which had been woven by a skilled craftswoman as a birth anniversary gift.

Vitaicus knelt beside the boys' bed and bent down to kiss their soft cheeks then beckoned Trasand to follow him. She too kissed them before blowing out some of the candles lighting the room, leaving two glowing dimly in the far corner with the fire in the hearth lighting up the rest of the room sufficiently for them to feel secure.

"What is it my lord?" Trasand asked as soon as they were out of earshot. "It's most unusual for you to summon me at this hour." Her face showed her concern.

"Come, sit with me," he replied and took her hand and led her down the passageway to his own bed chamber, a room Trasand only entered on his invitation.

"I'm leaving soon," he began hesitantly, "to an assembly of all rulers that will take place in the land of Iceni," he looked at her, gauging her response before continuing.

"I don't understand," she said, "why do you look so uncertain, so fearful of going to this assembly? Surely there's no reason for you to be so?"

She searched his eyes for an answer.

"It's not the assembly that worries me, but what will follow," he said simply.

Not understanding, Trasand waited for an explanation.

Vitaicus stood and stretched, then walked over to a shelf on the wall near the fireplace. He poured two goblets of wine and drank the first in a gulp, then refilled his goblet before returning to sit next to his wife. She took her wine from him and drank without speaking.

"At the assembly we must decide what to do about the Romans. We can't continue to let them threaten our land, our economic stability and wealth. We can't allow them to wipe out our priests as they have done in Gaul. We must attack them now while they are still over the sea where it's easiest for us to strike and surprise them."

"But surely, when the priests meet at this assembly and call on the gods, they will do this for you. Surely you, the kings, don't need to go to war, or at least if there is a war, you should send the warriors, the slaves, but you stay, you're needed here to rule," she ended softly, realising that her argument was shallow.

"If our people go to war and lose, there's nothing to rule. If they go to war without their kings, they'll surely lose."

"But the gods..." Trasand began.

"The gods will speak," Vitaicus interrupted with conviction, "but our most learned Druids are not here. Will these young priests who've been left in charge even understand what the gods want? We can't rely on them, we must take up arms ourselves and destroy the Romans."

His voice was rising with passion as he spoke and Trasand knew that further argument was useless, instead she asked, "What of boats and chariots, how will you fight without chariots and horses, or will you take those over the seas with you?"

"That's what we'll decide at the assembly. Each king and queen must give up what he has, put it together so we can fight as one, then we'll see if there are enough boats to take chariots. We shall have to see," he finished thoughtfully.

After gazing into the fire for some time he threw his empty goblet to the floor, startling Trasand, then took her by the hand and led her to his bed. "Come lie with me until it's light, for that is when I leave."

The suddenness of it all saddened Trasand, and she would have preferred to lie in his arms and talk softly through the night, but she knew her man and was content to let him vent his feelings as he made furious love to her, before falling into an exhausted sleep. All too soon and without sleep herself, Trasand saw the first lightening of the sky as the sun streaked it with pale shades of pink and mauve.

For once morning was unwelcome, Trasand would have preferred the night to last forever.

Chapter 15

AD 32
Winter

Dylan and Pren stood on either side of Trasand, holding her hands. Dylan's were chubby but strong, Pren's long and thin. They waved gaily with their free hands, and Trasand watched the pride on the face of their father as he waved in return. He looked briefly at her before turning his horse towards the gate of the courtyard, and then he was gone. Along the way they'd meet up with the many clients and clans who made up his kingdom. Wealthy men, noble men, chieftains and aristocrats, they would join with him and represent his kingdom at the assembly. Once again the mood was sombre, as if they'd already lost a battle.

It took six nights of hard travelling before Vitaicus and his men reached the large hilltop fort that was built after Caesar's first invasion. It was surrounded by a high timber fence, and was a cleverly designed and strongly built fortification. In front of the outer timber wall was a deep ditch and before the entrance a long twisting and complicated path then two sets of heavy gates. This strong fortress had been built in anticipation of the return of Caesar. It seemed an appropriate place to meet and discuss the ongoing problem of the Romans.

Three nights after Vitaicus arrived everyone was assembled, and during the time of waiting the young priests and priestesses sought the will of the gods. They sacrificed various offerings from fruit and vegetable, to animal and bird. They divined the future and read signs and their chanting could be heard day and night.

While they continued with their activities, the leaders of the land sat in groups and discussed the problem. They named that which they were prepared to give, chariots, warriors, boats, livestock, and as each new party arrived, they added to the growing inventory. Bards memorised their pledges of support, but as the days passed, there was mounting discontent. Kings in neighbouring lands questioned other's pledges, claiming that they held back, stating that they gave only half of what they had. Accusations were disputed and arguments broke out throughout the fortification. With fighting in their blood these men and women sparred and quarrelled, cursed and shouted. The accused refused to give more, their accusers refused to back down, and after days of disagreement they became locked in despair and sat in moody silence, waiting for someone, anyone, to break the deadlock.

Finally the priests were ready for them and the assembly waited attentively to hear what the gods had decreed in a matter in which the leaders could not agree.

The priest deemed the most senior of the novices, stood trembling before his audience. A fine lad of just seventeen years of age, he was overawed by the presence of the gods, and of these men and women. He began haltingly, but gained confidence as his enthusiasm for his task took hold of him. "As your councillors and spiritual leaders in the absence of your own priests, we've spent many hours consulting with the gods and divining their wishes at this perilous time, and it has become clear to us that we cannot proceed with this assembly, as by chance this gathering is in an inauspicious month. In reading the stars and setting out a pattern from the moon, the Vates have seen that this month is one with twenty-nine days, most un-fortuitous. Furthermore, by the time you were all assembled it was well past the second half of this inauspicious month and we are now into the period of the 'returning night'. To make any decisions during this time would be courting disaster, and it's our advice that we return again in the new month, one which we deem will be an auspicious one, and further that this assembly should take place under the full moon of the first half of the month, during the 'returning light'. Then the gods will be with us to guide us as to the question of the Romans."

Despite the age and relative inexperience of the novices that stood before the large assembly of leaders, despite the seriousness of the threat of the Romans or the number of days many of them had marched to be there, no-one questioned the word of the priest, but prepared to return to their kingdoms. The word of the Druid stood, the assembly was over.

As they readied to leave the fortification, someone noticed the dust trail of a messenger in the distance, and they all hurried to the western side of the fort to watch him. Heavy palls of smoke rose behind him and filled the sky, and as he drew nearer the smoke grew thicker and blacker, and the earlier mood of optimism immediately turned to one of distress. The smoke that filled the sky was coming from the west, from Cortiani, and the leaders of that land moved to the front of the gathering to watch, their faces frozen in masks of concern.

By the time the messenger had ridden his horse up the steep and winding pathway to the top of the fort, it was evident that the fire was enormous. The sun was obliterated and darkness overwhelmed the silent people.

The news from the messenger was almost unbelievable. During a fight between two clans of the Cortiani, one man set fire to another's farmstead, and a strong winter wind fanned the flames, quickly sending the blaze out of control. Initially the warriors continued fighting, while their women and children tried to fight off the flames, but they soon realised it was futile and rushed to where the men were setting on each other with sticks and clubs.

Seeing the extent of the fire, they laid down their weapons and took up buckets of water, wet skins, sand and branches. They worked furiously in a practised and organised manner for the remainder of the day and through the night, but to no avail. Eventually they sent riders out to neighbouring hamlets. By mid afternoon the following day and despite the arrival of hundreds of helpers, fanned by the continuous wind the fire spread over an area of hundreds of thousands of acres, decimating farms, homesteads, crops and livestock. The entire southern region of the Cortiani was wiped out. Scores of people were burned and injured, hundreds died and thousands were left destitute.

The large assembly of influential men and women listened to the devastating news. Knowing they were helpless and at the mercy of the gods, they stared at each other, not knowing what to do.

Finally, the priests roused themselves and began to chant in loud voices, calling upon Taranis, the God of Thunder to send rain upon the land of the Cortiani. Impressed by this wise move, the people joined in and the chanting and wailing continued throughout that night and could be heard for miles.

Just after midnight the first clap of thunder was heard and their pleading changed to thanksgiving as rain began to fall. It rained for three days from the west coast to the east, and although the fire was staunched, the misery of homeless people increased tenfold.

The messenger who'd been sent to inform the leaders of the fire was sent to fetch the man who'd started it. For the novice Druids, judging this man was the hardest task they'd yet to perform but by the time he'd been brought to them, they'd agreed on their course of action.

When the rain stopped the assembly broke up, and in a sombre mood the leaders of the country returned to their lands. As they filed off the hilltop, the sounds of the chanting Bards comforted them little as they picked their way in broody silence over the slippery terrain, leaving just three priests behind to deal with Vercd, the guilty man. He was put in a deep cave where he couldn't contaminate anyone else with his wickedness, and was guarded day and night until full moon. His crime was deemed serious enough for the man to be offered as a sacrifice and he was hung from a tree and once dead, burnt on a pyre as an offering to Esus, the Lord and Master, and the god who'd been offended most by his deed.

By the time Vercd had been sacrificed the full extent of the devastation of Cortiani had been seen. It was evident that they wouldn't be able to contribute anything to the impending battle against the Romans. The neighbouring peoples of the Cornovii, the Iceni, the Dobunni and the Catuvellauni, even the Trinovantes of the western regions of Britain would all need to help the homeless and farm-less Cortiani to survive, and they too would have far less to contribute to the cause. Almost everything they'd sworn to give up for the battle, they now gave to their fellow countrymen, all previous feuds forgotten for the moment.

Chapter 16

OBETACH had never been as pleased to see land as he was after the trip across the sea from Britain to Mona. He realised he was getting old, and the thought saddened him.

He'd enjoyed a good life on this earth and very much wanted it to continue. He wanted to see Dylan and Pren grow up and although he knew he'd spend the rest of eternity with them, leaving them while they were young would be hard. He was so much a part of King Vitaicus' life and household.

"Now I'm getting soft as well as old," he muttered to himself, as he lifted his sack of belongings and made his way across the pebbled beach towards the rest of the group that had been in his boat.

They faced a long walk to the Supreme Druid's residence, and then beyond to a sacred grove in a forest of oaks. This grove was set aside for the sole purpose of choosing a successor to a Supreme Druid and it had only been used twice in the past sixty years.

It was with trepidation that the priests set off in search of a place so difficult to find, so seldom used that no one even remembered its whereabouts. No human had passed that way for thirty-nine years, the path was overgrown beyond recognition to the handful of priests who'd been there previously.

Yet in the unerring way of the Druids, they followed the signs laid out for them by the gods, and found the grove and were ready to perform this sacred task, so far away from their own homes, on the Island of Mona, the place believed to have been the kingdom of Dylan The Great, sole survivor of the mighty flood.

Obetach sat musing about being in the land of Dylan for such an auspicious occasion. He pondered the significance of this in the life of young prince Dylan, having already been called by the gods to the great honour of Supreme Sacrifice.

He was forced out of his dreaming. The priests were forming a double line, the older Druids in front, followed by the senior Bards and then the Vates as they moved off in search of the focus of the ceremony, a tree growing mistletoe. As they marched in a solemn procession their voices could be heard across the island as they paid homage to the setting sun. As always in the way of the Druids, the leading priest took them to a tree deep within the forest that held the sacred green plant. This time there would be no sacrificial bull as the sacrifice would be the body of the Supreme Druid himself.

Following the procession were six young priests holding the litter that carried the body of the dead priest. He was wrapped in a golden cloak, each thread woven painstakingly by craftswomen who'd spent their entire lives mastering the art of weaving cloth with gold.

The golden torc around his neck was so large and heavy that his body wouldn't have held the weight in life, only in death could he wear it. His entire body was adorned with ornaments of the finest gold and silver, and loose diamonds glittered where they'd been sprinkled like snowdrops freshly fallen upon the leaves of a tree.

The face of the priest was serene, as death held no fear for him. He'd welcomed the release from his old and worn body and had secretly longed for the happy place in the west, the Otherworld. He'd died with a smile on his thin blue lips, as he battled to breathe his last breath.

As Oadde, the chosen Druid, began to climb the tree towards the mistletoe, golden sickle in his hand, the novices gently laid their burden on the ground. There was silence until the mistletoe was reached, then as the priest slashed at it with his sickle, the Bards began to chant, strumming at their lyres, praising the gods with one voice.

The Druids moved around the tree, hands joined together, ready with a fresh white robe, waiting to receive the mistletoe. With the precious leaves untouched by hands safely wrapped, they returned to the sacred glade.

Novices had gathered wood during the long walk and they set

up the funeral pyre. Although the Druid they were about to sacrifice was the highest ranking of all Druids, a Supreme Sacrifice himself, his pyre would be small. They weren't attempting to appease the gods, or atone for wrong doings, they were simply sending the Druid on his way into the Otherworld in a manner that would be pleasing to the gods who were waiting to receive him.

There was no need for a fire large enough to light the sky as a signal that the ceremony was taking place, for everyone of importance was present at the funeral. This would be a modest pyre, befitting the modest man the Supreme Druid had been during his life in this world.

The pyre was lit, the mistletoe lay round the old priest's face, his jewels, torc and cloak were with him and his golden sickle lay across his chest. He was ready to leave his body behind so that his soul could journey through lakes and fires on its dangerous journey into the Otherworld.

While the Bards sang and played their lyres, the Vates lifted the litter and threw it onto the roaring fire, and then the assembly sat in silent meditation, awaiting a word from the gods.

The fire died down, the acrid smell dissipated and the early glow of dawn could be seen in the sky, and still they sat in silence. Sounds of early morning stirred, birds sang, small animals scurried to and fro, a deer wandered into the glade, but startled by the last threads of smoke, bolted away, and still the priests sat motionless. The swirling mist lifted, the dew dried, and a watery sun attempted to break through the canopy of trees, although its meagre winter warmth never reached the men in the forest glade.

The sun moved across the sky, and the only sound was the occasional rumbling of a stomach, but the Druids waited patiently for a sign from the gods. Night fell early in the glade, the sun at its lowest point unable to penetrate through the trees and it was dark swiftly where they sat, waiting.

A freezing chill came up from the earth, and the ground they sat on became damp. There was no heat left in the remnant of fire and its smoke tendrils had ceased. Two hours before midnight an owl hooted in the distance, and a Bard began to chant. Swiftly the chant was taken up and the Druids rose to their numbed feet with one accord.

Although frozen stiff and hungry their only thought was the

task ahead of them. One hour before midnight the wind began to stir, gently at first in the topmost leaves of the trees above them, but as it gained in strength the breeze could be felt lower down where the priests waited. It was pitch dark, neither star nor moonlight reached them.

The Vates lit their torches and as if on cue, leaves began to fall from the trees, first one, then another, then two at a time as the Druids praised the gods with one voice. Four leaves landed beside four priests. These were four of the most learned and senior Druids and there was much murmuring and agreeing with the gods. Oadde addressed the assembly.

"We must decide between the priests who we believe will best serve the gods and the people as the new Supreme Druid?"

All heads turned towards the chosen four and everyone began to speak at once, each priest offering up his opinion and advice. Oadde listened as if with a hundred ears and after a long while raised his hands for silence.

"Of the four you have selected Obetach. He is held in the highest esteem of all Druids, however, his health is of great concern to many of you, therefore it seems prudent and is the opinion of the majority of you that Pantra – Arch Druid of the royal household of Queen Boudica, be appointed as Supreme Druid over all."

A spontaneous cheer went up and that was it, the decision was made and would never be questioned at any time. Once the priest Oadde had spoken, it was done.

A gown of gold studded with rubies and pearls and a torc of unequalled beauty were handed to Oadde. Although smaller and lighter than the torc burned with the previous Supreme Druid, it was far more valuable and magnificent.

The torc and gown were passed around and each priest touched and blessed them until they reached Oadde again. The priest placed the cloak around the shoulders of the newly appointed Supreme Druid, clipped the torc around his neck and lay prostrate on the earth at his feet. The other Druids followed suit. After some time they began their march out of the sacred oak glade and back to the residence of the Supreme Druid and welcome warmth.

Before the feasting could begin however, the remaining possessions of the dead Druid were offered to Teutates, the

Supreme God. Slaves had been busy during the time the Druids were away and had assembled his possessions on the side of the lake on the property of the great priest's residence.

As soon as it was light enough his chariots were wheeled down to the water's edge and pushed in at the deepest end of the lake. Every piece of furniture that belonged to the old priest was thrown in after the chariots. Then a boat was loaded with all the weapons that were owned by the Druid and members of his household. His slaves rowed out into deeper water, and so laden was the craft that it took a full hour's turn of the sun to throw them overboard.

Once the slaves returned to shore a second boat was rowed into the centre of the lake, and its contents were sent to the deepest depths to appease the gods who lived there. These were the most valuable of the Druid's treasures, the trumpets and lyres belonging to his Bards, the cauldrons and goblets used by his Vates, painstakingly crafted by the best artisans in Britain, each sunk to the floor of the lake. Then came a boatload containing his personal wealth.

Torcs of pure gold, others interwoven with gold and silver, ornaments and broaches, staves and goblets and wooden chests containing lumps of gold, silver, and bronze. Precious stones glistened in the early sunlight before they too sank.

All the while the Druids chanted the praises of their departed Supreme Druid. Finally the last of his treasures were gone, offered at great cost to the gods. The new Supreme Druid would be required to start afresh with his own following of priests, his own wealth and store of weapons and chariots.

All that remained to be done was for the last symbol of his reign, his slaves, to be set free. His priests came forward with tools to break the chains of the kitchen hands, garden workers, housekeepers and servers. The slaves were symbolically linked together as they'd been when they were first purchased. As each one was set free, their chains and tools were flung far out into the lake and with that symbolic gesture the slaves were freed.

And so it was with the death of the Supreme Druid that enormous wealth lay in the hands of the gods at the bottom of the lake in Llyn Cerrig Bach on the island of Mona.

Chapter 17

AD 33
Spring

Although she'd been summoned after dark and had covered herself in a man's cloak in an effort not to be recognised, someone did see Sebilus leave her mud hut at the farthest end of the hamlet where Vitaicus' servants lived.

They watched as she made her way stealthily through the yards, steering clear of the horses' stables lest they should hear her and snort. Leaving the path she took the long way so as not to be seen in the light of the fires that burnt in the servants' courtyard. She moved swiftly until she was finally in darkness under a moonless night.

She slowed to catch her breath before making her way directly to the main entrance of the king and queen's quarters, avoiding the kitchens and the staff entrance where slaves tended fires throughout the night.

There was little need for speculation. If Sebilus was summoned during the night, it could mean one thing only, the queen was with child, and with the first sign of daylight the news began to spread. With each passing on of the incident of the night before excitement grew, and within hours the people who'd previously been locked in despair over the severe winter and shortage of food, were revelling in the wonderful news that the queen was going to produce another heir.

King Vitaicus was riding Iorrach along the main thoroughfare through his kingdom, after having been away from home for three nights while he inspected his lands, and he was amazed at the changed attitude of his people.

Although he didn't know the reason for their merriment he found it contagious, and he turned for home instead of continuing on with his inspection so that he could share this bit of good news with his wife. His people were happy once again.

Trasand had her own news to give to her husband and as he entered her chamber, he knew instantly that she'd been affected by the same mood that had changed his people overnight. Bemused, he sat down and waited for her to explain.

When he heard that she was pregnant he fell to his knees and thanked the gods. Much as he loved and cherished Dylan who was growing daily into a fine strong lad who clearly had much of his father in him, Vitaicus longed for a child with his new love, the woman who stood opposite him beaming broadly.

Deciding not to try and stretch his mind far enough to understand how his kingdom knew something he'd just found out, and Trasand herself had only had confirmed a few hours earlier, he rose instead and held her as gently as a man of his huge frame and strength was able.

His joy was short-lived however as he made his way to his private chamber later that evening. He realised that he'd not been through his daily ritual for some time and he faced the task ahead of him with dread.

It was with a heavy heart and a goblet of ale for courage that he closed the door of the room and went to a large wooden chest that stood against the far wall. He heaved against its extreme weight, cringing as it screeched on the stone floor as he slowly managed to inch it out.

When it was far enough away from the wall for him to squeeze behind it, he picked up a sharpened blade that he kept hidden in a secret compartment at the back of the chest. He felt for the flattened stone on the wall where he'd been marking off the days since his son's birth.

Each day he scratched a stripe on the wall, and after every set of seven stripes, he scored them through with a straight line. Each group of seven had been counted until there were four groups, and they too had been scratched through with a double line, representing months. With deliberate precision he marked off the past three days, and scored them through to end yet another week, and then carefully counted and re-counted the months.

This day marked the end of the twenty-ninth month since the birth of Dylan. With the sunrise of the new day, the thirtieth month would begin. With tears streaming down his face Vitaicus heaved the heavy chest back into place and sat, head in hands in his chair beside the unlit fire.

He was exhausted and frustrated, weary of continually counting, watching, waiting for the day the gods chose to fetch his son. Would this the thirtieth month be the appointed time? Now that another baby was growing inside the belly of his wife, would the gods choose to take his first son?

He couldn't bear the thought, but immediately asked their forgiveness should they have read his mind. He reminded himself of the great honour bestowed on himself and his son by the gods. He thought of the happy place Dylan would be going to and chided himself for his selfishness in wanting to keep his child to himself, thereby depriving the land of a saviour.

Times were hard, the country was in dire straits, crops had failed, fighting was once again taking place everywhere, and there was the constant threat of the Romans. Perhaps a supreme sacrifice in these dark days was needed to set things in order.

Vitaicus couldn't bear the thought of a month long vigil at the side of his son and with a huge emotional effort he gave up his constant worrying, and determined to give in to the gods. If they would take Dylan now, well then let it be.

He reached for his goblet, but decided to go instead to the one person who could console him when his mood was this dark. He left his chamber calling loudly for his faithful servant, his priest and friend Obetach.

Dylan squealed with delight while Pren screeched with fear as they rode in their father's chariot, bare dusty feet dangling off the back end. Their small hands clutched tightly to the wooden handles, which had been nailed onto each side of its frame by the king's carpenter earlier that morning.

The chariot, although the same shape and size of a war chariot, had been made for the king when the boys were just a few months old, with them in mind. Even so the carpenter hadn't anticipated the king taking them out while they were still so young, and although he'd extended the wooden plat-formed floor to allow enough room for the boys to ride behind their father and his charioteer, he'd not put in handrails at a height the boys could reach.

The light wooden frame had sides woven from the reeds that grew alongside the River Medway. The centre pole, which had a yoke on either side for two horses, was carved with imaginative pictures of wild animals. The chariot had the usual two handles up front for the king and the charioteer to hold themselves steady, and the metal fittings covering the top of them had been crafted into the shape of falcons, the king's favoured birds. They appeared to be perched atop a tree, the main trunk being the wooden handle.

The charioteer anxiously tempered the speed to keep the ride as smooth and slow as possible for the young boys. Their constant companion, Sopa, scampered beside the horses, enjoying the outing almost as much as Dylan, and far more than Pren. The king was up front next to the charioteer, shouting directions to the highly competent and experienced man, as his own nerves showed through his excitement at this first trip with the boys.

Vitaicus was taking them to visit the blacksmith. All the recent talk of Romans and war had stirred up his spirits, and he was in a hurry to have his sons grow up and be warriors.

Although they were only two and a half years old, he was having a shield and a spear made for each of them. The shields would be lightweight enough for their young arms to hold, but strong enough to protect them from stabbing each other in error as he planned to teach them to fight.

He wondered why it was that the Celts taught their children the use of spears using shields for protection, but abandoned these useful guards once they'd mastered the art of duelling. Hand-to-hand duels were the way of honour among the Celts, and Vitaicus intended for his boys to be honourable and brave.

The thought crossed his mind that Dylan would be leaving him in a few short years to become a priest, and priests never went to battle, but, he reasoned quickly as he pushed the thought aside, he may not stay with the Order beyond his first degree. He may yet be a warrior and need the skill that only his father, a great warrior himself, could teach him.

Contentedly he continued to direct the charioteer until they pulled up outside the stone hut of Fludigat. The boys were helped down from the back of the chariot, although Dylan would have preferred to jump. With his face flushed and eyes shining, he flung his arms around his father's legs and gabbled excitedly in a language that only his brother understood.

Pren on the other hand, sat on the ground and wiped the dust from his dirty hands and ashen face on the edge of his robe, then closed his eyes tightly for a few moments. When he finally stood up he was looking less pale, but was still unsteady on his feet.

They spent the entire day with Fludigat, who had patience that came of being a father himself and he explained over and over again every move he made.

Throughout the day Dylan in particular would squeak "what's that, what's that?" and Fludigat would painstakingly explain the use of each tool.

"Why? Why?" was the question when he measured the boys for their shields.

"This is a funny thing," from Pren as Fludigat took hold of a piece of metal in his long heavy tongs and "hot, hot, hot," as the boys both neared the furnace. They giggled as he pumped the bellows, and covered their ears as the craftsman banged away at the red hot metal on his anvil.

Vitaicus sat watching his boys with a new fascination. He'd never seen them so inquisitive and talkative although he understood little of what they said. They preferred to jabber at each other in their own language rather than talk to adults. His pride in them was overwhelming and he had to work at keeping his emotions in control. Fludigat's apprentice came to the king's rescue when he sat beside him and engaged the king in a lengthy discussion of the Romans and the impending war.

The hours raced by with Vitaicus voicing his innermost thoughts on the problem to the young stranger who within the first hour seemed like an old friend.

"It is all the fault of Caesar," mused Vitaicus, "if he'd never set foot on our shores we wouldn't be faced with this problem today."

"Nay my Lord," the young man disagreed "even if he hadn't, Tiberius would have. The Romans are greedy. Look what they do to Gaul and the rest of those far away lands. They would have them all, and they've heard of our great wealth. Sooner or later one of them would have come, had it not been Caesar. They wish to rule the entire world."

Vitaicus thought on this a long time before agreeing.

They left Fludigat's fascinating workshop reluctantly just before sunset. The exhausted boys curled up on the floor of the chariot with their equally worn out dog snuggled up between them, and all three were lulled to sleep by the motion of the ride only moments after starting off.

Vitaicus felt mellow and content and looked forward to an evening of hearty eating and pleasant light-hearted conversation with his newfound friend and confidant, his wife and queen, Trasand. Had not thoughts of the child growing within her come to mind, he would have considered what the rest of the night might bring, but he banished them, as he feared hurting either the baby or Trasand.

He'd simply drink sufficient ale to make sleep come quickly, he told himself harshly.

Chapter 18

The king's contented state of mind, and the exhilaration of his kingdom were short lived. In his first duty as the new Supreme Druid, Pantra sent word to Britain of his decision regarding the aborted assembly and the Roman problem.

The news swiftly halted all feasting in the kingdom of Vitaicus and other kingdoms where there'd been reason to celebrate. The Celts would celebrate good crops, rains, a victory in battle, a blessing from the gods, whatever came their way to lift their state of mind. The mood swing was instantaneous as Druid messengers recited the decision of the Supreme Druid.

Having been to Europe and seen the enormity of the task that lay ahead, Pantra knew full well that any attempt to go to battle against the Romans across the seas would need not only the full blessing of the gods but also absolute cooperation of the kingdoms of Britain. They'd need to stand together and give up everything they could spare, every weapon, boat, and warrior as well as sufficient food to feed them all. Any attempt on their part with less than this would be suicidal.

Pantra knew that the deadlock between the royal clans and other chieftains wouldn't easily be broken and that the weather would only be in their favour for a few short weeks before winter set in. He instructed each ruler to recite to the messenger the entire inventory of their available resources, holding nothing back, neither weapon nor warrior, food nor beast.

Each messenger was to take with him a Bard to memorise the record, and return with the greatest of haste to Mona. Each king, queen and chieftain was told to be ready to meet once again at the fortification in Iceni, and warriors prepared to lay down farming implements and take up arms at a moments notice.

The priests went into the forests to their most sacred groves to call on the gods and to seek their assistance and blessing in bringing about a victory for their united land.

Although in a sombre mood, the people once again felt safe in the knowledge that something was being done, someone was taking charge. The senior Druids beseeched the gods on their behalf, and slowly almost imperceptibly the mood began to change to one of optimism, if not joy.

A few weeks after Fludigat delivered their newly made and highly polished weapons, Dylan and Pren were already adept at their use. Vitaicus wasted no time in teaching them how to hold their shields defensively, and how to thrust out with their spears, searching for an opening in their opponent's defence.

He showed them how to prance around the room, moving forward, feinting, and moving sideways. Being young and lithe and quick to learn, they delighted in the hours that their father spent with them.

Vitaicus told them time and time again that they could not use the spears unless he was present, and gave them blunted sticks to practice with in his absence. He would never be sure whether they'd not understood him, or had chosen to ignore him the fateful day he went hunting and left them at home practising with their shields and sticks.

As he mounted his horse that inauspicious morning, Obetach came hurrying out to the stables, looking extremely agitated.

"Will you ride with me on the hunt today Obetach?" the king asked the priest without noticing his pallor or demeanour.

"Nay, not today my Lord, for I've seen grave signs in my meditations today."

He hesitated before continuing haltingly. "My Lord, I believe you shouldn't hunt today, I see the spear as an ill omen. Please don't go!"

"As my priest are you ordering me to stay, or asking me as a friend?" Vitaicus looked at Obetach quizzically.

"Neither, my Lord, it's a mere suggestion that you don't tempt the gods when the signs are shown to me."

"I understand Obetach, my priest, and I respect your advice. However today I meet with Darwalt of Regni and we have long since planned this hunt. I'll take exceeding care, but why not join me, then you can spend the day pleading the gods for our protection?"

Obetach thought about this for so long, with eyes closed and face lifted to the early morning sun, Vitaicus thought he'd gone into a trance.

"I'll stay here and plead protection from the gods for your household, but will send one of my priests, Wyndem, to go with you."

Vitaicus agreed and left without giving the warning a second thought.

He arrived home that evening to a scene not unlike the one on the night his son was born and his Hilfuth had gone to the Otherworld. It was an evening that was certainly as traumatic and involved almost as much blood.

It took him some time to sort out exactly what had taken place and restore order to his household, then the words spoken by Obetach that morning returned to settle on him with a chill. He knew instantly that he'd angered the gods by not heeding the warning that Obetach had given him.

When he first entered his castle through the kitchens, leaving the pheasant he'd caught to be cleaned and roasted, he became aware of a deep wailing accompanied by intermittent and shrill screaming. As he neared the boys' room he heard Dylan crying above the other terrifying sounds. He reached the room at a run.

Trasand sat on the bed with Pren pinned down in her surprisingly strong arms, while Obetach and Gamenta worked frantically over the boy. Dylan lay on the floor sobbing, ignored by the three frantic adults.

Gamenta was chanting softly, while Obetach was pleading loudly with the gods, using strange words and incantations that Vitaicus had never heard before. He seemed to be in a trance, talking directly to the gods in a tongue that only they would understand.

As he approached, Vitaicus saw the blood and his own ran cold. He stooped down and picked up the devastated Dylan, hugging him tightly to his chest and carried him to the bed where Trasand held tightly onto Pren who fought her like a lion.

Vitaicus pushed Gamenta aside to he could see what was going on, as no one answered his frantic questions. He took in the dreadful scene with a gasp. One of the spears he'd so lovingly given to his sons lay blood soaked on the bed next to Trasand, and as his eyes followed the trail of blood he felt his stomach turn and he fought back the bile that rose to his throat.

Pren's left eye had been pierced through and in place of the once beautiful green eye there remained a mushy cavity filled with a mixture of blood, pus and tears which ran down the boy's cheek unchecked, and dripped onto the bed, further covering the already blood stained spear.

Vitaicus let out a bellow, half a cry, half a query, not sure himself what the noise was he fled the room and thrust Dylan into the arms of the first servant he came across. He stumbled to an open doorway where he was violently ill.

He shook his fuzzy head and slowly brought himself under control, stopping on his way back to the boy's room to drink the ale Flauston had poured for him. Feeling a little less shaken he returned to the ghastly scene where he gently pried Pren from the arms of his distraught wife, and ordered Gamenta to take her to her room and leave her in the care of her personal servant, Omilia.

"Has Lucet been sent for?" he demanded.

Lucet was the most learned priest in the art of healing, the one man able to treat such a hideous wound.

"Yes my Lord, a messenger is already on his way. He will be here soon". Obetach confirmed.

All there was left for them to do was keep the child quiet, plead with the gods, and wait.

The waiting was interminable but eventually Lucet arrived from the forest where he lived, many miles from the castle. He took charge with the quiet assurance of one who knows his skill. He had with him many different herbs and cloths, and he ordered Obetach to bring boiling water with which to make various poultices.

He worked over Pren until deep into the night, washing and cleaning the ugly mess, alternating hot and cold cloths filled with assorted plants and herbs, packing all sorts of healing leaves over the wound, until at last, just before midnight he placed the final dressing over the destroyed eye. He gave Pren a potion to drink which would ease the pain and cleanse the wound and left him to sleep.

As soon as he'd finished with Pren he gave the queen and Dylan drafts of the sleep inducing remedy, and they both slept until the sun was well up.

Vitaicus spent the night and the following day at the bedside of the weak and fever wracked child, not leaving his side for an instant. He neither washed nor ate, ceaselessly berating himself for his part in the tragedy.

Had he not left the boys untended with their shields, had he only concealed the spears better, had he never had them made in the first place, none of this would have taken place. If he'd only heeded the warning of Obetach, why the priest had even seen the spear as an ill omen but they'd both thought it the hunting spear.

He dreaded the moment when Trasand would arrive and he'd have to face her. His guilt weighed heavily on him, but he was less concerned about how she would feel towards him than how she'd feel about Dylan who'd inflicted this monstrous injury on her only son.

When he did see her he was astounded by her attitude and spent the remainder of his vigil thanking the gods for her placid acceptance of the accident. She assured him repeatedly that she blamed no one, least of all Dylan who was too young to have known the danger that lay in his mischievous routing out of the spears, to better play and practise the exciting game that their father had been teaching them.

The king felt a profound sense of relief as he looked at the fine and compassionate woman at his side, but he could see the ache in her eyes, the pinch of her lips and the strain that clearly showed in her brow as she fussed over her desperately ill son.

Pren hovered at the edge of the Otherworld for many nights while Lucet and other Druids came and went hourly, placing layer after layer of dressings over his eye and on his fevered brow. On the eighth night the fever broke, and Pren muttered and mumbled for the first time, not quite able to make himself understood after many sleeping draughts.

It wasn't until two weeks later when the Druids judged the time right to remove his final dressings that the real extent of his injury became apparent. Where Pren's enquiring wide green eye had been, a jagged scar had grown together to conceal the empty socket. The scar extended a short way down his pale cheek giving him an impish look once one became used to the unsightly appearance of the closed eye above.

Pren would never have full vision again, but with his bright and cheerful nature he was undaunted by his lack of sight or his appearance as he looked at himself in the mirror that hung in his mother's chamber.

Chapter 19

Vitaicus spent more and more time with Trasand as her pregnancy progressed, an entirely new experience for him. Although he'd endured Hilfuth's pregnancy, he'd done so from a distance. Hilfuth became reticent from the start, and when he spent time with her, she was moody. Sick day in and out, she was unable to keep down any food and seldom joined him at the table where eating was one of his favourite pastimes.

She refused wine, and seemed to sleep most of the day away. He was reluctant to lie with her at night, and although he still loved her during those difficult months, he became withdrawn and threw himself into hunting and fighting.

There'd been plenty of opportunity for that during the last few months in particular, as raiding parties from the Goidels had continuously hounded farmers throughout his land. As her time neared its end her company depressed him and he'd spent his free time with Obetach, drinking, talking and playing their favourite board game of Chelta.

With Trasand however, a fascinating change came over her and he was compelled to spend as much time with her as possible, even night times when she seemed unafraid, yes, even desired to have him come to her bed. Her appetite for him wakened and grew during those exhilarating months.

She was a constant delight to him as she blossomed. With each day that her belly grew, her pleasure in life increased and she pranced around, revelling in the fruit on the trees in the royal orchards and the showers of rain that fell during the day. The beauty of the summer sunsets and the moon that crossed the sky at night enthralled her. Her energy knew no bounds and she begged Vitaicus to walk with her through the fields as she picked wild flowers.

He found her in the kitchens preparing preserves for the winter, sending the slaves to their quarters while she worked. She called for him when she bathed so that he could see the baby kick inside her belly. She spent hours lying on rugs at his feet talking of their child and all the wondrous things that he'd do. She laughed and teased and tantalised him, until he felt he loved her more than life itself and was loath to leave her even to go and fight.

When Sebilus announced that her time was close, Vitaicus refused to leave her side. He wouldn't have the same fate befall her as his first wife. He ordered his priests to keep a constant vigil, doing everything in their power to appease the gods and keep them happy.

However, just three nights before the baby arrived, Obetach was summoned along with all senior Druids to join the Supreme Druid on Mona where they'd decided whether to go to Gaul to fight against the Romans or not.

Obetach was forced to leave immediately and both men knew it was an ill omen. Vitaicus watched his priest's reluctant departure, and as his chants became fainter, his large frame a mere dot in the distance, the king returned to his wife with a heavy heart.

The boys were almost three and they ran beside Vitaicus with Sopa dancing between their legs, tripping them up. Their gleeful shouts did little to raise his sombre mood. He'd felt the need of fresh air after three days bedside vigil and had given in to their constant nagging to go for a walk along the riverside.

He knew something was wrong as soon as they re-entered the courtyard a few hours later. The faces of the servants showed the concern he himself felt. There was much scurrying around, water was boiling on the fires and there was an air of expectancy in which he sensed dread rather than excitement.

Calling for Flauston to bring him a drink, Vitaicus hurried to Trasand's chamber. He found Gamenta spread out on the floor in a trance, his voice high pitched and pleading as he begged the gods to be favourable to the child, which Sebilus quietly informed him was about to be born on this most inauspicious day.

Nothing that the experienced and skilled midwife attempted could delay the birth beyond the turn of midnight to a more auspicious day. Vitaicus sat and held Trasand's hand, wiped her brow and agonised over her pain. He relived in minute detail every awful moment of Hilfuth's labour, until the time he'd fled to go and hunt. The sight of her dead body, the water, the blood, all these memories came flooding back, and he sat beside Trasand with his drink untouched, sharing her agony.

He silently pleaded with the gods to spare the life of this woman, if not the child.

Just one hour before midnight, the infant arrived, tiny and blue, but very much alive as was evident by its shrieks as it entered the world.

"A girl, it's a girl!" cried Sebilus, showing the bloodied baby to the queen as she coaxed the exhausted mother to put the infant to her breast.

Gamenta faced a dilemma and the responsibility lay heavily on him. Should this child born on the most unlucky of all possible days in the wrong half of a unlucky month, be allowed to live? He left for the forest where he could be at one with the gods, and spent three days in prayer, watching for signs, appeasing them with gifts and using every skill he'd learned in his twenty years of study to divine their will.

On the fourth day he returned and entered Trasand's chamber looking thin, weary and in need of a wash. The dust of his journey caked his bare feet, spoiled his white gown, and clung to his beard.

"What have you chosen to name the child?" he asked without preamble.

"She's to be Filethas," the queen replied softly not daring to look at his face, nor read from his tone the decision of the gods.

"I'll arrange her naming ceremony," he said simply, "she's to live."

And he turned and left the elated queen fiercely hugging her tiny daughter.

Chapter 20

Vitaicus had been waiting for days for the arrival of a merchant ship from Gaul. He spent hours scouring the roadway that led to his hilltop castle, watching for the messenger who'd been hired to bring news immediately the boat arrived. Rough seas from a storm must have delayed her passage, he thought grimly.

Vitaicus loved to trade and much of his wealth was gained from his keen eye for a bargain and his sound understanding of economics. The merchant he was expecting would be bringing in goods that he would use himself, but also items that he'd trade within his kingdom, further increasing his wealth.

He'd been setting aside goods for months to trade with the merchant, items that were needed across the sea, and would be sold to the Belgians, the Gauls and the Germans, probably even the Romans. He had a warehouse full of corn and hides and gold under heavy guard.

Aside from the horses in his royal stables he had several prize hunting dogs that he'd been breeding for the past two seasons and they'd produced eight puppies, perfect specimens, for the merchant.

Nine days later than the boat was expected, Vitaicus finally saw from his high vantage point the dust of a rider coming hard up the long drive that led to the castle gates.

The news was good, the boat and cargo had survived a terrifying storm. Leaving the messenger to wash and drink, Vitaicus and Gamenta went ahead to meet the merchant.

It was strange to be taking such a trip without his economic sounding board, Obetach, but Vitaicus decided that if Gamenta was to be the advisor of Dylan, the future king, then he needed to learn the art of trade first hand from a master.

Although anxious to reach port as soon as possible, they took time to stop along the way at various hamlets and farms where rent was due. The king bartered with his tenants and came to amicable agreements of the lease of his land for the ensuing months, adding to his mental list the quantity of items he had to barter with once he reached port.

The two men had only travelled fourteen miles when they became aware of a horseman riding hard behind them, shouting loudly. Vitaicus felt his stomach tighten in a knot as he recognised his servant Flauston.

The sweat stained man almost fell from his horse as he reined in and the look in his eyes scared the king more than any words he spoke. Vitaicus felt a sense of unreality overtake him, the situation was so similar to that dreadful day a few years earlier when Flauston had fetched him from hunting.

"You must return to the castle immediately," he said as he turned his horse and headed back the way he'd come.

Vitaicus and Gamenta followed without question, soon overtaking Flauston who was unable to keep pace with them. Flauston's horse, Noin, which meant noon for the hour the colt had been born, was already exhausted and he fell far behind as the dust of the horses ahead becoming less with each frantic mile covered.

Once back at the castle and after hearing in detail what had taken place, Vitaicus took time to calm himself, while Gamenta rounded up every priest that was on the vast property. When Flauston arrived he immediately sent slaves to summon the king's best generals. An hour was wasted while Vitaicus waited for them, pacing up and down the courtyard to the mournful sound of the priests' incantations as they prayed and pleaded with the gods.

By the time the first generals arrived, having themselves ridden hard, Vitaicus had formulated his plan. He gave the men no time to recover, but sat them down in the midday sun and told them what had transpired. They'd have time enough to wash their faces and drink of the cool pond water once he'd spoken to them.

"My friends and trusted warriors, I've called for you because the most grave fate has befallen me. My wife, the queen has been kidnapped."

Vitaicus stopped and took a long breath, afraid his voice would break. The generals stared at him in disbelief.

"It seems that Anandligat has been watching her these past weeks, waiting for the moment I left the castle to snatch her away. Since the birth of our daughter Filethas she's been unwell, and spent time each day walking in the fields, rejuvenating her body and mind by picking flowers for the castle, and wild mushrooms or strawberries for the kitchens. She's does this in the company of her handmaid and a number of kitchen slaves, but has often wandered off on her own, forgetting herself and her weariness in the fresh morning air."

He paused again, swallowing before continuing.

"It seems that Anandligat planned it well. As soon as Gamenta and I were away, he went straight to the fields where he had his horse tied up and waiting. The queen's handmaid, Omilia, heard her cries, but Anandligat must have placed a tie over her mouth as she called out only once. Omilia rushed to the edge of the field and saw his horse galloping away. She recognised his filthy, torn cloak."

The generals sat in stunned silence for a moment and then broke into an uproar, each offering his advice on how to handle the situation. The unanimous decision was to take warriors, kill the offender and reclaim the queen.

Vitaicus allowed them to vent their feelings before raising his hand for silence. The whole while the Bards continued to chant in the background.

"I appreciate your concern and particularly your loyalty and willingness to fight for myself and the queen, however, I've decided on my initial course of action."

His generals stared at him in confusion realising he was about to refuse their offer to go to arms immediately on his behalf.

"I fear for the life of the queen. Should we surprise this madman he may harm her before we kill him. I plan to go to his hovel with Gamenta and his priests in order to reason with the man. Once I have the queen safely returned, he will be yours to deal with as you see fit."

Although they were slightly mollified they would have preferred to go in fighting at the outset, however they prepared to take their leave and warn the warriors under their command of the impending action, knowing that Anandligat's friends and family would retaliate once he'd been slain.

Vitaicus was reluctant to waste further time and he and the

priests left the courtyard and his generals, with the king choosing to walk rather than ride his exhausted horse.

They arrived at the house of Anandligat in silence, not wishing to alert or alarm him in any way. Gamenta knocked on the door and called loudly to the man he prayed was inside.

"It is I, Gamenta, open up Anandligat, the king is here to see you."

"My home is too humble to admit the king," came the startled reply.

"Then come outside and speak to him here, he awaits your company."

After a few moments, Anandligat inched out of his doorway looking surly and defensive. He bowed low before the king, but looked in the direction of Gamenta.

"What can I do for you?"

Vitaicus opened his mouth to speak, but Gamenta raised his hand and spoke with authority.

"The king wishes to see if his wife is unharmed and take her back to the castle with him where her baby is hungry and in need of her."

"Please tell the king that the queen is here at her own request, and does not wish to return to the castle, or the baby."

Vitaicus lunged forward yelling, "You're lying. I'll have you flogged for this. Return the queen at once."

But again Gamenta restrained him, and bringing his skinny body between the two huge men he continued to play the diplomat.

"If you're sure the queen is here at her own request and is unharmed, you'll need to attend a council tomorrow at first light, and bring witnesses to agree with your statement." Gamenta warned sternly.

Anandligat nodded and returned swiftly indoors. Vitaicus stood numbed through as he listened to the sound of a heavy object being scraped across the stone floor and placed in front of the door. He turned on Gamenta, venting his frustration at the calm young priest.

"Why didn't you allow me to speak, to use my authority as king, why did you let him turn away from me after lying so?"

He spluttered, breathing heavily, stumbling over his words.

"My Lord, we could have come here with the generals and their warriors, but my Lord was afraid for the life of the queen. The man is unbalanced and if we threaten him, he may well harm the queen not caring about the consequences to himself."

Vitaicus knew that Gamenta spoke wisely, in fact repeated the words he'd himself spoken to his generals. He turned and began the grim walk home, not sure how he'd face the night ahead, but even more concerned about how Trasand would fare during the long dark hours in the hands of the monster who'd kidnapped her. Perhaps he should have taken his chances and let the generals do their best. What would Trasand think of him leaving her there for even one hour, let alone the entire night?

These and many other thoughts assailed him, making his mood deeper and darker with every footfall. By the time they reached the castle, Vitaicus had just the strength left to order Gamenta to prepare a council and witnesses for the morning before retiring to his chamber, not even going to the boys first who'd no doubt be stricken without their mother's presence for the entire day.

And what of the baby, should he call for Omilia to see that the baby was looked after, or would she already have done that?

He took hold of a flagon of wine and flung himself across his bed, where he lay until he'd drained every drop, tormenting himself all the while, until finally he slept.

Flauston found him in the same position when he called for him at first light.

Chapter 21

The king entered the courtyard before the sun had fully risen and the cold morning air was crisp. Birds chattered and chirped gaily at the start of what promised to be a clear autumn day.

Dew caused the sweet smell of grass to mingle with the fragrance of flowers that grew around the perimeter of the courtyard. Assembled were a large party of priests, the Bards already chanting and strumming their lyres, the Vates gazing at the sky reading signs in the rising sun.

Seated on the hard earth beside the pond were Omilia, six maidens, and five slaves. Some were from the kitchen, others were Trasand's personal hand maidens. All had been present the previous morning when she'd been kidnapped.

Gamenta rushed up the cobbled entranceway out of breath, curly hair awry, cheeks flushed, but grinning broadly. The king glared at him. There was surely little to smile about this morning when the fate of his wife hung in the balance, if she was indeed still alive?

Gamenta noticed the grimness of the king's look, the dark circles under his eyes, the weariness of his shoulders, but he continued to grin as he pushed his way past the priests. He didn't have the opportunity to enlighten the king as to his good humour as Anandligat entered the courtyard at that moment calling loudly to his twelve witnesses to follow him.

In the absence of Obetach, who was still with the Supreme Druid and was sorely missed by the king, Gamenta wasted no time in getting the session in order.

As judge in this council, Gamenta wore two white robes, the outer one fastened with a girdle. He wore two official rings on his right hand and around his neck hung the breastplate of judgement, which he pressed against his breast from time to time. The breastplate was made of a thin single sheet of gold adorned with various ornaments in the shape of stars, the sun and moon, suspended by a chain of gold. The front of the plate had two small conical pillars of solid gold so highly polished they glistened in the early morning sun light, causing Vitaicus to avert his eyes.

Dressed in this splendid outfit, he almost looked the part of an arch Druid and judge, save for his unruly red hair and beard which grew down to his breast and obscured some of the ornamentation and the inscription "the gods require sacrifice."

Ominous words in front of a guilty party, ones that generally ensured that the truth was told.

Gamenta ordered Anandligat's witnesses to be seated on his left hand side. On his right he placed the queen's witnesses. Twelve priests were positioned a few feet in front of him, while the king, who was neither witness nor council member, had no say in the court-case and was left standing at the side of the yard, feeling out of place, an unwanted party in his own castle.

Gamenta raised his hands and the Bard's lyres fell silent. The queen's maidens and slaves had been quiet from the start, intimidated by the presence of the king and the Druids, overwhelmed by their responsibility in this awful situation, they'd not uttered a sound the whole time they'd been waiting. Only Anandligat's men were noisy and even after Gamenta called for silence, they continued to be ribald and rowdy.

Gamenta looked directly at Anandligat and said in a quiet but stern voice, "if your witnesses don't obey me, the judge in this proceeding, I'll cancel the matter and send the king's finest warriors to retrieve the queen while you sit here laughing together."

Anandligat ordered his cronies to be quiet, his face ashen at the threat.

"It is your testimony Anandligat, that Queen Trasand, wife of King Vitaicus and mother of Prince Dylan, Prince Pren and Princess Filethas, faithful to the gods, the priests, and this royal household, left the castle willingly and of her own accord, without force or violence, to seek sanctuary with you!"

The last of his words were almost spat from the mouth of the usually diplomatic priest, his meaning obvious by the inflection placed on the word 'you' disgust and disbelief clear on his honest face.

"That is my testimony." Anandligat replied without bothering to rise. Vitaicus wanted to rush forward and order the man disciplined, but knew he couldn't interfere.

"Do you have twelve witnesses to bear testimony to this?" Gamenta asked. Anandligat waved in the direction of the friends he'd spent the night rounding up.

"Stand up and speak, one at a time," Gamenta ordered with growing impatience. One by one the men stood and told their version of the story, as requested by the rogue who sat grinning at them. The payment he promised them tantamount in their minds, they'd not learned the facts well and contradicted each other, left details out and added others to make their testimony more colourful.

After a night of drifting from hamlet to hamlet, drinking at each home, Anandligat was still inebriated sufficiently not to notice this, and imagined things to be going splendidly. Once each man had spoken, Gamenta turned to the queen's witnesses.

"In the absence of the queen, and without her having had the opportunity to coax or coheres you into telling anything other than the truth, I ask each of you to give testimony to what you know with regard to the queen's disappearance?"

Once again his emphasise on the words 'coheres' and 'disappearance' left little doubt as to what Gamenta believed, and Anandligat glared at him with open hostility.

Although Gamenta could imagine what the man was thinking, he continued, showing no fear. There was a handful of men across the land who had no fear of the Druids or the gods, and Gamenta sensed that this was one of them. Men like him had killed Druids before and although the gods always avenged their deaths in the most spectacular way, it hadn't convinced the likes of Anandligat of the power of either the gods or the priests. Gamenta knew his life was in danger, but continued with the council.

The maidens spoke first, divulging every detail of the fateful morning, delighting in telling the audience of every flower picked, where the strawberries were found, and how the queen had moved some distance away in search of fatter, riper ones. The slaves told the identical story.

The last witness was Omilia and she began by telling the council of the queen's love for the king, her children, her home, even her servants and slaves. She told how the queen would never have conceived of the idea of running away, especially not to a ghastly man like the one present today.

As she said these words, she turned and spat at Anandligat to the amazement of everyone present.

No matter how foul the deed, a man had the right to a trial, and to be treated in a civil manner until found guilty. After that, well he could be ripped apart by everyone present and no one would care, but until that time proper procedure and behaviour was expected.

The king placed his hand over his mouth to conceal his shocked grin, he wished he'd done the same.

Once the gasps from the crowd ceased and Anandligat had gathered himself together, having been restrained from hitting the young girl by two of his cronies, she continued as if nothing had happened.

She told the council how she'd been just a few feet from her queen when she heard her scream, not once, but twice, and that the second time she called out the words, "leave me."

After that there'd been some muffled sounds, then silence. She'd run to where the sound came from and seen the filthy torn cloak of Anandligat as he fled on horseback. She'd also seen the queen bundled up in front of him, a cloth tied around her mouth and she feared that the queen would fall, so quickly did the man flee.

After her testimony there was shocked silence. Anandligat hadn't told his witnesses that he had in fact abducted the queen, but had said that she'd been willing. He'd also neglected to mention that she'd screamed. In their testimony each had said how they'd seen the queen come willingly and although with different versions, they all testified to the same theme.

Turning to the queen's witnesses Gamenta asked, "Do you swear an oath that your testimony is true, bearing in mind that if it's not, you'll never see the Otherworld, but will forever wander the outer planes with your spirit trapped?"

The witnesses nodded solemnly.

Gamenta turned to the twelve witnesses that Anandligat had rounded up, and asked the same question. A few of the men squirmed uncomfortably and made the sign to ward off evil behind their backs as they nodded. Gamenta asked all twenty-four witnesses to repeat a solemn oath after him.

The men mumbled incoherently, hoping that the gods wouldn't take theirs as a true oath, but recognise the fact that they withheld some of the words and not force them to wander forever after their death on this earth.

Gamenta and his priests moved to the far side of the courtyard to consult with each other. They were in a precarious position and Gamenta wished that the older and wiser Obetach were present. However, when they returned to their positions he addressed Anandligat with a genial smile.

"It's the testimony of your witnesses that the queen came to you voluntarily. It's the testimony of the queen's witnesses that she did not. As is the practice in this land, one testimony cancels out the other and so no judgement can be made, therefore you and your friends are free to leave."

With that he turned and walked towards the king whose face had turned a deep crimson, and Gamenta feared he would collapse on the spot. Anandligat couldn't believe the pronouncement, he fully expected the Druid to rule in favour of the king despite the law in the regard of witnesses.

He sat in stunned silence for several moments before his men dragged him to his feet and fled before Gamenta could change his mind, or worse still the king ordered them captured.

They didn't get far. Vitaicus still hadn't spoken and his servants were fanning him and forcing him to drink some water, when the first awful sounds from beyond the courtyard rose on the morning air.

Gamenta had anticipated what would take place at the council and had also been busy during the night. He'd visited each of the generals to whom the king had spoken the previous day.

They'd selected a handful of their best warriors who were positioned in the trees just off the king's property, ready and waiting for the evil Anandligat and his men to leave the castle. They spared not one, but mutilated each man beyond recognition, not even saving their heads as trophies, they left them for the wild dogs and birds of prey. By noon only their bones remained, and the warriors returned and burned the clothing and other items the men had in their possession.

The queen was rescued and returned to the king before he fully realised what had taken place.

Dylan missed the queen least of all, not because she wasn't his blood mother, but because his young life was filled with adventure, his mind so inquisitive, his already athletic body so active that he seldom sat still for any length of time, certainly not long enough to notice that she'd not been fussing around the boys that day.

Pren however had become listless and weepy and flung his arms around her with more force than she believed the skinny child capable of.

Although her return to the castle was celebrated with a hurried feast, Trasand was withdrawn and pale. She'd missed her boys and the king dreadfully, but it was baby Filethas that had been her undoing. In the dark hours she'd spent locked up, bound to a hard wooden chair and all alone in Anandligat's damp hovel, she'd thought of little else and as the hours passed and her swollen breasts continued to fill with milk, she pined for her baby and made herself more distraught at the thought of Filethas' hungry little mouth searching out her mother's breast.

By the time Anandligat returned in the early hours of the morning she was burning with milk fever and her distress was so great that even he was alarmed.

Her fever ran for five days despite the ministrations of Sebilus and numerous priestesses, and by the time it broke and she felt fit enough to nurse her child, her milk had disappeared. She'd been depressed before this turn of events, now she was distraught, and as Omilia brought a wet-nurse for her to meet, she cried bitterly sending her away without a second glance.

As the days and weeks passed, Trasand never regained sufficient weight to give her a healthy appearance. She seemed to be perpetually tired and seldom smiled. Vitaicus was extremely concerned about her, but the many priests he consulted with were unable to bring about a change to her body or mind. Even more worrying to Vitaicus was her absolute obsession with the children. She dreaded them being out of her sight, and while Filethas was no problem and Pren too was happy to spend his hours playing in front of her, Dylan wanted his freedom to explore and run free.

A few weeks later the king had an idea that finally allowed the boys some time away from their over-protective mother. He decided it was time for them to begin riding lessons and sent Gamenta in search of a pony for each of them in celebration of the third anniversary of their birth, which was imminent.

Obetach finally returned from Mona and was shocked to hear what had taken place in his absence. When Vitaicus finished his tragic tale, Obetach told him that the Supreme Druid and his council had declared that there were simply insufficient resources available to launch an effective attack on the Romans. They had no option but to wait, relying on the gods to protect them during this time of uncertainty.

The king took the boys, with Sopa in tow, to Fludigat to have helmets made in preparation for their first riding lesson. Each helmet was a work of art, an exact replica of those worn by warriors going to war, with miniature horns so that the boys resembled Cernunnos, the God of Hunting, whenever they wore them.

Chapter 22

AD 33
Autumn

Gamenta was readily granted permission by Epona, the Goddess of Fertility, to take two ponies from the forest. Epona had a special relationship with and guarded all the wild horses of the land and no one ever took a horse without her permission.

Gamenta wanted the boys to go through the ritual of getting their horses from her even though he'd already been given them. As one of the most important creatures in the life of the Celts, acquiring a horse was something one didn't do lightly. Once a Warrior chose a horse for riding he'd keep it for life, and select a separate horse for drawing his chariot. His riding horse was not only part of his wealth, but was treated with the same regard and respect as a member of his family.

In order to make the ritual as realistic as possible, Gamenta left early one morning with the ponies and took them back into the forest where he tethered them to a tree, leaving food and water within their reach. He sang all the way back to the castle, unable to contain his excitement.

The boys were ready and waiting, their anxious mother waving until they were out of sight. They soon grew tired and stopped frequently to drink from the water skin that Gamenta carried, and to investigate every item of interest that Dylan spotted from a hare scurrying across their path, to an ant hill against the trunk of a tree.

They reached the forest as the sun reached its zenith, and stopped in the shade to eat cheese and apples before continuing the short distance to where the horses waited. While the boys finished their meal, Gamenta hurried ahead and loosened the ponies, hid their food and water and ran back to the impatient princes.

Gamenta let the boys run ahead and they soon spotted them. They stopped in awe, waiting for the priest to join them. He showed them how to call for the Goddess Epona to come and sit with them and they closed their eyes and chanted the unfamiliar words, then sat in silence until Gamenta whispered, "she's here."

They opened their eyes eagerly and in their strong desire to see her, imagined they did. Following Gamenta's lead, they asked the Goddess if they might choose two of her horses and again waited in silence. It wasn't long before one of them brayed softly and Gamenta shouted for joy. "She's agreed, she's agreed."

They ran forward and selected their own. Pren immediately went to the smaller of the two, the only way the ponies could be told apart. Gamenta gave them a small cauldron of holy water, and showed them how to walk around the ponies three times in each direction chanting softly in order not to frighten the young animals. They sprinkled the holy water over their gifts and sang praises to Epona for allowing them to have such beautiful creatures.

They left the forest bursting with excitement, leading their ponies and happily discussing names. After much chattering Gamenta suggested that Pren choose Tuath-Reul meaning North Star, as he was an avid astronomer and always the first to spot the stars as they came out at night.

To Dylan he gave the name Luath-Reul, which meant Swift Star, as the youngster loved the feel of speed as he rode in his father's chariot. Dylan loved the name and knew he'd soon coax his pony to ride swiftly for him.

Gamenta found the boys the following afternoon at the stables where they'd spent most of the day with their ponies. It was growing dark and he took Dylan by one hand, with Pren firmly clasping the other and led them to the courtyard to a fire that had been lit for them by the slaves. They sat on skins, legs crossed in imitation of Gamenta.

He'd told them on the way that he had a special story to tell them and they listened intently as the priest solemnly related the tale of the dreadful yet fortuitous night of Dylan's birth. They sat still without losing interest, although they understood little and were happy when they could race back inside to eat and play before bedtime.

Vitaicus spent less and less time with the queen during the difficult months following her kidnap, but preferred to pass his free hours teaching the boys to ride, although he went to her on those nights when he was unable to sleep as the affairs of his kingdom weighed heavily on him.

He was nevertheless shocked to learn that she was with child again. The news wasn't unwelcome, but he was concerned about her health and her fragile mental state. He determined to spend more time with her in an attempt to lift her spirits and encourage her to eat more and rest often.

His treatment worked and in the final months of her pregnancy she once again blossomed and became something of the Trasand he'd first grown to love. As her attention grew daily towards the impending birth, she spent less time fussing over the boys, and young Filethas, who was growing into a charming creature.

Chapter 23

AD 34
Summer

Obetach promised to be present for the birth of the baby and gave the king a daily update on the pleasure or displeasure of the gods. He told Vitaicus each morning whether it was an auspicious or inauspicious day and as the time grew near, Sebilus and her assistants attempted in vain once again to induce an early onset of labour on an auspicious one, and tried equally hard to prevent it when it did come naturally on an inauspicious day.

The king ranted in the courtyard, calling on the gods to be merciful to his unborn child. Obetach found him sitting in the hot sun raving like a lunatic and ushered him inside, calmed him down and sent him to sit with his wife who was in desperate need of him.

He assured Vitaicus that every available priest across his kingdom was in urgent prayer and supplication for the life of the child and the queen herself. However, as the day wore on and Obetach continued to meditate and read the signs, he grew increasingly convinced that the gods were not in favour of this birth.

Gamenta found him brooding near the river late in the day, the very river that had burst its banks on the night Dylan was born, but which now ran quietly along the eastern border of the king's castle grounds. Gamenta came to tell Obetach that he too believed the gods desired this as yet unborn child. The priest was forced to face Vitaicus.

They returned to find Sebilus holding the infant that had been hurriedly wrapped in a cover not large enough to conceal its blue colouring from the priests. The queen lay in a dead faint on her bed, where Omilia attempted to revive her. There was no need to ask if the baby was dead, the look on the faces of both women confirmed what the priests already knew.

"Has the king been told?" Obetach asked the midwife.

"The king was summoned as soon as the baby was delivered," she whispered, "and he held his daughter briefly, covering his robe in blood. He himself handed the baby to the queen. She only held it long enough to kiss its tiny face before fainting. The king fled to his trophy room and asked that you go to him as soon as you return."

She was clearly exhausted and emotional as she respectfully addressed the priest with her head bowed.

Vitaicus looked up as Obetach and Gamenta entered his private sanctuary, nodded towards a cauldron of berry wine and took a long drink from his own goblet before he spoke.

"The child is to be called Kwethin. That is the name the queen chose should it have been a girl. Please arrange a funeral for her. The queen hasn't the energy and I haven't the heart."

He dismissed the priests, knowing that it would be done.

As the leaves changed colour on the tress in the orchards, and autumn made it presence felt, the king heard that trouble was brewing in his kingdom and a fight was imminent and his heart sang with joy for the first time in weeks.

A band of Celtic warriors from Gaul, who were fleeing the brutality of the Romans, had successfully sailed across the channel and landed in Britain. After resting overnight they moved westwards along the coast where they waited for more of their clan to join them twenty miles from the hamlet of King Vitaicus. Once assembled they planned to pillage the land and win over the kingdom for themselves.

They moved northeastwards further into Canti and headed towards Vitaicus' own property, where the king ruled not only his own clan but hundreds of other families too.

"That's exactly what we need," he told himself joyously, "a good hard battle."

Since the death of baby Kwethin, his people had been in mourning, their mood dark and despairing, and he knew that nothing short of victory in battle would raise their spirits.

He waited anxiously for Obetach to return from the holy glade where he and his priests and priestesses were meditating about the impending battle. They'd spent the night in the forest and taken a young deer for a sacrificial offering to Modron, the God of War. Novices prepared the pyre on which to burn the animal and a Vate sprinkled holy water over it, then stabbed it skilfully just above its midriff.

The doe fell soundlessly to the ground carpeted with fallen leaves, and the Druids watched the convulsions of its limbs and the direction in which its blood and entrails spilled from the dying body with a practised eye. Satisfied with their findings, they ordered the carcass to be flung onto the fire where it burned until no trace of the once graceful creature remained.

Obetach reported to the king that they'd indeed seen a battle in their divinations and that the gods would go with them to the battle grounds, but would only instruct them further once there. The king would need to wait until the men were assembled and ready to fight.

Spirits lifted immediately word went out to the farms across Vitaicus' kingdom. Men laid aside their sickles and farming tools, took up their swords, wheeled out their chariots, mounted their horses, or fell in on foot to join the growing lines of warriors. Many women joined them, and with their hair oiled and spiked, they chanted and screeched themselves into a frenzy as they supported their men going to battle. The men washed their hair in lime and when it dried out it too stood up in sharp spikes and was snow white in colour. The sight of these male and female warriors was enough to scare any faint-hearted enemy before a battle even began.

They met up with the first small party of raiders on the outskirts of the kingdom. It was a scouting party and although well armed, was no match for the force of eager warriors with Vitaicus. His men and their women made short work of mutilating the plunderers, and with mounting glee after their period of mourning, they hung the heads of their foe onto their already well-decorated bridles.

Vitaicus saw two men escape and knew they were on their way to warn their compatriots, but his warriors had already marched ten miles before the skirmish, and he allowed them to rest for the night where they celebrated wildly, leaving only the sentries, and Vitaicus and his priest sober. Vitaicus longed for the fight that would surely take place at first light, and looked forward to the spoils he would take home with him.

Obetach roused the king from slumber before dawn. Although he and the other priests wouldn't fight, they accompanied their king to battle to provide him with the final word of the gods before fighting began.

Vitaicus dispatched scouts who returned quickly and said that the enemy lay sleeping seven miles south of them. Close to their encampment they'd found an ideal area for the fight, they reported. Vitaicus sent them to rouse the warriors who were ready to leave camp by the time the sun had risen.

The march to the designated battleground took until midday, slowed down as they were by their chariots, but the men were in high spirits despite the delay. They were anxious to get the fighting underway before rain that was threatening in the sky to the east arrived to spoil their victory.

The pillagers from across the sea also roused themselves at first light and marched to the place picked out by the king's scouts. They knew their enemy would come to them, and spared themselves the energy they'd have used to march. They lay about in the autumn sun throughout the morning, waiting patiently for the battle that would ensure them their own land in this safe haven, free of the Romans who persecuted them.

As Vitaicus and his leading warriors came into sight, battle pendant flying proudly in a light breeze, the Gauls roused themselves and formed their battle lines.

Vitaicus stopped his warriors long enough for them to drink, and to allow their horses to blow and rest briefly, before they too took up their positions, facing the enemy positioned one hundred and twenty feet in front of them. With battle lines drawn and both sides ready, the outcome was in the hands of the gods.

Obetach stepped forward and stopped in front of their most senior Druid, Lunobeaux. Both he and Obetach had a group of thirty or forty priests lined up behind them. They greeted each other with respect. Without a further word but under an unspoken agreement and act of protocol, Obetach gave the sign for the Bards to begin to chant. The mournful sound of their voices could be clearly heard by both armies.

The Vates from both countries scoured the skies, awaiting a sign from the gods as Obetach and Lunobeaux walked up and down the line between the waiting armies. Despite swords being drawn on either side, even though blood pumped furiously through the veins of the warriors, every one of them would respect without a murmur the decision of the gods. They waited breathlessly.

The priests continued to march up and down, while in the background the Bards chanted and the Vates watched and prayed. The day wore on and the storm moved off. The warriors were tired and thirsty once again, their horses restless, snuffling and stamping their hooves. But these were men of great patience, born to the way of the gods and they continued to stand and wait.

Vitaicus was beginning to think the battle would have to be halted until the following day should the gods not speak soon, as the sun was close to setting. 'Perhaps that would be the best course of action,' he thought, as his warriors were tired. He'd hardly finished his train of thought when he became aware of a stirring among his men.

Obetach and Lunobeaux were standing with heads thrown back, watching the path of a flight of geese. As they approached the battleground their squawking could be heard, growing in intensity as they sensed the mass of bodies far below them. Their curiosity roused, they turned towards the assembled armies, and swooped lower and lower, until the flap of their large wings could be felt on the bare arms of the men.

The noise grew until it was quite deafening and the horses became agitated. Both armies were distracted, shuffling around, quietening their horses, talking amongst themselves, tired sword arms dropped to their sides. Only Obetach and his compatriot never stirred, but continued to watch the geese, determining the will of the gods.

It seemed a long time, but was only moments before the geese were out of sight and silence fell. The Bards ceased their chanting, even the horses were quiet now that the geese were gone.

Obetach picked up a sack that he'd placed between the lines earlier in the day and carefully undid the knot in the thread that kept it tightly closed. Without any visible sign of fear he turned the sack upside down and out tumbled an adder. The snake had been tied up for hours and was frightened and angry. It hissed and slithered around his ankles, not sure where to vent its fury. Obetach stood perfectly still, and after a moment the adder chose its course of action. Sensing the presence of horse and man in every direction, it curled itself up and lay still.

Obetach raised his left hand in which he held his golden sickle. He stood facing the sinking sun with the army of the Gauls on his right, King Vitaicus and his warriors on his left.

He brought the sickle down and touched the earth with it and in a voice loud enough to carry to his king and the chief of the Gauls, he boomed, "There will be no fighting. The gods have spoken."

He turned to Lunobeaux, bowed slightly and walked away. His priests fell in behind him chanting a song of praise as they went. Once they were clear of the battle line, King Vitaicus ordered his standard bearer to raise his flag. He looked directly across at his enemy, nodded and turned, his army following him.

The Gauls remained where they were, but at ease, waiting for orders. Their chief respected the will of the gods in this particular battle, he knew there'd be others where the gods would favour them. They would find other land, take it by force and occupy it.

Gamenta went in search of the boys one morning the week before Dylan's birth celebration. They were happily playing at the riverside, catching fish in the icy water with their bare hands. The priest watched for a while, smiling, before calling them to sit with him on a sheep skin covering which would protect them a little from the cold rising from the earth.

They chatted idly for a while, telling Gamenta of their failed attempts at fishing, until Pren curiously asked Gamenta why he'd come for them.

"You know the kingdom is preparing once again to celebrate the anniversary of your birth as the royal son, Dylan, and it's my duty as your priest to prepare you fully for your future."

The boys nodded.

"Do you remember just before the last celebration, I told you both the story of your birth?" The boys looked at each other and shook their heads, neither remembered that evening. Gamenta smiled fondly at them.

"Well, you were both quite little then, not as big and clever as you are now, so I'm going to tell you the whole story again."

"Oh good, I love stories," shouted Dylan.

"Yes, me too," echoed Pren.

They settled comfortably on either side of the priest, who they thought to be the wisest person they knew, wiser even than their father or Obetach. Although they didn't understand the full implications or even absorb half of what Gamenta said, they knew how important it was for them to pay attention and try to remember the story.

Pren listened with great interest and kept repeating to himself every detail. Dylan listened with fascination. Although so young he knew in his heart how important his birth had been.

As Gamenta continued to tell the brothers of Dylan's future and how he would someday become a Supreme Sacrifice to the gods, the little boy felt a sense of glee, and he puffed up his chest with self-importance. Pren shivered but said nothing when he saw how delighted Dylan was with this piece of horrific news.

They lay in bed that night, discussing over and over again everything they could remember, helping each other to learn the story by heart. Still not understanding it all, they memorised it as best as their four-year-old minds allowed.

Chapter 24

AD 35
Winter

IT was unusual for Flauston to be in a fluster and it affected the entire royal household. By mid-morning he'd upset enough of the staff to have Trasand up in arms. She went in search of the king, something she seldom did lately in her withdrawn state. She found him in discussion with Obetach and waited patiently for them to complete their conversation.

Not one to be hurried, Obetach continued to tell the king of the trade ship that arrived the previous evening, and of the many goods these merchants were looking for to trade with the Romans. The list was endless and included much of what Vitaicus had stored for just such a day. He was in a high-spirited mood when Obetach bowed and left him.

"My beloved wife, how very pleasant to see you this morning," he took her painfully thin hand and kissed it lovingly.

It had been some time since he'd last held her close, and he breathed deeply of her own special aroma, filling his lungs. Just the touch of her after such a length of time made his senses reel. He was immediately aroused and wished to carry her off to his chamber.

"My husband, I'm distressed to have to trouble you with unimportant issues when you have a kingdom to oversee, but it seems that Flauston is unwell."

"Unwell, how so?"

Vitaicus was immediately concerned and already making his way past her, all previous thought forgotten at the thought of his manservant being ill. 'Why he is almost as valuable to me as

Obetach is' he thought unhappily, 'what can it be that ails him?'

Trasand held onto his arm to stop him walking away.

"My Lord, before you go in search of him, allow me to tell you more."

"Of course," he said hurriedly, wondering if Obetach had left the castle yet.

"He has already, at this early hour of the day, upset the entire household, had Omilia in tears, and banished the kitchen hands to the gardens to pick vegetables, when the stores are full to overflowing. He's barked and bawled at everyone he's seen, and is most unpleasant to be around."

She trailed off as she noticed the king's face, not sure if he was about to explode with anger or mirth, she backed off slightly. Unable to contain himself, the king burst out laughing. He laughed until he was forced to hold his sides. Upset, Trasand turned to walk away.

"No, no," he called after her, "come back, I apologise, it's just that, well, I was panic stricken when you said he was unwell, and what you've just said means that he's at least not so unwell that he's taken to his bed. I'm sorry, I didn't mean to laugh, it's just my relief, forgive me," he ended sheepishly, took her hand and went in search of his wayward servant.

Flauston was in the trophy room where a slave was wiping the dust off the king's trophies with a soft leather cloth. He was berating the slave for not having completed the task earlier in the day, for being lazy when there was much to be done, for being ugly and insolent, and breathing the air the king needed to breathe.

As Vitaicus strode into the room, still holding Trasand's hand, the slave bowed so low her head almost touched her knees. Flauston turned around startled.

The king motioned to him to dismiss the slave, who inched out of the room, never turning her back and keeping her eyes to the ground. When she was well out of earshot, Vitaicus motioned Flauston to the open window. He stood in companionable silence with his servant, taking in the crisp fresh air, and the stark bareness of the leafless winter trees sprinkled with a light covering of snow that had fallen overnight.

He said softly, "Isn't it a glorious day Flauston?"

"Indeed," was the sullen reply from the disgruntled man at his side.

Trasand pulled herself free of the king and sat in a comfortable chair watching the pair with an interest she'd not displayed in some time.

"Pray tell me, what ails my good man on a day such as this?"

Flauston flinched and turned to the queen with hurt betrayal shimmering in his pale blue eyes. He brushed a grey lock of hair from his face, pulled his shoulders up and said with great dignity, "tis not a matter for the king to concern himself over."

"That may well be, however, when I find maids, slaves and servants either banished or in tears throughout my normally orderly castle, I find it has become a matter for grave concern."

Vitaicus was trying hard to sound stern and had to look away from the distraught old man to prevent himself from laughing again.

"My Lord, it grieves me much that this matter has come to your notice, and I'll put it right immediately. I apologise that you've become distressed and your household is in disarray. You need not concern yourself any longer, but consider the problem solved."

He began to move away as he spoke, head bowed respectfully.

"Out with it man. You've been my manservant all the years I've been king, you needn't be afraid of me, nor keep things from me, or you'll find reason to fear. What is it that has brought about such calamity?"

This time he had no need to hide his mirth as it was fading fast, and he felt immensely frustrated instead. He, the king, should be able to ask any question and be given an immediate and straight answer.

Flauston hesitated only a moment before plunging right in, not wishing to upset the king further but sensing the change in his mood, he said quietly, "three of the king's slave girls have run away, fled in the night with their lovers, two of them freemen, the other a slave of King Rehobadd." He finished without looking up.

"And?" bellowed the king, even more frustrated that his question hadn't yet been answered.

"And, this has put much pressure on me to get the remaining slaves to do additional work. They are unwilling, lazy, stupid ...."

Vitaicus cut him off before he completed his tirade.

"For the love of the gods, man, go out and purchase more slaves. Don't make the lives of the entire household, even that of the queen herself a misery. Take a cow and go to the market, and don't return until you have three more slaves."

“But sire, what of those that ran away, you paid a price for them and now they’ve cost you that price by deserting.”

Vitaicus looked across at his lovely young wife, and although too thin lately and not as bright and cheerful as she was four years ago, she was still beautiful and his loins ached from their earlier encounter. He knew he loved her, and at this moment had great need of her.

“Let the slaves go to their lovers, wherever that may be, for they’ll find hardship enough to repay themselves for leaving my household. Let them be, take the princes and teach them how to choose the best slaves. Go, leave us.”

Flauston left the room hastily, calling for the princes as he went. He didn’t hear the king close the door behind him as he took Trasand in his arms and carried her to the soft floor covering that lay before the hearth.

There he gently disrobed her, and gave vent to all his feelings of joy in the beautiful winters day, his desire for the woman who lay beneath him who’d been distant from him for so long and his yearning for what was gone and past and would never be again, and he made love to her with a passion and emotion she’d not felt from him since the very first night he took her to his bed.

Chapter 25

The visit to the market was one of the most exciting days in the life of the young princes. Dylan loved the ride in the chariot more than almost any other adventure, and even Pren had become used to the bumpy and often hazardous journey.

For Sopa, anything the dog did with the boys was exciting enough to keep his tail wagging at a furious pace until he was too exhausted to move, and then he'd lie at the feet of the princes and sleep, regardless of where they were, or what they were doing.

They arrived at the marketplace, dusty and hoarse from shouting at each other as they pointed out all the interesting things they saw on the way, and jumped down from the chariot with wide eyes. They'd never seen slaves chained together before, but here before them in the busy and noisy market were several hundred slaves, young and old, male and female, all naked except for the chains around their necks that bound them together in lines of twenty.

There was no hurry to choose the slaves, they needed to wait for the cow to be driven to the market by Andethon, a slave himself. Gamenta took the boys by their hands and they began to walk slowly up and down the rows of chained men and women, in amongst the many other merchants who were there.

The market was dry and dirty, and incredibly smelly. Dylan wasn't perturbed by the stench, but Pren wrinkled up his delicate nose in disgust as they passed the more sweaty males. Aside from the rank smell of perspiration, there was a strong uric smell as the slaves had been standing for hours without relief and had urinated down their already filthy legs. On at least two occasions they passed slaves who had diarrhoea, and then even Dylan wrinkled up his nose and motioned for Gamenta to move on quickly past the offending person.

After the first cursory walk up and down the rows, Gamenta went back to the half dozen young girls he'd previously made a mental note of. He stopped at the first of them, and asked her to lift her arms. He examined her hands and nails, looked at her legs and asked her to open her mouth. He took a long time gazing down her throat and examining her teeth before pulling up her eyelids, and asking the girl to look left, then right.

Satisfied, he continued down the row to the second girl he'd marked. He repeated the process, then went behind the slaves until he came to the first girl. He asked her to bend, which caused the other slaves in the line to shuffle closer and lose their footing.

The girls on either side were on their haunches and completely off balance when Gamenta asked her to stand erect. Obeying instantly, she pulled them upright as she straightened her back, and the chains around their necks pulled taut. Gamenta nodded and smiled as he noticed the ripple of muscle. He repeated his request behind his second choice, but she was unable to pull up the slaves that over-balanced beside her, and Gamenta passed by her and began walking up the second row of unfortunate victims.

The boys tripped along happily beside him, listening intently as he explained his every move.

"It's important to see whether they've worked before," he explained, "and you can see that by the state of their hands. You tell their strength by looking at their arms and legs to see how muscled they've become. The condition of their teeth and eyes will tell you if they're healthy. No good choosing someone who'll be ill all the time."

By the time they'd repeated the long process on the sixth girl, Gamenta was well satisfied with his choices. He strode across to the market overseer and pointed out the three girls he'd chosen. The man unchained them, meticulously re-chaining the entire group together again.

He'd just completed his task when Andethon arrived with the cow. Now it was the turn of the overseer to examine the cow to determine if it was a valuable enough animal to exchange for three prime slaves. As the cow was chosen from the king's stock, she was a magnificent beast, well fed and brushed that morning until her hide gleamed. He was entirely satisfied with the bargain and thanked Gamenta for his trade asking for the gods' blessings upon himself and his household, then hurried off to his next customer.

Gamenta returned to find Dylan and Pren happily chatting to the overawed and shy girls he'd purchased. They knew better than to reply, and dare not even look in the direction of the princes unless given orders to do so. Sopa was bounding around, licking the girl's sweaty hands in turn, rushing back and nudging the boys, before searching out another sweaty palm.

Gamenta ordered Andethon to begin the walk back to the castle with the slaves, while he attempted to get his unruly party loaded onto the chariot for the ride home.

The boys sat on the floorboards with their legs dangling over the edge. Sopa ran as hard as he could to keep up. They chatted animatedly the entire way, while Gamenta smiled at the content of their conversation. They couldn't believe how many slaves they'd seen and were astounded when Gamenta told them that Caesar had once bought fifty thousand slaves.

Neither boy could imagine what five thousand slaves chained together would look like, after having seen just a few hundred today, the enormous number that Gamenta mentioned meant little to them. This had been a memorable occasion for Gamenta too and he looked forward eagerly to the years he'd spend with the bright and enthusiastic young men in his charge.

Chapter 26

This time, no one saw Sebilus either enter or leave the castle, so the king himself had the happy task of announcing that the queen was once again with child. Obetach dispatched his novices to spread the news throughout the kingdom while he and Gamenta arranged a fitting feast.

Everyone was on edge as the time of birth grew near, Vitaicus most of all. Trasand seemed resigned to her fate while Obetach and Gamenta spent hours chanting and supplicating the gods, and the servants and slaves tried to keep themselves invisible as they went about their tasks.

When the due day did eventually dawn, it was an anticlimax to all. The birth took place shortly after midnight when everyone was asleep, including the king, and the baby was so tiny that he slipped out of his mother without much fuss and little pain to the weary but relieved queen. Her labour had been just three hours long, and Sebilus hadn't yet sent for the king when the first cry was heard.

The tiny creature was named Roulst and as soon as they were awake, Dylan, Pren and Filethas were fetched to see their newest brother Although the scrawny child grew quickly, he was sickly and remained thin and pasty all his life. He preferred the company of his mother and sister to that of his father or brothers, and try as he might, Vitaicus never had any affinity towards him. He knew in his heart that he loved Pren better than Roulst who was his own flesh and blood. Even though Pren was himself a thin scrap of a boy, timid, shy and not inclined to take the risks that Dylan would, he somehow had more spunk than Roulst and was at least willing to leave his mother's side.

For her part, the arrival of another child set Trasand back immeasurably, and this distressed Vitaicus and gave him more reason to resent his youngest son. His behaviour towards Roulst over the following years caused Trasand great pain and she became even more quiet and withdrawn. Her faithful handmaid Omilia often spoke of her as a flower fading away at the end of the summer. Vitaicus got to hear this and had reason to believe it was true, his lovely wife appeared to be fading away before his eyes.

"My Lord," Obetach greeted the king respectfully as he entered his chamber.

"Obetach, is it time to leave already?" The king asked startled, as he peered out of the window to see the position of the sun.

"Nay, my Lord, it's still early, but I must speak with you before we leave." Perplexed, the king sat down again and waited. Obetach shifted around the room, picking up objects up and putting them down again before speaking.

"I don't believe we should be taking Dylan with us today when we meet with your generals."

He paused long enough to see if Vitaicus would protest, but the king remained passive.

"He'll never be a warrior, as he's to be a priest and besides he should be spending less time with you." He explained. "He needs to be with Gamenta. They should be spending time together in preparation for leaving here, for going into training." Vitaicus nodded thoughtfully.

"You'll not see the prince for many years, you need to prepare yourself too."

Vitaicus felt his stomach knot at the words but knew the truth of them. He needed to prepare himself for a long separation from his son, but preferred to spend every available moment with him instead. He would deal with the separation when the time came. "There's wisdom in what you say Obetach, but …."

"It is the will of the gods." Obetach interrupted, and that was that, the matter was closed. They left for council without Dylan.

It was some days before Vitaicus saw his son again and as he stood before him, the king noticed how the boy had grown, how strong his young body looked next to that of Pren. He tore his eyes from the appealing young face and looked once again at the priest standing before him and tried to focus on the matter at hand.

Gamenta was politely asking the king's kind permission, while

Dylan was begging and pleading loudly, even Pren was quietly entreated the king to allow them to go hunting in the woods for a few days.

Vitaicus was reluctant, not because he was afraid of the trip or what might transpire, but because he desperately wanted to go too, but knew that it was time, that it was probably as a result of his recent conversation with Obetach that Gamenta made his request. He also knew in his heart that he had to obey the gods, but it was without good grace that he gave his permission, giving each boy a lengthy lecture before turning to the unusual looking priest before him and glaring at him long and hard.

He strode from the room, hearing the squeals of delight behind him as he went in search of Trasand to inform her of his decision. 'Perhaps she will be willing to spend some time with me and ease this ache in my heart,' he thought miserably, as his son tore past him on his way to the kitchens to pack their provisions.

Although the boys could ride their ponies well, Gamenta decided they'd be travelling too far for the small animals to carry them, and so they left in a chariot with his horse, Leigh, at the rein.

Dylan rode next to Gamenta in the place of the charioteer, while Pren sat on the floorboards in the position with which he was now comfortable. With his arm round Sopa, he sang a merry song and pointed out all sorts of strange sights and sounds to the dog as their long journey progressed. There were two other chariots behind them, one carrying two servants and their provisions, the other, two priests of Gamenta's age.

They passed through several hamlets before they stopped to rest and eat, and hadn't been on the road long again when they neared one of the hamlets on the northern border of the kingdom of Vitaicus. Gamenta had been feeling uneasy since they'd begun the second leg of their journey, and had seen more than one ill omen. He'd been quietly beseeching the gods to protect them when a flock of birds, startled into flight, swooped past them.

Gamenta immediately stopped his chariot and called for the priests following him to draw alongside. They too were uneasy and had seen the hurried flight of the birds as a sign of something untoward.

Before they'd time to discuss what action to take, they heard the distinct sound of warriors marching. The noise that accompanied them became clearer as they neared, and the little party by the side of the roadway could make out the sounds of singing and cheering, shouting and bantering. It was clearly a victorious group of fighters that was approaching.

Gamenta pulled their chariot out of the way and held tightly onto his charges as the first horsemen came into sight. The noise grew louder until it was difficult to separate the sounds, and a huge cacophony assailed their ears. The princes were at an impressionable age and they watched the returning warriors with differing feelings.

Dylan felt awe and pride in these brave and victorious men. Pren felt horror and disgust as their horses carried the spoils of war, the heads of their foes dripping blood along the dusty road. By the time the group of fifty or so men had passed them the blood and gore had mingled with the droppings of the horses and the rank smell blended with the stench of urine and of death. Pren felt bile rise to his throat and tore his hand free of Gamenta so that he could be sick away from his brother who was clapping his hands with delight at the sights and sounds of war.

On the last horse, draped carelessly over its back was a seemingly lifeless form. The horse was being led by a woman who walked slowly, wailing loudly. She saw the priests and stopped, fell to her knees in the filth and begged them to save her husband.

Gamenta went to the injured man and recognised him immediately as Luchrad, one of the king's finest warriors. The priests lifted his inert body from the horse and laid him on the verge of the roadway. One of the servants had already collected Gamenta's sack of medicines from the chariot and the priest got to work immediately, cleaning out the man's deep wounds and stuffing the entry holes with a preparation of herbs before sealing them with Sphagnum moss. The wounds were serious and bleeding profusely.

The herbs would staunch the flow and the incredible absorption of the moss would soak up the remaining blood and pus preventing the wound from festering. Gamenta bound each moss covered laceration tightly with strips of clean white cloth. While he worked the woman told the priest what had happened.

She and her husband lived in the hamlet that Gamenta and his party were approaching. The people living there were from two different clans and had lived peaceably together for many generations, farming corn in the huge fields they jointly owned. In the centre of the hamlet, next to the large communal bread-making oven was the granary, the woman explained.

While the men gathered corn, the women baked bread that they traded in other hamlets for vegetables. The granary was the largest in the land of Canti, and every child living there knew better than to play near it, she continued.

Yesterday morning however, two boys just a bit older than Dylan and Pren climbed to the top of the tower and peered in. One of the boys had fallen, or been pushed, and lay at the bottom in the pile of corn, bleeding from a badly broken leg and crying wildly. The other boy, afraid to admit that he'd been at the top of the tower, ran home and hid. Eventually someone heard the boy's distressed wailing and he was rescued.

However, she went on, he must have suffered further injury than was evident, for he died during the night. The dead boy was her son, she sobbed, and so her husband gathered his clan and called his neighbour and onetime friend, the father of the cowardly boy who'd hidden, to come out and fight. Although her husband lost the battle, the head of the offending boy's father hung from the horse of the man who'd slain him. Many of her clan were dead and her husband wounded and she was afraid that he too would die.

Dylan and Pren listened wide-eyed to the tale. The excitement of the events preceding the battle, the thought of the battle itself, the sights and smells roused something deep within Dylan, and he knew he was born to be a mighty warrior, not a priest. He felt like grabbing a spear and running wildly with it, slashing and cutting at anything that moved. He felt a war cry bubbling up inside him and wanted to shriek and dance and challenge Pren to a duel. He looked across at his one eyed brother and remembered with deep regret their last duel, and some of his adrenalin subsided.

Pren watched Gamenta's hands as he worked swiftly and skilfully on the wounded warrior lying so lifelessly before him. He too felt many emotions. He desperately wanted to be a Druid and knew he had it within him to be a healer, like Gamenta. He knew that he could compose and sing beautiful songs, and would be the best Bard in the land. He so badly wanted to be eight years old right now, so he could go to the forests and learn all the wondrous things that Druids learnt. He didn't want to be a warrior, and as a Druid he would be safe from fighting forever.

Gamenta came to the last and worst wound the man had sustained. An arrow had pierced his side and as soon as the priest bent to sniff at it, he knew the arrow had been poisoned. Although he dressed it in the same manner as he had the other injuries, he knew there was only one cure for the effects of a poisonous arrow.

He asked his priests to gather all the druids attached to the hamlet while he finished working on Luchrad, giving him a potion to drink as he called on Sulis, the God of Healing, to assist him. Gamenta knew that King Vitaicus would want him to save this warrior, and he'd do everything in his power as a priest and healer to ensure that the gods let him live.

It wasn't long before a party of priests arrived, fifteen in all. A senior priest approached Gamenta and reported to him that the battle had been lost through the fault of the novice priests who'd performed a chant incorrectly as the warriors were going out to fight.

Gamenta realised instantly that this was the ill omen he'd felt all morning, but it was too late to change that, the novices would be dealt with later. It was his task to work against the poison that was slowly killing Luchrad.

An ancient and well known Druid named Trostan had been told the secret of healing poison by the gods, and this knowledge had been passed down to Druids for generations, taught to them during their years of training. It was a ritual Gamenta hadn't performed before and he knew that the young priests standing before him wouldn't have either.

Nervously he ordered them to gather fifty white hornless cows, ready for milking. They were to be milked simultaneously and the milk was to be brought to Gamenta along with the cows. The priests looked at him with astonishment, but didn't question him. They hurried to the hamlet and gathered the cows and returned as the sun was setting, herding the cows. Behind them came the people of the hamlet carrying the buckets of milk.

At midnight Gamenta told them to milk the cows again, and they filled the buckets further. At dawn Gamenta ordered that the cows be milked for a third time. The clan carried the buckets of milk to the battlefield of the previous day. Gamenta and three priests lifted the wounded man and carefully carried him to the centre of the battlefield where the heaviest fighting had taken place.

Gamenta ordered that the area be cleared of debris and a hole dug. A fly infested horse lay where it had fallen, the headless body of a man whose family hadn't yet bothered to collect him lay close by. A number of broken swords littered the ground, caked and covered in mud and strips of clothing. The task of clearing and then hollowing out the area Gamenta required took some time and while they worked the injured man lay groaning and muttering in an unconscious state.

Gamenta told the men to hurry and when he was satisfied with the hollow he commanded the women to pour the milk into the ground where it formed a pool while he began a lengthy incantation to the God Sulis. As soon as the last bucket was empty Luchrad was stripped naked and placed in the bath of milk. Gamenta, in his bare feet, held the man's wounds under the milk and bathed his feverish body. Three times he lifted Luchrad out and three times placed him back into the hollow and bathed him in the swiftly decreasing pool. Satisfied at last, Gamenta told his family to take him home.

He asked the priests of the hamlet to re-dress the wounds daily for a week and assured them that Luchrad was healed of the poison. The wife thanked Gamenta and the gods profusely before helping to carry her husband home.

Drained from the day's ordeal, Gamenta and his party followed. As a Druid, he had the right to anything he required in the land, but even had that not been so he would have been warmly welcomed for his ministrations to Luchrad. As he walked beside his horse, he thanked the gods that they'd chosen to name her Leigh, which meant healing, and that those healing powers had flown out from her today into his own body, allowing him to minister to the deathly sick warrior.

A hut was hastily vacated for Gamenta and the princes, and room made for their priests and slaves. They were given ample to eat and drink and were all asleep before the sun dropped below the horizon, Dylan to dream of being a warrior, Pren of becoming a priest.

The following morning when Dylan woke, he lay thinking over the events of the previous two days and remembered with a start that he'd never be a warrior, he was destined to be a priest.

Pren too lay thinking, fearing in his heart that his mother wouldn't allow him to leave her and become a priest. He would no doubt have to be a warrior. Dazed and disheartened, the boys asked to go home, they no longer had any enthusiasm for the hunt, and Gamenta reluctantly returned them to the relative safety and comfort of the castle.

Chapter 27

AD 36
Summer

Vitaicus sat watching his wife dress Filethas. She was a pretty three year old with long curly hair, which Trasand combed vigorously, making the golden strands shine in the sunlight. Obetach disturbed the quiet moment as he hurried into the room.

"My Lord, I'm ill at ease," he said hurriedly. "I've just completed my meditations and saw an ill omen."

He motioned for Vitaicus to follow him from the room, but the king commanded him to continue.

"Very well," he said glancing anxiously at Trasand,

"I had a vision in which I saw many boars, but each one was crippled and unable to walk on all fours. Each had a broken foreleg, and hobbled about feebly. It seemed to me too that they were blind, as they knocked into each other and bumped into trees. My flesh crawled as I watched the vision, and I fear for the prince."

Vitaicus shot out of the chair he'd been sitting on.

"How many boars where there?" he demanded, "how many?"

"Not as many as thirty my Lord," said Obetach, knowing instantly what the king was thinking.

"Come, we must find the boys."

He bowed to Trasand and left the room quickly with Vitaicus trailing him, sweat breaking out on his brow as he realised his son faced a new danger, probably at the hand of the gods.

It took some time to find the princes, and at first it didn't appear that anything was amiss. They were playing at hiding from each other and Pren had gone into the weaving room. Dylan heard the heavy wooden door shut and followed Pren as soon as he'd waited long enough for his brother to conceal himself.

The weaving room was large and filled with wonderful hiding places. There were two huge looms to hide behind, tables to hide under, and bales of wool to crawl inside. The boys usually hid inside a bale of wool, and often it was their sneezing that gave them away.

This time Pren chose to hide behind a loom, but tried to make himself as small as possible and to keep his body flush up against the wooden frame. He crept along the base and at the edge, put his arm through the side beam to keep his balance. It was a tight squeeze and he was not sure how he'd free himself. He hoped Dylan would find him quickly.

Dylan didn't want the game to end in a hurry and took his time, making a great show of examining each of the bales in turn, talking loudly as he progressed.

"I'm going to find you Pren, I know where you are, I can smell you, I'm getting closer, I'm coming to get you."

Realising Pren wasn't where he expected, Dylan stopped and looked around. He spotted the edge of Pren's robe peeking out from behind the loom. He went down on his belly and crept forward, coming up behind Pren silently, and once he was directly behind and below him he yelled out loudly, "got you!"

Pren got such a fright he jumped, yanked his arm, lost his balance and fell off the base of the beam, but his arm was jammed and he dangled in midair, all his weight on his shoulder. He heard the sound of something tearing before he felt any pain, and then thankfully fainted.

Dylan wondered why Pren hadn't responded to his shout and stood up. He looked at Pren, dangling from his right arm, his good eye closed, his face pale, and tried to fathom what had happened.

It was at that moment that Vitaicus and Obetach pushed open the door and took in the scene. Obetach knew instantly that his vision had been about Pren rather than Dylan, but felt no sense of relief at the tragic sight.

It took many weeks for Pren's arm to heal enough for him to be able to use it again, but its use was limited. He could wiggle his fingers, clench his fist and move his wrist and elbow, but his shoulder would no longer rotate and he could barely lift his arm a hand's width from his body.

Secretly, and despite the constant nagging pain, Pren was

delighted that his arm, his right arm, was useless. He'd never have to hunt again and he'd never be a warrior. He'd hoped when he lost his eye that his father would accept that he couldn't hunt, but Vitaicus had been undeterred and taught him to sight his prey and hold his bow ready with his remaining eye. However, without the use of his right arm, he simply couldn't hold a bow or a spear and would never fight or hunt. Now he really could become a priest.

Vitaicus too realised that Pren wouldn't be a warrior, and prepared to give up both his boys to become priests.

Dylan was horrified by this second devastating accident to his little brother. Although the same age as Dylan, Pren was a head shorter, and much slighter and lighter and ever since Pren had lost his eye, Dylan had felt protective towards him. Those feelings doubled with this fresh disaster, for which Dylan felt entirely responsible just as he'd been for the accident with the spear. He loved Pren deeply and made a covenant with himself to spend the rest of his life looking after him.

With only two years to go before they turned eight, the magical age at which they'd disappear into the forests, Pren felt contented with his life and the tragedies that had befallen him.

Chapter 28

AD 36
Autumn

As the anniversary of the birth of the princes drew nearer, Pren looked forward to the celebrations almost as much as his excitable brother. For Dylan all activities from fishing to festivals, picnics to a birth celebration, were wonderful occasions and he greeted each new day with the exuberance of youth and the energy of a seasoned warrior. For their sixth birth anniversary a huge feast was planned and the servants and slaves had been busy preparing for weeks.

Dylan knew he wouldn't be able to sleep the night before the celebration and was delighted to see Gamenta appear at the doorway of their chamber. He nudged Pren over roughly and made room for the priest to sit on their bed.

Gamenta had come to fulfil his duty and relate the story of the birth of Prince Dylan. They both knew the story well by now, but listened wordlessly as Gamenta related it yet again, marvelling at his memory as he repeated word for word every detail. When he'd finished they fired questions at him.

Understanding better the tragedy of Hilfuth's death, Dylan wanted to know about her as a mother, and Gamenta told him all he could remember. He asked questions he'd never have the courage to ask his father. Once satisfied that she'd been a good person, as good as his mother Trasand, he settled down to daydream until he fell asleep.

Pren wanted to know more about Obetach's decision to kill the queen and save the baby, and why he'd felt it necessary. Gamenta longed for the day the boys would join the Order of the Druids, where they'd learn the ways of the gods, and better understand his answer, which he realised wasn't satisfying the enquiring mind of Pren.

Once he felt he'd explained Obetach's actions to the best of his ability, he tucked the boys tightly under their covers and left them to talk before falling asleep, the excitement of the following day no longer the focus of their attention.

Shortly after the feasting and celebrations, Obetach announced that it was time to prepare for the Festival of Samain. Samain marked the end of the warm season and was a Fire Festival dedicated to all the gods in times of uncertainty and potential danger, such as at the start of another winter season. It was the one time of the year when the veil between the reality of the people and that of the Otherworld was most easily penetrated. The priests were needed by the people to placate the gods as they faced the winter ahead with its accompanying dark, cold and hunger.

There was great trepidation throughout the land as every tribe planned to appease the gods and plead for a merciful winter, one with sufficient food and warmth for the people to survive. For the priests, the celebrations that lay ahead were to be holy and crucial and they were anxious not to offend the gods in any way. The novices were nervous of chanting incorrectly and the senior priests watched them like hawks, lest the entire land suffer at their inexperienced hands and at the displeasure of the gods.

The queen was heavily pregnant once again and Omilia wondered if she'd last long enough to make it to the celebration. The day of Samain dawned and Trasand was feeling well. There was no evidence that the birth was imminent, but Sebilus had moved into the room next to the queen's chamber as a precaution and kept a constant vigil.

The day passed uneventfully and Trasand was in a bright and cheerful mood as night fell and the festival was due to begin. Despite the protests of Vitaicus and Obetach, Omilia and Sebilus, the queen was determined to be present at the ceremony.

Vitaicus finally gave in seeing that his wife was in higher spirits than for some time, and ordered his finest carriage to be brought into the courtyard so she could ride in comfort most of the way. The final passage through the thick forest before reaching the open glade would need to be made on foot, but at least she could cover the first part of the journey seated on soft cushions.

This chariot was large enough to carry four passengers and Sebilus sat next to the queen, opposite her was Omilia, and beside Omilia sat a priestess who kept up a constant supplication to the gods for the protection of the unborn infant and the queen as they made their way towards the forest.

To Trasand the walk over the last part of the journey was stimulating. She seemed to abound with energy, and once beside the large fire she sat transfixed on a soft pile of cushions as the first day of the familiar festival played out before her.

Although it was many hours later, it seemed like no time at all that Omilia was beside Trasand helping her to stand. Her body was stiff from sitting still watching the ceremony unfold. Omilia and Sebilus rubbed her aching legs and coaxed life back into her frozen feet.

The walk back to the carriage in the early hours of the morning was less pleasant and Trasand realised she was exhausted. She leant heavily on Omilia and Sebilus who did their best to support her under each arm as they made their slow way out of the forest. Her waters broke before the first pains assailed her, and she stood dumbfounded while the warm liquid ran down her legs, and then with the first contraction she was forced to sit on the damp earth and breathe deeply until it passed.

As soon as she was able to rise, the panic stricken women raced her to the carriage. The contractions came fast and furiously on the ride back to the castle, and by the time the panting horses stopped in the courtyard, Trasand knew the baby's head was crowning. She was unable to stand up. Omilia raced into the castle screaming for help. Four male slaves carried the queen into her chamber, as no one else had arrived back from the forest.

By the time Trasand was settled on her bed the baby was well on its way and Sebilus didn't stop to put her birth coverings over the queen's woollen blanket. The infant arrived in a swift messy moment, ruining the beautiful wool, staining it forever with the blood of the newest princess.

When Vitaicus arrived at the castle an hour later he was told he had a guest waiting to see him.

"Bring him in!" he said dismayed, as it was almost time for the sun to rise. He was sitting at his worktable resting his head in his hands when Omilia stepped in so quietly that he didn't hear her.

"My Lord, meet Mellund, your daughter," she said softly, offering him the tiniest bundle he'd ever held.

Chapter 29

AD 36
Winter

Trasand ran straight into Obetach as she rushed out of the children's chamber in search of the Druid. "Oh thank the gods you are here!" she sobbed.

"What is it my Lady?" Obetach asked seeing the concern on her thin face and sensing her hysteria. He followed her into the room without waiting for her reply. Mellund, only a few weeks old, lay sodden through in her wooden basin. Trasand had stripped her clothing from her and a damp cloth lay on the floor where she'd flung it as she ran in search of help. The baby's body was red with fever and perspiration shone on her tiny face.

"Fetch Gamenta and bring him to me in the courtyard," he ordered the queen as he picked up the infant and left the room, taking large hurried steps.

Once outside he plunged the fever hot baby into the cold spring water pool in the centre of the courtyard. When Gamenta and Trasand arrived a few moments later, her body was cooler and more normal in colour, but shortly after they had her back in the castle she began to cough, a piteous sound that alarmed Obetach.

He'd heard wet coughs such as this many times in his years as a priest, and knew instantly that the child was deathly ill. He knew he had only one course of action, he had to call on the Goddess who ruled the springs and wells and holy water of the land to use her healing powers.

Many summers previously a number of Druids from Gaul had fled the Romans and crossed over into Britain, where they'd met Obetach and told him of their Goddess Sequana who lived in the

River Seine in that far away land across the sea. The Druids from Gaul believed that she'd come with them to Britain and had testified to her wonderful healing powers. Obetach prayed they were right as he prepared the queen and the sick baby for the journey into the land of the Atrebates, to Aquae Sulis, where the priests had settled.

Along the River Avon were many small tributaries and pools that flowed into the great river. One of these tributaries came from a spring in the heart of a thick forest, where a sacred pool had been dug. The crystal clear water that flowed out of the rocks was the holiest water in Britain and it was where Obetach was headed with Mellund. He hadn't seen the pool before but instinctively knew where it was and led the chariot carrying the queen and her child straight to the forest, where they met three of the Druids from Gaul.

They left the royal chariot and went deeper into the forest on foot. Still weak from this latest birth, the long and arduous journey, and the many other trials that had beset her since becoming the wife of the king, Trasand stumbled along the rough pathway, crying softly as she followed the priests into the unknown place. Once they neared the sacred pool, Trasand was allowed to sit on a rock and rest, while the priests took the baby and went on.

Although Obetach was permitted into the holy place, he wouldn't play any part in the ceremony. He'd brought with him offerings for the Goddess Sequana of fruit, wine, vegetables and honey. The Gaulish Druids told him that he could take a cauldron of sacred water back with him with which to bathe the baby, but the Goddess required the offering of a young animal in return and Obetach cursed the evil gods that had brought about this calamity in the season when there were no young to offer.

The priests took the gifts that Obetach brought, and walked around the healing pool praying and chanting to the goddess. Then they took baby Mellund and walked into the ice-cold clear water with her. One by one the priests took her and dipped her into the pool. The screams of the frozen child drowned out the sounds of their chanting.

Trasand sobbed as she listened to her baby's distress, but it lasted a few moments only before Obetach was back, giving Mellund to her. She hurriedly wrapped the shivering baby in a covering then placed the infant under her own cloak against her warm flesh, as they began the long walk to their waiting carriage.

Obetach was subdued on the return trip, unsure that the Goddess Sequana had been present and even if she was, not convinced that she'd be willing to heal this baby who was not from her own land.

It didn't take long for all to see that the healing waters had not healed, and Mellund grew weaker daily. Her cough increased and became wetter, until she choked constantly and was unable to drink from her mother's breast. Four days after returning from the land of the Atrebates, she made her journey into the Otherworld, to join the gods and her sister Kwethin.

A week after the death of Mellund a messenger came riding into the courtyard. He looked weary but not flustered and it didn't appear that he'd ridden hard, and so Flauston sent him to wash and refresh himself before taking him to the audience chamber where the king would see him. The news the man carried was not critical, but it left Vitaicus thinking long after he'd left.

Disaster had struck the city of Rome and she was suffering a financial crises. A fire on the Aventine had destroyed a large area of the city and the relief fund needed was enormous. The treasury was bankrupt and Emperor Tiberius had came to the aid of the city and its people and lent them an enormous amount of money, around 100 000 000 sesterces. As Vitaicus questioned the messenger further, he learnt that Tiberius had already lent the treasury a similar amount from his own personal wealth to alleviate financial crises three years previously, and even this was not the first time that he'd saved the treasury. Nine years earlier a wooden amphitheatre had collapsed at Fidenae and over fifty thousand people were either crushed to death or seriously wounded and mutilated.

The relief fund needed then had been staggering and Tiberius had come to the rescue. Vitaicus could barely imagine a crowd of fifty thousand people, and had never seen an amphitheatre, so the picture in his mind of the devastation was vague.

"In his earlier years as Emperor", the messenger continued, "Tiberius provided large subsidies to permit the price of grain to be lowered."

He appears to be a generous man, if nothing else, thought Vitaicus. As the Celts still bartered, he had no real concept of the value of money, but the man before him said that in terms of livestock or barter items, Vitaicus' entire wealth would have been a quarter of the sum which made Vitaicus realise how generous Tiberius was even though he could no doubt afford, but could he keep on lending this kind of money to Rome? Surely if Tiberius continually needed to do so, it implied that the treasury was always empty. The obvious place to come looking for additional wealth was as ever, the mystical land across the sea, the land of Britain.

Vitaicus was right to be concerned. Like Augustus before him, Tiberius continually gave the impression that a conquest of Britain was imminent, knowing how popular an expedition into that country would make him, however Tiberius was unable to proceed as he once again became seriously ill. As he suffered epileptic fits he was often unwell.

So far, all penetration into Britain by the Romans during Tiberius' reign had been peaceful, but Roman influence throughout the country was becoming marked, and Vitaicus felt that it was inevitable that the Emperor would come eventually, this time to conquer and annex! Even if he once again forced the Celts to pay tributes to Rome, that would surely swell his coffers.

As Vitaicus thought these things through, he became deeply depressed.

Chapter 30

AD 37
Winter

After the death of Mellund, Trasand withdrew from life almost entirely and seldom left her chamber. Not even the younger children could bring her out of the dark world where she brooded day and night. Filethas was three and a half and Roulst a little over a year and they both needed their mother, but she seemed unable to respond to them.

Vitaicus couldn't bear to see Trasand, but couldn't cope without her either, until he couldn't stand it any longer and sent Flauston to bring one of the slaves to be his mistress. He'd watched her working around the castle, admired her muscular body, her ample bust and short bouncy brown hair. He was fascinated with her.

She was entirely different to Trasand and he'd become aware of a growing lust for her with each passing day. He couldn't go to his wife for fear of impregnating her again, besides which she wouldn't allow him to touch her. He had a desperate need of a woman and the young slave filled his dreams more with each passing day.

The younger children were less aware of the subtle changes in the castle, but Dylan and Pren were keenly aware of what was taking place. They knew their mother was beside herself with grief and didn't want to be with her children or her husband, but this didn't disturb them. They'd seen their father take the slave girl into his chamber, and even that didn't worry them.

What did upset them was the lack of interest either of their parents took in them, combined with their erratic behaviour. One day Vitaicus would laugh with them and ask them to sit with him and then stare off into the distance. The next day he'd banish them from his chamber. They'd visit their mother who'd ask them to talk to her, and then not listen to anything they said, but cry silently into her hands until they crept away unnoticed.

The king took to shouting at the servants, the queen to sending uneaten meals back to the kitchen. The atmosphere in the castle became unbearable and the boys began leaving as soon as they'd eaten their porridge in the morning, returning only at nightfall. They'd catch fish in the river, amble through the forest picking strawberries, or ride their ponies, Tuath-Reul and Luath-Reul until both horse and boy were exhausted, then they would find a sheltered spot to huddle together and talk.

They'd spent every moment together almost from the day of their birth, and although different in every way, they'd become soul mates and were at an age where they could play happily for hours or enjoy conversations in which they discussed adult things. They talked of war and of trading. They fantasised about the lands over the seas and planned to visit them one day. They discussed the Romans and retold each other all the stories they'd ever heard, but their favourite topic was their future as priests.

As tensions mounted in the castle, they knew that life there would never be the same, and they longed for the sanctuary of the forests, and the relative peace and tranquillity of the life of a Druid.

Having come to terms with the fact that he'd never be a warrior, Dylan looked forward to the harsh living and the intensity of the learning. Fascinated with all aspects of life he wanted to know simply everything.

Pren longed to learn of medicine and be a great healer. He looked forward to the time when he'd compose and sing songs in his sweet voice.

Each day spent discussing their futures was a delight to the boys, and they made a pact to be together until the great day when Dylan would be called by the gods, and even then, Pren promised to follow him into the Otherworld.

The aging Emperor Tiberius had been living on the Island of Capreae for some years, ruling his ever growing Empire from there, but he'd become ill yet again. Fearing rightly, that this was his last illness, he left for Italy at once.

He died at the Misenum on the 16th day of the Roman month of

March at the age of seventy-eight. Although he'd been an austere and gloomy emperor and one who suffered from a serious temper, he'd also been reserved and generous, and hadn't troubled Britain unduly. When word reached Vitaicus that Tiberius was dead, his greatest concern was who his successor would be.

By the time the news arrived, the new emperor had already been named. He was Gauis Caesar Caligula, son of Germanicus and Agrippina. It was with amusement that Vitaicus learned the background to the name Caligula a few months later. Apparently the new ruler enjoyed dressing up in a miniature soldier's uniform when he was young. The little sandals that he wore with this uniform were the reason for the nickname 'Little Army Boot' or 'Caligula', being given to him. He kept the name, and what Vitaicus learned was that he was a good choice after the gloomy years of reign by Tiberius.

He was a handsome, young and athletic man, whom his people loved. However, within a short time Caligula too fell ill and became a changed man. His wit and charm turned to surly and suspicious cruelty. Obetach felt certain he'd been struck by an evil god, as his personality changed daily. His behaviour became more curious as he decreed that he should be worshiped as a god before his death, while he could enjoy it. His senators were made to bow before him, kiss his feet and worship him. Those who disobeyed were sent to the arena, where they fought to the death against gladiators. Caligula executed thirty-five senators and almost three hundred equites who displeased or disobeyed him. Vitaicus was bemused at the news. He worried over the potential trouble a madman such as this could cause to his own country.

Rather than turn to Britain for wealth during his fading years, Tiberius had levied extortionate taxes to build up his treasury, and at his death it was reported to be somewhere between 2 700 000 000 and 3 300 000 000 sesterces. Caligula began to spend this enormous treasury on games to entertain the people and at the same time on building up his army, and each report that Vitaicus received concerned him deeply.

Chapter 31

AD 37

Spring

Dylan awoke early to what he thought would be an ordinary spring day, and was surprised to find Gamenta standing beside him, calling softly. He flew out of bed, and taking hold of Gamenta's hand tiptoed across the room. Pren slept peacefully on, oblivious to the whispering close by.

Gamenta had come to take Dylan riding and planned to go to a special forest a long way from the castle, a journey that would take them the entire day. Still early in spring, the days were lengthening, but were much shorter than they'd become once summer arrived, and they needed every daylight hour. Gamenta wanted to take Dylan only, but the prince begged and pleaded for Pren to be come too. Eventually after Dylan confided to Gamenta about the pact that the boys had made to always be together, he relented.

The priest had already prepared provisions for the day, and waited patiently while Dylan and Pren dressed. They washed their faces and wet their hair in the cold water of the pool in the outer courtyard, then picked a strawberry from the vegetable garden to rub and clean their teeth with as they followed Gamenta towards the stables.

Dylan's, Luath-Reul, snuffled as he smelled the boy come close, and he gave the pony a piece of apple to eat. Tuath-Reul became excited by the smell of the fruit, and moved closer too, pushing his wet nose and mouth into Dylan's hand, until Pren gave him a piece of the apple too. The ponies weren't suitable for the ride that Gamenta planned, and the stable hand had colts ready for them. They were the smallest horses in the stables, and the boys could ride them easily. Pren was given Tara, a slight but majestic horse named after that far away land where Dylan's ancestors originally came from.

Dylan was given Fion, who was slightly larger with a high-spirited nature. She loved to canter, as did Dylan. With growing excitement they mounted the horses. They'd spent many hours riding them in the fields around the castle, but had never ventured out as far as Gamenta planned to go.

Their excitement increased as the morning wore on and they rode further from the safety of the castle into country they'd never seen before. Up hills, down dales, and through streams and forests they went, until Gamenta could see they were tiring and they stopped beside a river for midday food. The boys ate quickly then began playing a game with acorns, while Gamenta tended the horses. They rested for some time before the boys begged to go on. Gamenta wanted them to see the forest where he'd been trained when he was a novice, and they approached the outskirts in silence.

Gamenta wouldn't allow them to enter the glade for fear of interrupting other novices in training, but just being there in that hallowed atmosphere had the boys whispering in awe to each other as they walked their horses through the thickets. They could barely contain themselves as they discussed their future, possibly in this same forest. Pren saw himself as a Bard, singing and composing the songs that filled his head, while Dylan imagined himself learning to be a fully fledged Druid, staying the twenty years necessary to learn all the many things required.

Gamenta listened to them with amusement. He too could hardly wait for the time ahead to pass.

It took some persuasion from him to tear the boys away from his forest and begin the long ride home, but it was a pleasant journey filled with tales from Gamenta of his own days of learning. They travelled slowly enough to talk most of the way and were still a few miles from the castle when the sun began its rapid descent. Gamenta knew they'd need to speed up if they were to arrive with any daylight left, and as the boys weren't experienced at riding full grown horses and were already tired from the long day, he didn't want to risk their having to find their way on treacherously uneven roadways in the dark.

He spurred his horse into a faster pace and the boys followed suit, eventually letting their horses gallop, and Dylan and Pren shouted as they felt the wind blow through their long hair, cool now as the sun lost its warmth, it stung their cheeks and brought bright pink colour to them.

Gamenta kept looking back to see how they were faring, and didn't see a snake slithering through the sand in front of his horse. She only saw it as she passed it, and shied slightly to the right. Gamenta looked forward to see what had startled Leigh, but he was already well past the reptile. Feeling his horse's tension, he slowed her and looked back again in time to see the snake rear up in front of Dylan's horse. Pren managed to force Tara off the roadway and skirt Dylan's horse through a clearing in the bushes on the left where the snake had been moments before.

Tara just missed crashing into Fion as she came to a standstill, whinnying. Fion raised her forelegs, shying away from the loathsome creature that swayed in front of her. Dylan clung to the back of his terrified horse with all his strength, but could feel his sweaty fingers slipping down the mane as she continued to buck and kick out at the snake. One of her hoofs connected with the swaying adder and it fell back, recoiled and reared up again, lashing out viciously at the huge object in front of it. Fion reacted to the backward fall of the snake and brought her forelegs down, intending to crush the creature that terrified her so, but the snake was too quick, and was upright again as the hoofs crashed into the soft sand.

As the snake lashed forward, her fangs bit into the foreleg of Dylan's colt, and she squealed, a sound that made Gamenta sick to his stomach. He was frozen to the spot during the split seconds that the scene played out in front of him, but with the sound of the horse's agony ringing in his ears, he turned Leigh round and charged back towards the snake and Fion. Sensing danger from behind, the snake dropped to the ground and slithered into the bush with astonishing speed.

Fion, already petrified and stricken with growing pain, saw the charging horse and reared up again. This time Dylan couldn't hold onto the mane and was flung backwards from a height twice that of his own body. He landed with a heavy thud on a rock and even above the noise of the horse and Dylan's own cry, Gamenta heard the crack of bones.

He brought Leigh under control, leaving Fion to run off into the bush. Pren was beside him and off his horse by the time Gamenta dismounted, and together they knelt next to Dylan who'd bitten through his lip in order not to cry. Blood ran down his chin, and into the sand where he lay on his side, not daring to move as the pain in his back was so sharp.

It was well after dark when Gamenta and Pren led the horses into the stables. They'd walked the horses home with Dylan lying on the back of Leigh, and although in great pain, he remained conscious and brave throughout the awful journey. Apart from his bleeding lip and badly broken ribs on his right side, he'd suffered bruising down his back, but no other injury. Nevertheless the royal household was in an uproar, led by a formidably angry Obetach.

Dylan wasn't quite sure who Obetach was angry with, himself, Gamenta, or the evil gods who'd allowed this to happen, but one way or another, he was very angry. It was his charge to keep Dylan perfect until the day of his Supreme Sacrifice, without blemish, now he had a broken bone and even though it would heal, he'd never be perfectly whole again.

Obetach ordered an immediate ceremony to appease the gods, and a bull was fetched from the grazing fields to be sacrificed before midnight. Priests and priestesses were brought to the castle from far and wide. With torches lit, their incantations began as soon as the word spread. A bonfire was built in the courtyard beyond the pool, and Dylan was carried out on a litter and placed at the head of the ceremony. Obetach and Gamenta spent the night, begging the god's forgiveness for allowing this catastrophe to befall their charge, and calling upon Sulis to mend the broken bones.

Dylan spent the night being prayed over and sprinkled with holy water. He'd been given a large draught of medicine to ease his pain, a draught that made him sleepy. Added to the exhaustion of the long day the potion made it almost impossible to stay awake, but each time the he began to drift off, a priestess would wake him with more cold water over his face.

Eventually the priests agreed they could do no more. Every conceivable prayer had been said to every known god. The bull had been slaughtered, its blood drained and the carcass incinerated in the large fire. The child had been prayed over and sprinkled with holy water time and time again.

The priests were exhausted, their legs lame from dancing. The Bards were losing their voices and their fingers were numb from playing their lyres. The priestesses could no longer keep Dylan awake, even with cold water, and so they carried him to his bed by the pale pink light of the new day.

Chapter 32

It was several months after Vitaicus first took Ashannon to his bed that he felt guilty for the first time. Guilty that he'd betrayed the queen and guilty that he'd neglected Dylan and Pren. His other children never crossed his mind. Although Filethas was a charming little girl, she was a girl, and held little interest for him, while Roulst was a puny and whiney child who he simply did not like.

Vitaicus decided to make amends and went to see Trasand. Over the past weeks she'd heard that her husband had a mistress and had been interested to learn that it was the slave girl Ashannon whom Gamenta had chosen from the slave market two years earlier with Dylan and Pren.

The news didn't come as a surprise to her, but neither did it upset her. She was afraid to become pregnant again and was content to spend the rest of her life as queen of Vitaicus but not as his wife, and so when he came to see her for the first time in many weeks, she smiled at him and motioned to a nearby chair. Vitaicus was unsure what to say to her but commented on the weather and the health of the children. Trasand said little and they spent an uncomfortable few moments together before the king took his leave and fled.

He went in search of the boys and eventually found them wading in the river, attempting to catch frogs in their hands. They were laughing gaily when he approached but stopped as soon as they saw him and with eyes downcast waited for him to speak. Vitaicus was so saddened by the sight that he determined to spend every available moment with them from then on. The boys found his company unsettling and inhibiting and dreaded being with him. They tried every trick they could to avoid his daily trips with them riding, hunting and fishing. The only enjoyable day they spent together was the day he took them to order a gift for their mother.

Vitaicus was spending a little time with Trasand each day, after which he rushed into the ample arms of Ashannon. His time with Trasand had become more pleasurable and he realised with relief that he still loved her and wanted to get her a special gift to ease his guilt and her pain.

The chariot ride to Mananius was exciting as always, with Sopa trotting behind trying to nip at their feet every time they slowed enough for him to get close. Once at Mananius they were quiet and subdued until they saw what their father had ordered.

Mananius had been working on it day and night for weeks and the boys stood wide eyed, not daring to touch the magnificent object. It was a large cauldron of bronze with the entire life of the queen depicted round its base, from the time she'd come to the castle, through the birth of her babies, and included the journey into the Otherworld of Kwethin and Mellund.

Each depiction was surrounded by swirls and tendrils, all vague images, fading from one fantasy to the next and all showing a happy, laughing Trasand. At the front of the cauldron was a section of enamel, which had been specially prepared in pale blue, Trasand's favoured colour. Inset into the oval shaped panel was a large ruby that shone brilliantly in the morning sunlight. The top of the cauldron thickened into a wide brim overlaid with a torc like ring, interwoven with silver and gold and on either side was a handle of gold, cast into the mould of a bird in flight. The detail in the two small creatures was so intricate that even their eyes had been set with precious stones.

So magnificent was the gift that when it was presented to her, Trasand felt compelled to leave her chamber and set it on a large table in the evening room, where the family used to sit and talk, a room that hadn't been used for many months. Trasand sent Filethas to the gardens to pick flowers and she arranged them in the cauldron. That evening the family sat around the display and talked much the way they used to.

Ashannon found the king's bed empty that night. He lay in the arms of the women he truly loved and thanked all the gods for her return to him.

Chapter 33

AD 38
Summer

IT was many years since Trasand's first husband Midamail had been sacrificed to the gods following the death of queen Hilfuth, but his brother Moulton had never come to terms with losing him. Although he was content with his wife and had a fine young son, he missed the company of his only kin. Their parents had departed for the Otherworld when he was young, and he had no other relatives.

He lived with his wife and son in a small hut in a hamlet not far from the castle. They worked hard to keep themselves fed, but never seemed to harvest enough food and hadn't been able to get any livestock of their own. They owed a large debt to their landlord, which Moulton knew he'd never be able to repay.

When Moulton returned home from working in the fields one early summer's day, hungry and ready to eat, and found his wife lying on the bed cradling their son who was very clearly dead, he did what he knew to be the only sensible thing. He drank a draft of the poison he kept to kill rats and before the effects of it overcame him, asked his wife to torch the house.

The distraught woman hurried to the landowner and told him that Moulton would pay what he owed him in the Otherworld, thanked him for his patience and returned home. The landowner enjoyed his evening meal comforted by the knowledge that his debt would be repaid to him once he too ventured to that place.

When the wife arrived home Moulton was already dead. Without hesitation she put a brand in the fire and flung the flaming torch into the straw roof. Once the hut was well on fire without any chance of dying down or being put out by some well-meaning neighbour, she threw herself into the flames and joined her family on their journey

When Vitaicus heard of the triple tragedy, he was angry that the man hadn't come and seen him first. Having taken Moulton's sister-in-law to be his wife and queen he would have been happy to give the man some livestock, perhaps even settle his debt for him, if he'd only asked. It never occurred to the king that he could have allowed Trasand to keep in touch with her family, or even kept abreast of their welfare himself. It also didn't occur to him to tell her what had taken place. In his mind her family ceased to exist the night she'd come to the castle.

As it was, Trasand showed no sign of emotion when she overheard the slaves talking the following day, her world revolved around her own tragedies and it seemed as if she was unaware of the fact that these people were once her kin.

Vitaicus and Obetach sat talking quietly in the king's chamber, drinking ale and eating bread with goat's cheese and large black grapes. It was the first time in a long while that they'd spent an evening together enjoying each others company without discussing affairs of the land or worrying about the ever present threat of war from other tribes or the Romans. However, despite the pleasant and light-hearted conversation in which they were engaged, Vitaicus sensed that Obetach had something on his mind. As always, he knew the priest would speak in his own good time and so Vitaicus stopped his idle chatter and waited.

Obetach, who'd been staring at the night stars during the silence, finally turned to face his king.

"I feel it's time my Lord," always one to talk in riddles, Vitaicus waited for Obetach to explain exactly what it was time for. "All the signs point to it. It's time for Dylan to go…."

Vitaicus gasped and choked on the chunk of bread he'd just put into his mouth. He began to tremble and felt his face grow red. After all these years of waiting and watching he'd finally released his son into the care of Gamenta and he felt he'd let go enough to cope with Dylan's impending leave taking to the forests to become a Druid.

He'd stopped his constant vigil of waiting for the gods, counting signs, watching for omens, waiting for the dreaded thirty that would take his son from him, and had grown complacent. Now, on a beautiful evening like this when all was quiet in the land, and peace had settled in his heart, the gods had reared up again and were here to take his firstborn, his only son from his beloved, departed Hilfuth.

He stood up as he coughed and spluttered and felt tears fill his eyes and spill onto his cheeks. Obetach slapped the king violently on his back causing him further distress. Once he'd quieted enough for Obetach to be heard, they sat again, and while Vitaicus wiped his eyes and regained his composure, Obetach continued with his interrupted sentence.

"It's time for Dylan, the name, to go – for it to be replaced by his own chosen and permanent name. The gods have been giving me signs and showing me that the time is now."

Vitaicus looked at him without comprehension. He felt a sense of relief, but couldn't fathom why. He took a long drink and a deep breath, and then replayed in his mind the last sentence Obetach had spoken. Time for the name to go, his temporary name, time for it to be replaced!

He began to laugh, a deep chortling laugh that emanated from the very depths of his being and he laughed until he once again felt tears dripping off his cheeks into the twirls of his long and bushy moustache, but these were tears of relief and joy.

Chapter 34

AD 38
Autumn

Dylan was beside himself with excitement. He'd hardly slept and was up at first light, ready and waiting for Gamenta to fetch him. They were going hunting, but this trip was to be different. For the first time in his almost eight years, he'd be hunting alone with Gamenta.

Although he was once again enjoying spending time with his father, and hunting together was an exciting adventure, he felt over shadowed by the great man and afraid of him lately.

He knew in his heart he could have caught many of the deer, rabbit and fowl that his father told him to leave. He knew too that much of the game brought back to the castle would have been his trophies had his father not always had first choice and kept the more difficult shots for himself. He'd longed to ask permission to try some of them himself, but it would show lack of respect and his father would have refused, for if Dylan failed, the game would have been lost.

Today he'd finally have his chance to prove himself without his father, free to choose his game and his shots. All trophies brought back today would be his. He puffed his chest up with pride at the thought of all he'd shoot. He let his imagination run wild during the long hours of sleeplessness, and imagined himself bringing back bigger and better catches than had ever graced the royal kitchens.

For once, Dylan wasn't concerned that Pren wouldn't be coming. He knew Pren wouldn't enjoy the day and was relieved when his brother happily agreed to stay home. Even Sopa would be staying behind on this unique occasion.

Gamenta too was in high spirits. He'd also longed for the day when he'd be alone with his special charge, not overshadowed by Obetach or the king, but able to impart his knowledge to the prince in his own way. Gamenta knew he was very different to Obetach but he also knew he was just as wise, if not as learned. He had much he wished to teach Dylan in a manner he thought would be more appropriate to the boy's age and upbringing.

They were deep in the forest after spending the morning talking, laughing and discovering a newness to their relationship. Dylan realised he wasn't missing Pren or Sopa. The sun was high and warm, even through the canopy of trees and although they hadn't even begun to hunt they were both sleepy. They spread a sheepskin to sit on while they ate their bread and fruit and drank goats' milk.

It wasn't long after they'd eaten that Gamenta grew silent, and Dylan realised that he'd fallen asleep. Too charged with excitement and the thrill of being deep in the forests alone, Dylan knew he couldn't sleep and crept off the sheepskin. Making his way silently from the glade where they rested, he moved into the woods in search of game. After his grand dreams he couldn't, wouldn't, return to the castle empty handed.

He hadn't gone far when he was aware of a noise behind him, perhaps a hare, he thought. He turned and crept back, listening intently, trying to distinguish the various sounds of the forest, separate them from each other and work out what it was that he was hearing. He stopped for a moment as the leaves under his feet crackled and added to the confusion of sound. Barely daring to breathe he waited, all senses sharpened. Although young, his father had taught him well and living in this harsh land had added to his learning.

He hadn't realised how close he was to where Gamenta lay sleeping, but now he was sure he could hear him breathing deeply. He also believed he heard the buzzing of a thousand bees, but even those two sounds, separated and set aside was not the noise that originally alerted him, he wouldn't have heard either from where he was a while earlier. He lay still and waited with the patience of an experienced hunter, shutting out all other distraction, even that of Gamenta's heavy breathing and the bees' high pitched buzzing.

The sound came again and he knew instantly what it was. It was the deep growl of a fox and with the chilling sound of it, he heard even louder buzzing and breathing.

Feeling afraid for the first time Dylan inched forward. Willing the leaves to be silent beneath him, careful not to place his body over a twig that could snap, he made his way painfully slowly to where he could peep into the glade where Gamenta lay. The sight before his eyes left him frozen with fear. The sweet fruits they'd been eating had attracted the bees and the swarm that was before him was the largest Dylan had ever seen, but they weren't what caused sweat to break out on his forehead.

The left over food that they'd carelessly left beside them as they lay talking had attracted a fox. Fast asleep and unaware of the danger, Gamenta hadn't heard the animal approach. It was only once the bees began to attack the magnificent red haired creature, stinging him on his nose and ears, the only places they could get through his thick fur, frightening him with their frenzied buzzing around his face, in his ears, even his eyes, that the fox began to growl.

It was the growl of an animal about to strike that woke Gamenta and he saw the danger he was in. As the bees tormented the fox, so it looked for something to vent its anger on, and its eyes fell upon Gamenta. The sudden movement of the Druid alerted the previously oblivious animal to his presence and he was poised ready to strike, seeing Gamenta as the object of his pain and misery. He growled deeply once more and made ready to pounce.

Dylan took in the horrific scene in an instant. Once the fox landed on Gamenta, the sacred bees would begin stinging the exposed skin of the Druid. Dylan had seen a fox kill a rabbit, and in his mind it would be a race to see which killed the priest first, the jaw of the fox, or the sting of a thousand angry bees.

Without further thought Dylan knew what he must do. He couldn't attack the bees because they were sacred and he feared angering the gods, and he knew he had no chance of driving them off, as they were working themselves up into a deeper frenzy with every sound and move the fox made. He had to attack the fox and draw it away from Gamenta who lay helpless, the animal just a foot from his exposed throat, his sword out of reach beside their food basket.

With a bloodcurdling scream Dylan charged the fox with all the speed his young legs carried. Startled by the noise the fox turned mid stride, and although he landed with his legs across the hapless priest, his head was turned in the direction of this new attack, his jaw wide open, teeth bared in a deathly grimace, teeth that moments earlier were poised to strike the jugular of Gamenta. Dylan came on screeching and panting, calling the gods in a jumble of confused pleas. Not too sure whether he should be addressing the hunting god, or the supreme god, perhaps some other mightier one, he shouted more to the fox and the bees than anyone else.

The noise he made was confusing and frightening, to Gamenta, to the fox, and even the bees for miraculously they took flight and swarmed off, in a dark cloud and a swishing wind as they passed close by his face on their way back to their hive and safety. Dylan realised that he'd only the fox to contend with and his chances were greater. In the fleeting instant he'd seen his only course of action, he'd imagined his fight against the fox becoming weaker from the poison of the bees that would begin stinging him the minute he attacked. He'd hoped that by then Gamenta would have been able to get to his feet, regain his spear, and come to the fight.

Dylan had been quite sure he wouldn't be able to save himself, but found instant solace in the thought that he may save his mentor and friend before succumbing to the will of the gods, and leaving this earth to join his mother in the Otherworld. All these thoughts raced through his mind as he lunged at the fox with every ounce of strength he possessed. The many hours spent training with his father in the art of spear fighting, the hours on horseback, the time spent lifting an assortment of weights, carrying heavy objects around the courtyard, and the races the priests encouraged between the children in the kingdom combined to strengthen his body beyond its age.

His anger and fear further fuelled him and he held his spear firm and true, and struck at the heart of the fox. With the momentum of his lunge he felt the shaft pierce through flesh and muscle, brush past a bone, and sink deep into the chest of the creature that lay pinned beneath him. He heard a gurgle of air escape the wound. A spurt of blood rushed out of the dying animal and ran down his arm, and he was aware of the last breath from the nostrils of the fox against his cheek like a light breeze on a hot summer's day.

His tears mingled with his sweat as the life drained out of the warm heaving body beneath him and he slowly became aware of Gamenta, pinned under his body and that of the fox, anxiously calling his name.

Frozen by fear and by the enormity of what had taken place, Dylan was unable to respond. He felt revulsion for what he'd done, killed the most magnificent of all the creatures of the land, mingled with relief that he'd surely saved the life of Gamenta. A whole range of emotions assailed him and he sobbed, loud heaving sobs that assured Gamenta he was alive and all right.

The priest lay patiently, his legs already numbed, but his years of harsh training had taught him how to submit to all things and he neither flinched nor attempted to move, but prepared to wait for as long as it took for the prince to calm down and sit up.

When he finally did, Dylan felt totally drained. His face was stained with a mixture of tears, blood and dirt. His body ached and his heart felt as though it had been wrenched apart. He got up as gently as he could, lifting the fox to his chest. Gamenta emerged unscathed, although stiff and dirty and almost as blood stained as Dylan.

They laid the still warm fox on the sheepskin and stood looking at it, feeling different emotions. Gamenta hadn't the heart to tell Dylan how unlikely it was for the relatively small animal to kill him, but began to chant, giving thanks to all the gods for the gift of the fox and the gift of his life. Finally he gave thanks for the strength and wisdom of his charge, the young man by his side, for he surely was a man from this day forward.

Dylan too began to give thanks, but his thanks were for the strength and wisdom his father had given him that allowed him to save the life of the grateful priest. He also asked forgiveness of whichever god chose to give it for having killed this magnificent animal, something he'd never have done during the hunt.

When they arrived back at the castle some hours later, dirty, blood stained and at a walk, with the fox carefully wrapped in the sheepskin and lying across Dylan's horse, the king and almost the entire household rushed out to greet them, consternation on their faces.

It was all Dylan could do to clean himself and climb on his bunk to sleep, without supper or the energy to pull up his sheepskin. The king covered his son that night, standing beside the sleeping child, pride swelling his heart until he felt it would surely burst. Gamenta had related the entire day's adventure as he, the king and Obetach settled down with a meal and some mead, much needed by the exhausted priest.

Vitaicus knew of only one way to still his charged emotions and he tore himself from his son and went in search of Trasand who was anxiously waiting to hear what had taken place during the hunting trip.

Obetach was smiling broadly when he entered the king's chamber the following morning. Gamenta was a pace behind him and the king looked surprised at their unannounced visit.

"Didn't I tell you it was time for Dylan to go?" asked the priest smugly. Vitaicus nodded and waited for him to continue but it was Gamenta who spoke next.

"Yesterday the young prince became a man. It was the day the gods chose for him to have his own name, and they have truly chosen well."

Vitaicus waited with bated breath. This was a solemn occasion in the life of his son, and he knew without doubt that the gods had smiled on him. They'd given him supreme strength and wisdom and chosen him above all others for a great purpose. They'd been leading his life from the moment of his birth and for the first time since that long ago day, Vitaicus felt entirely at peace with their hold over him.

"From this day forward your son the Prince will be known as Lovernios, the Fox, for not only did he slay this beast but he used the guile and wisdom of a fox in doing so. It's a fitting name and one he's earned with his cunning, strength and bravery. He'll no longer be Dylan the Great, but Lovernios the Fox, the most clever and noble of all creatures."

Vitaicus felt overcome by emotion and sat down heavily on his bed. His pride in his son knew no bounds and he couldn't wait to see the boy's face when he told him of the great honour, but the pleasure of this thought was dashed immediately.

"Tonight at a special ceremony, Gamenta, the chosen priest for the great Lovernios, will give him his name. My Lord, he's not to be told before the ceremony, restrain yourself, and your overeager heart. This is in honour of your son and the gods, not for your pleasure," Obetach told him sternly.

Knowing the king so well Obetach knew he was ready to rush

in and wake Dylan. Disappointed beyond words, Vitaicus nodded. His son, his precious first-born, blood of his own blood, indeed belonged to the gods and his own right to him had ended, if not the day he was born, then this day.

The king waved the priests away and sank back onto his bed in a fit of despair. He lay there for many hours, until he heard Trasand speaking softly and lovingly beside him, easing his dark mood in the way only she knew how, and as it was one she seldom used, he appreciated it all the more.

Chapter 35

When Dylan was led into the courtyard just before sunset, he had no idea what was in store for him. He'd spent the previous hour with Pren and Gamenta as they went through the ritual retelling of his birth story.

With each passing year the meaning of it became more significant, and he'd gone from a feeling of glee when he was younger, to one of pride as he understood more. He'd questioned Gamenta about his mother previously, now he wanted to know about the gods and their requirements.

Although Gamenta couldn't answer all his many questions, Dylan felt comfortable with the knowledge that he was special to the gods, that they wanted him one day. He knew he'd be leaving home to go with Gamenta and Pren to join the priests in a few months time, and if the gods called for him then, he wouldn't mind, but he secretly hoped that it wouldn't be before then. He loved his life so much at the moment, even the thought of that far-away place in the west couldn't make up for the happy place in which he lived right here.

As he looked around the courtyard Dylan wondered what the occasion was, aware that it wasn't festival time of any sort, he was confused. The central fire had been lit and the entire courtyard was decorated with flowers and branches of trees. Candles and braziers were flickering in the fading light, and every priest and priestess under the training of Obetach was assembled in the courtyard.

Dylan was led into the centre by Obetach, where cauldrons of holy water stood ready. As the ceremony began, Dylan, who'd witnessed many name giving ceremonies, recognised this as being the same and was even more confused. There were no children in the royal household who'd not been named but as Gamenta approached him, a full thick and shiny fox skin draped across his outstretched arms, Dylan understood what was about to take place. Although he'd no idea what name had been chosen for him he realised it had something to do with the previous day's events.

Being given a second and permanent name was the way of the Celts, he knew in the back of his mind that at some stage in his life, he'd receive his own, earned name. He felt a twinge of regret that he was losing the name of Dylan. Having heard the story of his birth on the anniversary of that day each passing year, he'd grown to love it and the reason he'd been given it. He was proud to be Dylan the Great and honoured that it was largely because of his mother's departure. In some strange way it was an association with her that he didn't want to lose, but the Celt in him knew this was how it must be and he waited with the same expectant air as the rest of the assembly.

Gamenta placed the fox fur in front of Dylan, spreading it out carefully so that it lay flat, its red fur gleaming in the firelight, as the last rays of sun dropped below the height of the stone wall surrounding the courtyard. Dylan noticed immediately that there was a piece missing, cut out carefully from the side of the animal's belly. He saw too the tear where his spear had pierced the heart of the brave creature which had died at his hand, and he winced.

Gamenta caught his eye, held it steady, and his manner said, 'it is well, be still.'

Dylan pulled himself together and tore his eyes from the skin. He kept his gaze on the strange but beloved face of the priest in front of him. The Bards began a chant, giving thanks to the gods for the life of Dylan, repeating in verse the events of the previous day. During their long ballad they sang the praises of Dylan, the fox and the gods themselves. For those assembled in the courtyard, the slaves, servants and friends who'd not yet heard the story, no detail was left untold, and at the end a roar of approval and applause filled the fast falling night.

Obetach finally held up his hands to quieten the crowd and they obeyed instantly. The silence was eerie after the noise, disturbed only by the crackle of fire and the hoot of an owl out early for the nights hunting.

Gamenta took from the folds of his voluminous robe the missing portion of fox fur. It had been neatly cut and measured into the perfect size for an armlet for his charge. Gamenta placed the armlet around Dylan's upper left arm and a seamstress came forward and stitched the fur snugly into place with such speed and precision that she'd returned to her seat against the wall before the king realised what was happening.

Gamenta took the cloak from around Dylan's shoulders, lifted it above his head and began an incantation to the gods, thanking them for the protective covering they'd placed around their son over the past seven and a half years, promising to return it to them as they'd provided him with a new one. He walked towards the fire and the crowd fell silent, the Bards stopped their chanting, even the owl was silent.

With a swift and practised move, Gamenta tossed the cloak up and it fell into the waiting flames. It burned easily, and not a single eye of those assembled moved from the sight until the last fibre was burnt. Then they again looked at Gamenta who walked back to where Dylan stood, apprehensive and shy at being in the centre of attention.

Gamenta stooped to pick up the fox fur and in the same lithe movement, draped it around Dylan's naked torso.

"From this day forward, you will wear the cloak of the animal you have slain, and in honour of that great and wily beast, a beast of intelligence, magnificence and honour above all other, in honour of the slaying of this creature in order to save the life of a priest of the gods, you will be know as Lovernios – the Fox."

The crowd at first gasped, then applauded and shouted with one voice as the great honour bestowed on the young man before them sank in, and they shared in the glory of the moment. They shared in the pride of the king, and in the pleasure reflected on the fine face of the prince who'd heard his name for the first time – and loved it.

Later that night, as midnight approached and all was still in the royal household, Dylan, who was now Lovernios replayed over and over again in his mind the events of the past two days.

His life had changed immensely and he realised the importance of it all. He was no longer Dylan the Great, son and prince of King Vitaicus, he was Lovernios the Fox, Son and Chosen One of the Gods. His fate was sealed and he was at peace with it. He'd been prepared for it all his life and he longed now for the seminary, the training, and for his ultimate, Supreme Sacrifice to the gods with the resultant journey into the Otherworld.

The honour given him, the thought of seeing his blood mother, a life spent in that eternal and happy place, all these thoughts prevented the overexcited and contented Lovernios from sleeping that eventful and life-changing night.

Part Two

Chapter 1

AD 38
Autumn

"LOVERNIOS! Lovernios!" Totally lost in thought it took some time before the prince turned to see Gamenta calling him. Although he'd been Lovernios for a few months and was quite accustomed to it, at times like this when his mind was elsewhere he simply didn't hear himself being called.

It was the night before his eighth birth celebration, and Lovernios had grown into a strong good-looking boy with amber red hair that shone in the fading sunlight.

"Where is Pren?" Gamenta was asking now that he had Lovernios' attention.

The prince roused himself from his pleasant daydream. In a few days time he and Pren would leave home to stay with Gamenta for a short while before their induction into the Druidic Order at the first new moon of the following month.

Lovernios went in search of Pren who was taking care of their siblings, telling them a story that had them enthralled. He stood unseen in the doorway and watched for a while. Pren was a natural when it came to storytelling, he was able to change his voice easily to match the characters he was portraying, and his scarred face gave him far more expression than any other storyteller. He was still a slight, rather thin and gangling boy, pale in complexion and with colourless hair. He had long thin fingers and feminine hands, even his face resembled that of his mother in a remarkable way and he had her soft nature, which was why Filethas and Roulst loved him so.

Lovernios had no doubt that they loved him too, but in a different way. It was to Lovernios that they came when they wanted to rough and tumble, which was seldom. More often than not they'd be at Pren's side, listening to all he knew about plants and trees, animals and the stars – his favourite subject. He'd taken over the evening story telling from his mother and faithfully spent time with the children before they went to bed, telling them the history of the Celts and the Druids.

When Pren was with the younger children, Lovernios took time to learn from his father as much as he could absorb about being a good warrior, and leader. He was determined to know as much as possible about life outside the Druidic Order, so that he was not totally ignorant once he'd graduated and came back home again, hopefully to take over his father's role and lead their kingdom, if the gods so ordained.

Pren looked up and smiled, and Lovernios felt his heart lurch. He loved his brother fiercely, more than he loved either of his other siblings, probably because he'd twice been the instrument of Pren's misfortune, but as he saw his brother's good eye twinkle and wink at him, he was thankful that Pren had never held him responsible.

Lovernios looked at Filethas and Roulst in turn and knew he'd never feel the same about them. He'd not miss them when he left home, but he smiled at them now and they ran to him, begging for a ride across the floor on his back.

"Gamenta is waiting for us," he told Pren. "We have to go, now!" he said to Filethas and Roulst as he shook himself free.

The boys knew it was time for the annual ritual of Lovernios birth story. They also knew that this one would be different, the first time the story would be told of his naming as Lovernios the Fox, and they looked forward eagerly to hearing Gamenta relate his version of that fateful afternoon. As they sat before the roaring fire in the courtyard, waiting for Gamenta to begin, Lovernios rubbed his fur armlet and pulled his cloak over their legs.

Neither was disappointed at the tale as Gamenta brought back to life the traumatic event, and even the reminder that the gods still required him didn't dampen Lovernios' high spirits, if anything it heightened them.

As they made their way to bed later that night, eagerly discussing the eventual sacrifice, Pren once again promised to join his brother on his journey to the Otherworld when the time came.

Chapter 2

THE first thing Lovernios saw were the girls, and he pulled a face and tugged at Gamenta's robe.

"Surely we don't have to live with them?" he asked the priest in disgust. Gamenta smiled inwardly but outwardly remained severe.

"Only if you misbehave."

Now what did that mean Lovernios wondered? He was totally disenchanted with the whole idea of belonging to the Druidic Order and wanted to go home and the sight of the girls only made things worse. He didn't like girls, in fact he didn't like boys much, only his brother Pren, and he wasn't here and Lovernios missed him and he didn't want to be a priest anymore.

He felt like crying but bit his lip and followed Gamenta and the other boys who were headed for the initiation ceremony, stifling a sob and stumbling along as his eyes watered. If it hadn't been that the girls might see him, he may just have thrown a tantrum and lain down and cried. Instead he fought back his hurt and anger and continued down the path laid before him, one set long before he was even born and over which he had absolutely no control.

Everything had been fine until the day before the boys were due to leave home. The nights following their birth celebration feast had been filled with talk, and they'd been too excited to sleep. Then Trasand visited them in their chamber, something she seldom did. They'd been surprised and nervous and sat side by side on their bed waiting for her to speak.

The queen looked round the room as if she'd never been there before, fingering things, picking them up and putting them straight down again.

Finally she'd turned to Pren. "You're not going to the forest with Lovernios – you're not to be a priest."

The boys sat dumbfounded as she turned and left without another word. In their hearts they both thought this might happen, but as the years passed and nothing was said, and indeed as this year passed and the entire kingdom was in a state of excitement as boys and girls from all over who'd reached the age of eight prepared to leave for the Order, and still nothing was said, they'd felt certain that Pren was to go too.

Often children elected to be priests or priestesses, sometimes parents chose from among their children those they thought were best suited to the life and sent them.

Among aristocrats and royalty, children were sent for the education even though they knew their children hadn't the makings of a priest. Many left the Order along the way, having learnt enough to satisfy themselves and their parents, others found that they'd been called by the gods, and stayed twenty years.

There'd been no indication from either Gamenta or their parents that Pren wouldn't be going with Lovernios, and as the news sank in, the boys jumped off the bed simultaneously and went running in search of their father.

The king was busy in his workroom and Flauston sent them away. They hunted down Gamenta instead. He was in the kitchens having the cooks prepare food for the coming days that he and Lovernios would spend alone in the forest.

"Why can't Pren come with me, why?" wailed Lovernios before Gamenta had even seen them.

"I want to be a priest." Pren added quietly.

Gamenta sighed and led them into the courtyard where they sat under a tree.

"These things aren't always up to us," he began… "Sometimes the gods ……."

"But it wasn't the gods, it was mother," shouted Lovernios.

"Calm down!" Gamenta replied sternly. "The gods may have spoken to the queen. In any event, she feels…. she doesn't want…… She's afraid to let Pren go!"

"Afraid?' asked Pren, "afraid of what? Why?"

He looked at Gamenta searchingly, wanting to understand so that he could change her mind.

"She's lost too many children, she cannot bear to lose you too. You know she prefers not to let you out of her sight, and with your various accidents, well, she feels that you're too... too vulnerable."

"Oh that is just awful," cried Lovernios. "We have to make her change her mind, we have to. Come Pren, let's go and wait for father, he'll talk to her, you'll see."

The boys sat outside the king's work chamber the entire morning, and when he did finally see them, he wasn't prepared to talk to Trasand. He knew her fragile state of mind, understood what losing Lovernios was going to mean, and wasn't prepared to have her in a worse state over Pren. He fully supported her position and so the matter was closed.

The boys went to their room where they remained for the day, going to bed without supper and refusing to speak to anyone, even Gamenta. They held each other and cried. They pleaded with the gods, and then made plans to run away, then discarded them knowing the gods would come in search of them.

They decided to kill themselves and go straight to the Otherworld together, now, but were afraid that Lovernios would be rejected, being the Supreme Sacrifice required of the gods at their demand, not in Lovernios' chosen time.

Eventually exhausted, they slept in each other's arms and Vitaicus found them that way, with tear stained cheeks, when he came for them the next morning. Their parting tore at his heart, but he too didn't want to see Pren go. It was such a wrench for him to say farewell to his son, his pride and joy, that having Pren waving by his side was some compensation and he determined to make it up to the boy.

He'd spend as much time with him as possible, perhaps teaching him to hunt a little despite his one eye and poor arm, not realising that hunting was the last thing on earth that Pren wanted to do. Unaware that he only wanted to learn, and to sing and compose songs, the king led the heartbroken boy away to a life of despair.

Lovernios too was heartbroken as Gamenta took him by the hand as they left the castle. He and Pren waved until they could no longer see each other, and even then he continued looking back hoping that Pren had been allowed to run along the roadway to wave some more.

Lovernios too was starting out on a new life, and although not one that he'd dislike as Pren would, it was to be the harshest of times with twenty long years ahead of him, and during the first six years he wouldn't be allowed to see his family. That thought was the hardest for him to bear. Six years without seeing or speaking to Pren.

The previous evening he'd said his formal farewell to the household. The staff lined up in the courtyard and he walked past each one, shaking hands with them, slaves included. Lovernios, with his lively nature, wonderful sense of adventure, and friendliness to all, made him the favourite of the king's children, and the entire household was sad to see him go. They knew that life would be a lot quieter for them all with Lovernios gone.

Once back inside, the farewells continued over a magnificent meal. The king and queen invited everyone of importance in the kingdom to attend, and over three hundred people were fed and entertained during the long night. Lovernios made his way round the huge room, saying his goodbyes to people he didn't even know.

Just before the sun rose, he stood before his parents and siblings who'd been wakened to see him leave. He hugged Filethas and Roulst in turn, then shook his father's hand solemnly, but without word, and bowed slightly in front of Trasand with whom he was too angry to speak. His father pulled him back as he tried to walk away.

"You'll not leave us like this my son, say your farewells properly, or you'll be disciplined by Gamenta."

Lovernios turned reluctantly back to Trasand who leaned forward and hugged him. For a moment he was lost in the embrace as he felt her familiar warmth, and he knew how much he loved her, how he'd miss her, despite his hurt and anger, and he wanted to cry again for a host of different reasons. He hugged her back, kissed her cheeks that were wet with tears, and then turned to his father again.

His father too hugged him and this time Lovernios felt a tear slide down his own cheek. He loved this huge man more than he believed and suddenly felt very scared. He wanted to stay here where it was safe and secure, he no longer wanted to go to the forest, he was too young for this, he simply couldn't do it.

Gamenta, sensing the change in his charge, stepped forward took him by the hand, looked him in the eye, and said so softly that only Lovernios could hear, "you can do it, the gods are with you, as am I. You're strong, you're Lovernios the Fox, you can do anything."

The boy nodded, wiped away his tears, and walked swiftly to his chamber to collect his cloak and fox fur. Pren followed him and they hugged one last time, saying nothing. All that could have been said had been and each knew exactly how the other felt. They walked together to the courtyard where Gamenta and the family waited for them. Lovernios' final words were to Pren as he and Gamenta walked out of the courtyard into the rising sun.

"Blood brothers in this world and the next. Blood brothers to the end."

"To the very end," responded Pren, in a broken voice, as he waved and waved.

The words cut deeply into Lovernios' heart as he remembered the first time he and Pren had said them three months earlier. The king wanted to do something special for the Festival of Lughnasa – the choice festival of the God Lugos, and decided that the boys were old enough to have their own swords. Proper swords, ones that they'd keep throughout their lives. They'd been excited as always as they climbed into their father's chariot, with Sopa bounding round beside them. The trip to Fludigat was filled with laughter and shouting, as they greeted people they passed.

Fludigat was waiting for them, all other work set aside as he patiently spent the day teaching the boys the art he'd learned as a youngster himself. The secrets of the craft of metal working had first been taught by the God Ucuetis to his favoured priest, and he'd in turn taught his son and so the knowledge had been passed down from generation to generation.

Fludigat showed the boys how to shape red-hot iron on his anvil, giving them each a lightweight hammer with which to practise. While he worked away at the swords their father ordered for them, they worked on their own pieces of metal, each making a special memento for the other. Pren fashioned a crudely shaped star, while Lovernios managed to make a lump of iron resemble a fox. The ornaments were small enough to be worn round their necks, and Fludigat helped them re-heat the metal and pierce each one with a sharply pointed spoke. The holes were for a leather thong to fit through, and they were eager to get home and try them.

That night, long after the household was asleep, the boys tiptoed out of their room and raced down the passageways to the kitchen, where they begged the slaves tending the fires not to tell on them. They ran out into the warm evening and charged down to the rivers' edge to their favourite hideout under a large apple tree. They'd brought their works of art with them, as well as the sharpened blade that Vitaicus used to shave off his beard every second day.

Once they'd stopped giggling and caught their breath, they became solemn. This was something they'd planned to do for a long time, and now that the moment had arrived they were nervous and not sure how to begin. Pren eventually took the lead.

"Lovernios, you're my brother in this life and the next, and I solemnly swear to be with you always. When you leave this life, I'll go too."

"Pren, you're my brother in this life and the next, and I solemnly swear to be with you always, to watch over you and protect you, and I welcome you coming with me when I leave this life." Lovernios answered.

He picked up their father's blade and sliced into the vein on his right wrist. The blood pumped out faster than he imagined it would. Seeing it, Pren quickly took the blade and sliced his own right wrist in the same manner. They held their arms together, their blood mingling and dripping onto their legs. After a few moments they pulled apart.

"Now we're blood brothers," announced Lovernios. "Blood brothers in this life and the next. Blood brothers to the end."

"To the very end," responded Pren.

They placed a covering of sphagnum moss over their wounds and wrapped each other's wrists with cloth, then took off their necklaces. Lovernios hung the fox around the neck of Pren.

"To give you strength and protect you always, I give you the fox, the strongest and wiliest of all creatures. Also to remind you of me, so that we'll never be apart, even if we are parted."

Pren felt the cold metal against his chest and knew it would always be a comfort to him.

"I give to you, my blood brother, the star that will guide you, so that you'll always know where you are, and where I am, and always come back to me, if we are ever parted."

Lovernios grinned at his brother and they hugged and collapsed on the ground laughing. We'll always be together, always and forever they thought happily as they made their way home under the light of the stars above.

As they trudged along the rough pathway that led deep into the forest where Lovernios would spend the next two weeks with Gamenta, he'd thought about these things, his mind flitting from one occasion to the next. He was incredibly excited but at the same time enormously sad. He'd never before felt such a range of emotions and it left him exhausted.

He spent a large part of the next two weeks sleeping, and relying heavily on Gamenta to comfort him and help him to understand and work through his emotions. The priest didn't let him down. He was patient and gentle and let the boy talk all he wanted.

He listened to him rant and rave, reason and argue, and even cry. And then, when he was feeling better, they talked of other happier things, particularly the year ahead.

Chapter 3

BY the time the two weeks were up and they were ready to leave for his initiation, Lovernios was feeling better and they left the quiet forest filled with anticipation. The long walk was pleasant and they passed the time chatting about nothing in particular. Lovernios finally accepted the situation and was feeling quite relaxed when they arrived at the grove where the ceremony was to take place. Then he saw the girls and his earlier mood changed immediately.

The sight of the girls reminded him of his sister, which reminded him of Pren, and all of a sudden he was scared again and homesick and he didn't want to be a priest, he wanted to go home, but it was too late. As he stumbled along blindly behind Gamenta, he'd not seen where he was going, and when the priest stopped and Lovernios looked up, he was already standing in front of the senior Druids and waiting to receive him into the Order, was Obetach. It was truly too late.

Obetach was smiling, pride and expectation written all over his face. If Lovernios let him down, he'd be letting everyone down, his father, the gods, Gamenta, perhaps even Pren himself. He pulled himself together with an effort and allowed himself to be led through the ritual, trying hard to understand and enjoy the proceedings as the initiation began. A hush fell over the expectant crowd as Obetach raised his golden staff. This was one of the most solemn ceremonies held each year and Druids of the highest rank were officiating.

The first order of the ceremony was for an oath to be undertaken. This was an extremely solemn oath where the candidates vowed not to reveal the mysteries into which he or she was about to be initiated. The children stood beside their appointed Druid, in groups of three. Gamenta was in charge of Lovernios and two other boys who Lovernios had seen before at feasts and festivals, although he'd never spoken to them.

One was the son of a warrior, the other the son of a wealthy farmer and landowner. Obetach chanted the solemn oath and each boy and girl repeated the words, swearing allegiance to the gods, and promising before the assembly that they'd never divulge the secrets of the Order.

Once the oath was completed the novices were led to a large circular cave a few miles deeper into the forest. As soon as they were assembled at the entrance of the cave, the children were asked to hand over their clothing and were given instead a robe of white, blue and green, these colours representing Light, Truth and Hope.

Over this was placed a sky blue robe with a hood that they'd wear during the Bardic years. This blue robe was representative of Peace. Both garments were made with full-length openings in the front and before the actual initiation began the candidate opened both robes so that the officiating priest could be assured of the child's gender.

Obetach walked up and down the long lines of male novices, glancing briefly at them while a senior priestess inspected the girls. Once their sex was verified a crown of ivy was placed on the head of each child.

They were ready to enter the cave. The children were overwhelmed and afraid. The cave was huge and dark, but they had little time to think, as the first trio were led in and the rest followed swiftly behind.

Each candidate passed through a large rock that had been rent in two by the gods at the beginning of time. This was a symbolic purging of sin. The novices followed the lead of their priests and priestesses and chanted to the gods, begging for forgiveness and cleansing. They entered an enormous cavern where hundreds of priests and priestesses waited.

One by one the candidates were presented to the assembly by name then they were blindfolded with a thin white cloth. The Bards chanted a hymn dedicated to the sun, calling on it to bear witness as they placed the novices into the charge of druids already nominated to them.

As the novices continued to be led in, the Vates lit the sacred fire. Still blindfolded, each candidate was led nine times round the sanctuary, moving in circles from east to west, to the loud clanging of musical instruments and joyous chanting of all the Druids. The fire was burning brightly by the time the last novice had completed their ninth circuit. Obetach once again signalled the assembly to silence by raising his golden sickle.

With only the occasional crackle of dry wood the silence was eerie, and the darkness intense beyond the flickering light of the fire. Lovernios shivered. Obetach called for a second oath to be sworn, an even more solemn and serious oath than the first where each candidate promised to be faithful to the Order. If they should at any time break or violate the oath, the penalty was death. Death without the gods that would result in their spirit wandering for all eternity, never reaching the Otherworld.

Once each child had sworn the oath, their blindfolds were removed and they were led through a narrow opening at the back of the cavern into a tunnel.

Lovernios was more afraid than before as they stumbled along but after a few hundred feet he sensed they were nearing the end. The darkness round him seemed to lighten and the air became a little fresher. They turned a corner and exited the tunnel under a moonlit sky. The assembly of Druids left the chamber by a different and shorter tunnel and were already waiting at the edge of a narrow river.

Wearing just their white initiation robes, the novices were led into the river and fully immersed in the ice cold water, then helped onto the opposite bank where they put their new blue robes back on.

Then they were presented to the Supreme Druid Pantra, who was seated on a chair used for initiation ceremonies only. It was made of gold inlaid with precious stones of many colours. Pantra wore the apparel of highest office and looked splendid and godly as he greeted each child with a kiss on the forehead. Some of them were afraid of the impressive figure, others felt safer in the presence of the Supreme Druid.

Lovernios wasn't sure what he felt, as a mixture of emotions ranging from fear to excitement then loneliness assailed him. He wished Pren had been here to see and share in all these strange rituals.

The initiates sat on the bank of the river in front of Pantra, huddled together to warm themselves, while the Supreme Druid explained to them the symbolical meaning of the various ceremonies in which they'd taken part. He had a soft and melodious voice for so large a man and the youngsters immediately felt comforted, and it was with reluctance that they left him to start their new life in the forest where they'd remain for many years.

Chapter 4

PREN spent the first three days after Lovernios' departure in a state of semi-trance. He'd never felt anything like it before and was quite sure the gods were trying to communicate with him.

He remained in his room, neither eating nor sleeping, but slipping in and out of this trance-like state for hours on end, as he stared out of the window at the stars by night and the passage of the sun by day.

He felt an over-whelming sense of foreboding. The past eight years had been such happy ones and now they were over, but that didn't seem to be the cause of his consternation. He knew in the deepest part of his soul that the gods had called him and they were angry that he'd not gone with Lovernios to join the Druidic Order.

Trasand was concerned about her son, but felt sure it was just childish pouting and that he'd become hungry or bored and leave his room eventually, and then he'd begin to play with his siblings and forget all about being a priest.

Vitaicus was far more concerned, noticing the strange faraway look in the boy's eyes each time he went into Pren's chamber, which became more frequent as the days passed and he became more and more concerned. Eventually he called for Obetach.

The moment he saw Pren, the priest was alarmed. The boy was definitely in a trance and as he'd not seen the child for a few days, his pallor and obvious weight loss were immediately noticeable. Rather than startle the child, he led Vitaicus out of the room to the king's day chamber, where they sat pensively.

"I need to confer with the gods straight away," the priest said. "I fear for the child, he may be in the clutches of an evil god, or it may be that our gods are speaking to him. I'll return as soon as I've an answer for you, in the meanwhile don't allow anyone to disturb him, lest his spirit take fright and leave him. Guard him well."

Vitaicus was afraid and rushed back to Pren, where he took up vigil until Obetach returned the following day.

"I have news," he said as he sat beside the exhausted king. "It's not evil that keeps him in a trance, but Esus the Lord and Master who is communicating with the child. The gods are angry that Pren didn't join the Druidic Order and as it's too late now to send him, they have to be appeased. I'm afraid they'll take vengeance on the queen. I'll continue to make peace offerings on her behalf and perhaps with time they'll forgive her, but you need to know that they hold Pren in their hands. He'll be theirs even while he remains in your household." He sighed sadly. "They'll continue to talk to him and through him, using him as their medium. Pren will never be a normal boy again, and although never a priest, he'll be something close to that. Somewhat like a Vate, he'll see and hear the gods, and you must never hinder him or disbelieve him. He will develop powers too as he gets older and as the gods choose to use him. He's been blessed and given high privileges, but unfortunately for him will live neither the life of child or adult, nor the life of a priest. He is bound somewhere in-between!"

After the initiation ceremony, the boys were taken into a forest on the left bank of the river, while the girls were led away in the opposite direction. Lovernios was relieved.

The novices had been instructed to maintain absolute silence during the long walk to their new home, and now that the daunting ceremony was over and it was too late to do anything about being a priest, Lovernios was relaxed and eager to know about his companions.

All along the way, priests with their three novices turned off into secluded spots that would become home. Gamenta and his novices were almost the last group still marching well into the night, when they too turned off the pathway and went deeper into the forest for a few hundred feet.

They finally stopped and Gamenta gave them permission to speak, but they were too exhausted and found themselves a hollow in which to lie down and were asleep within minutes. Nestled together for comfort, not knowing each other but being so young and vulnerable that they needed human contact, they slept as one. The following days were wonderful for the boys as they set up their home, building a shelter from tree branches and reeds, hollowing out sleeping places, and helping Gamenta as he skilfully wove them sleeping mats. They dug a cooking area and filled it with flat rocks, then fetched clay from a nearby stream to build an oven, which they left to bake and harden in the sun. They fashioned pots and buckets from clay for gathering water and food.

Each morning they chewed grass and ate wild berries. Gamenta showed them which were safe to eat and which to avoid. In the evenings they hunted for hare and duck, small game or birds. They sat around the fire that they took turns in making, roasting their meal and talking until exhausted, and then fell into their sleeping hollows once again.

The boys took to each other instantly. Obetach and the priests who were responsible for organising the novices into trios had done well. They were strong, healthy and well-built lads, and Gamenta watched them for the first few days with mounting pride, knowing that they'd do well.

Delinius was the son of a famed warrior and had his father's intelligence and fearless nature, while Mardial, the farmer's son, was hard working and strong. Lovernios was a mixture of the two and they were already functioning well together, complementing each other. Gamenta looked forward to the days ahead when they'd compete against the other novices intellectually and in sports, for he felt sure that these three would do exceptionally well.

On the fourth morning in their new home Gamenta woke them as the sun began to lighten the sky. This was the time of day they would rise in future and the sleepy boys rubbed their eyes yawning and moaning in protest.

"Today is the start of your schooling," Gamenta told them. "No more getting up late. From today onwards, you'll be expected to learn everything we do and say. By the time you've completed your twenty years you'll have learnt twenty thousand verses. You'll know everything there is to know about your history, the land, the stars, medicine and economics. Listen carefully and remember everything."

The boys looked at him with astonishment – twenty thousand verses, how would they learn so much? But before they could ask, Gamenta was telling them to hurry up and get ready as they were to meet with the other novices at the river before the sun rose.

There their lessons would begin.

Chapter 5

Vitaicus sat long after Obetach left him, thinking about his wife and the tragedies that had befallen her. He loved her dearly, but was angry with her. Angry that she'd upset the gods, angry that she'd not let Pren go with Lovernios, yet he understood why she hadn't.

In fact he was pleased that she'd made the decision, glad that he himself hadn't had to, causing the gods to be angry with him instead! But that was a cowardly thought and he wasn't a coward. He was fearful for her too, knowing well what the gods could do to her, wishing there was something he could do to protect her from them, but accepting that there wasn't.

As these conflicting thoughts ran through his mind he became depressed, and longed for the company of Obetach who'd gone to seek the gods in an attempt to appease them on the queen's behalf. He'd no intention of going near Trasand for fear of what he might say or do, so instead called for Flauston to bring him some wine.

A few months earlier he'd traded five of his prize hunting dogs for flagons of Roman wine. Rome produced a fine wine that was made from the grape, unlike British wine, which was produced from the rowanberry, a celestial fruit possessing powers of longevity.

Once Vitaicus had tasted grape wine he'd felt a burning passion for the nectar, but it cost dearly. If he'd traded directly with the Romans he might have bartered for less, but he didn't want to be seen to be a friend of his enemy and so left it to his faithful servant Flauston who found a man trustworthy enough to trade on the king's behalf. He had six-dozen flagons hidden in his stores that he was keeping for a special occasion, and he asked Flauston to bring one to him at once.

It didn't take him long to finish the fiery drink, however his mood only became deeper as the unfamiliar fermentation took hold of his brain and made it muzzy. He called for another flagon and this time Flauston sat with him, trying to slow the king as he emptied the contents rapidly. So drunk was he that half an hour later Flauston had to help him to his bed, but the king wasn't there long before he stumbled off in search of the reason for his depression.

He found the queen asleep and in his drunken state didn't even wake her. He climbed roughly into her bed and began ripping her nightclothes from her thin body. Trasand woke with a start and stifled a cry as she realised what was happening. In the present mood of the king she knew better than to resist him and so she bit her lip and allowed him to vent his anger, using her frail body to do so.

Pren watched his father's drunken passage from the shadows. He knew where the king was headed. He went to his own room where he lay and listened to his father's grunts and groans. He visualised the scene, having watched countless animals mating, and he cried silent tears for his frail mother, trapped beneath the huge man for what seemed an eternity.

As he lay with his head under his covers, trying to shut out the noises, Pren knew that something awful was going to come of this. He knew this had to do with him, although he didn't fully understand what. It seemed as if the gods had granted him wisdom beyond his years, and he had no doubt that Vitaicus was punishing his mother, but sensed that the gods would punish them both in turn. He desperately wished Lovernios was with him, and he cried out to the gods to protect his brother and keep him safe until they could be together again.

For their first lesson the novices were together, including the girls. They looked a little different to Lovernios today, more like priestesses in their blue robes and less like the sister and other girls he'd left at home. He, Delinius and Mardial nudged each other and pointed at the prettier ones, whispering and giggling until Gamenta told them sternly to be quiet and behave like priests.

Obetach took the lesson for the day, the only lesson he'd take until the first of the four graduation ceremonies that they'd undergo during the course of the next twenty years.

For this first lesson they were taught the meaning of the word Druid. It was a Celtic word with 'Dru' meaning 'oak', and 'wid' meaning 'knowledge' or 'to see'. The Celts acknowledged the Druids as being men and women with superior knowledge, having acquired the wisdom of the oak – the oldest tree, and possessing supernatural sight.

One would only gain this knowledge, wisdom and sight through years of learning and much time spent with the gods understanding their ways, so that one could be attuned enough to divine their every wish and whim.

It was because of this stringent training and the enormous knowledge that Druids obtained during their studies that most Celts sent their children to the priests to be educated. Even the Druids from Gaul acknowledged that the Druids of Britain were more knowledgeable and better trained than they and frequently sent their own priests to study with their superior counter-parts.

The second thing that Obetach taught the novices was the moral doctrine of the Druids.

"You are to be pious against the gods, not to do injury to anyone and to practice bravery. Once you are a priest, you are to teach those under you to worship the gods, to do no evil, and to be valiant in battle."

The novices were made to repeat this over and over, as they would do with everything they learned from that day forth.

After they'd eaten at midday, Obetach patiently explained to them why they were required to learn so much. Some of the children had already learnt to write basic Greek lettering, as many of the wealthier and more influential Celts were being taught to read and write.

However, the Druids believed that if they wrote things down, they'd lose the use of their memories and more importantly, they wouldn't be able to protect their secrets from becoming common knowledge.

The novices were forbidden to learn to write and those who already knew how were warned against doing so on pain of severe punishment and banishment from the Order.

Once Obetach finished tutoring them, the youngsters were taken to their own shelters where they built a fire, and the priests and priestesses in charge taught them how to dance. The ritual dances of the Druids were many and varied, and mostly required dancing on one leg as they traversed the fire from east to west following the course of the sun.

The novices would spend hundreds of hours in the coming years dancing and the Druids knew from experience that it took a long time to build up muscles and bones to the extent where they no longer ached after a ceremony that could last for hours. The boys went to bed that night with stiff backs and aching legs, and Lovernios felt that he hadn't slept at all on the hard ground when Gamenta woke him for the next day's lessons.

From then onwards, each morning started with the novices repeating the verses learnt on the previous day, and as they learned more, this time became longer and longer.

As the months passed, Gamenta woke them even earlier so they could finish in time to begin the normal chores of the day before starting new lessons. They weren't allowed to eat, drink, wash or relieve themselves before they'd recited perfectly all their verses, and they soon realised that diligence in learning would save them agony in the mornings.

Vitaicus listened patiently to the latest messenger to visit his castle. The news he brought was interesting, but not worth much, perhaps three or four cow hides.

"Drusilla, the favoured sister of Emperor Caligula is dead," the messenger said.

Caligula had previously named her as heir in his will, but with her sudden death at an early age, he'd ordered extravagant honours to be paid to her instead. Rumour in Rome was that he'd had incestuous relations with both his sisters, and was therefore more attached to her than was natural. He was reportedly devastated at her death.

Vitaicus wondered if this turn of events would have any impact on Britain, and fretted for days as he attempted to take a reluctant and unhappy Pren hunting with him.

Eventually he gave up and went alone, brooding all the while.

Chapter 6

AD 39
Winter

Trasand knew something was wrong the moment she tried to stand up one fateful morning shortly after the Festival of Imbolc. She lay down again and called for Omilia. Seeing her pallor and obvious pain, Omilia immediately sent for the midwife Sebilus, but she arrived too late.

During the months following Lovernios departure, Pren watched his mother closely and realised she was with child again even before she herself did. She hadn't told the king for fear of what he would do. His moods had been unpredictable since the night he'd last gone to her all those months ago, ranging from depression to uncontrollable anger.

Occasionally he seemed to take hold of himself and then he'd treat her with a sweetness she'd forgotten, but mostly he avoided her.

He spent more time with Pren than before, which pleased her, although not Pren. When he wasn't with Pren he was hunting or seeing to the affairs of his kingdom and Trasand seldom saw him, but knew he was around when she heard his ranting and raging.

It was due to the knowledge the gods had given him that Pren became aware of her pregnancy, and he foresaw disaster and heartache ahead. He stayed close to his mother, sometimes playing with the other children in whichever chamber Trasand sat, but mostly sitting quietly by her side in the trance-like state they'd all come to accept, as he learned to hear what the gods were saying. He soon realised that he needed to get outside and read the signs the way Gamenta had taught him, and he began to accept his father's invitations to accompany him on hunting or riding trips, taking this as an opportunity to be where the gods could speak easily to him.

Of late he'd seen many things in two's and wasn't at all surprised when Trasand produced twins. What did shock and repulse him was their half formed state. They'd only grown in her womb for four months, and were tiny, blue shapeless creatures.

Sebilus told him secretly later that night she believed they had many deformities, and had they lived they would have been hideous creatures, an ill omen indeed. As it was she was unable to determine the sex of either of them, and they couldn't be named, a second ill omen. Due to this the pathetic creatures couldn't be given a funeral. For them there would be no great pyre, no celebration as they joined those who'd gone before them into the Otherworld.

Instead they were taken by Flauston in the dead of night and buried in a deep hole on the opposite bank of the river, on property that didn't belong to the king. With all this ill fortune upon them there was a dark cloud hanging over the castle, which remained through the whole of summer and into the long weary winter. No one laughed, hardly anyone dared to speak, and Trasand remained in her chambers the entire time. Vitaicus was seldom seen or heard.

Shortly after the loss of the twins, Sebilus plucked up the courage to visit the king. She'd been to see the queen and was in the castle when Vitaicus walked past her on his way to his workroom. She followed him and stayed in the doorway until he looked up and saw her.

"What is it?" he asked wearily.

Sebilus walked towards his large wooden table with her head bowed. She didn't want anyone to hear what she had to say, but also didn't want to get too close to the king, of whom she was afraid.

"What is it?" he repeated impatiently.

"My Lord," Sebilus began. "I feel it's my duty to the queen, and to yourself," she added hastily "to tell you that, well, should the queen become pregnant again, I fear..... I fear she'll die my Lord. The queen must not become pregnant again, ever!"

Vitaicus stared at her, at once admiring her courage, but also resenting her audacity. To tell the king that he must never lie with his wife again, how dare she? Yet in his heart he knew she was right, and he nodded slightly and waved her from the room. Should anything further happen to Trasand, physically or emotionally, she would surely die.

He accepted the loss of yet more children and the loss in spirit of his wife, along with this new turn of events, as his punishment from the gods for doing what he'd done to her. He acknowledged it as the queen's punishment for not allowing the gods to have Pren.

However, although he acceded to it, he still avoided Trasand and his household as he felt every eye was on him, accusing him of having brought about this new calamity to their fragile queen and having caused her to suffer further. He brooded for a few days then called for Flauston. "Fetch Ashannon," he commanded.

When Flauston returned with the slave, Vitaicus continued talking as if his servant had never left the room.

"Give her that piece of land on the river bank opposite, the one I can see from my trophy room. Take whatever you need and have slaves build a house for her. Give her some livestock and vegetables to plant."

He looked at the slave. "Ashannon, you're no longer a slave. I grant you your freedom provided you remain in the house I'm building for you, ready for me to come to you whenever I wish. You'll never marry or leave here, however you are free in your own home and on your own land. Go now, I'll come to you shortly for I can no longer bear to be in my own castle with whispering and stares all round me. Be ready and waiting."

Chapter 7

Lovernios was unaware of what was taking place in the castle as the novices weren't allowed contact with their families during their first six years of training for fear that they may be influenced in any way.

He was suffering enough of his own misery and would have been horrified to hear of theirs. Each night he lay in his sleeping hollow and pined for Pren. He rubbed his sore legs and hips and tossed and turned to try and relieve his aching back. The prancing around on one leg was proving the most tiresome of the difficulties he was going through physically, and missing Pren was the worst problem emotionally.

Without Pren he felt he'd lost a part of himself, his kindred spirit had been removed from him and he was half a person. He enjoyed his new companions enormously, but they would never replace Pren in any measure.

He lay awake most of the night before his ninth birth celebration, knowing that this year there'd be no feasting, no presents, no ceremony, and he wondered what would be taking place at the castle. Would there be a feast for Pren? Would anyone continue the ritual of the retelling of his birth story? He doubted it, but wished he knew and was feeling immensely sad when it was time to get up long before sunrise, knowing that this day would be so different to celebrations of past years.

As it was Trasand was so deep in her misery that she gave no thought to her children. Pren's birth anniversary never entered her semi-deranged mind. Even Vitaicus forgot about it, although he did remember it was the time when Lovernios had been born, simply because he remembered that a year had passed since his son had left the castle. He spent the day with Ashannon and never gave

Pren a thought.

Pren brooded the entire day too, not about being forgotten, but about his brother and how badly he missed Lovernios. Finally he went in search of Flauston.

He spent the remainder of the short day telling Flauston of his dreams and visions and of the things that the gods said to him. He confided to the king's servant that he desperately wanted to learn to write these things down so he could share them with Lovernios one day.

He couldn't ask Obetach for help, but knew that Flauston was influential among the traders. He was sure that Flauston would know of someone who could secretly teach him to write Greek. Flauston had felt sorry for Pren all year and was only too pleased to assist. He knew just the man and promised to get word to him immediately. Pren went to bed that night feeling better than he'd done for months.

Lovernios also went to bed feeling better. The day had passed much the same as others with the recitation of all they'd learned previously, followed by food and then a further lesson. After their midday meal they walked through the forest to an open area where they'd met with hundreds of other novices, boys only, Lovernios was relieved to see.

The afternoon had been filled with games, something new and wonderful for them. As youngsters growing up they'd all taken part in sport, but this was the first time they'd done so during their training. The games were designed to improve their ability as priests, and many of them consisted of throwing objects. Some were to build up stamina, such as running races and at each event Lovernios excelled. His father had insisted throughout his childhood that he be strong and quick and he'd beaten the children in the hamlets surrounding the castle at everything he tried.

Now, as he competed against boys from the remainder of the land of Canti, he was up against many he'd never seen before, but as in the past, he won easily. He was well built and muscular, which was definitely to his advantage, but as he lay sleepless later that night, he knew he had his father to thank for his inner strength. Never being allowed to give up, always fighting to the end, he'd been made to practise over and over until a skill was perfect. His love for the outdoors, which the king had passed on kept Lovernios tough and ready through all weathers, and now it paid off.

He was crowned champion at the games and he was thrilled. As evening began to fall, the priests lit a fire and the exhausted novices were allowed to rest and warm themselves, as their seniors served fish and bread, followed by warm milk to their hungry charges.

Once they'd eaten Gamenta stood and raised his voice loud enough for every one present to hear. To Lovernios' delight he began to tell the story of the king of Canti, of his son Prince Dylan and the auspicious day of his birth. The boys listened in absolute silence. As Celts brought up with story telling, they'd missed hearing tales such as this. They loved hearing Gamenta tell of the gory birth of the baby and death of the mother.

The significance of the gods being present struck them all, especially Lovernios, after months of intense learning of the whims of the gods. However, Lovernios was a little disappointed when Gamenta began to relate the tale of his given name Dylan, but the boys all exclaimed as the story proceeded and there was obvious envy that he'd been given such an illustrious name.

When he'd finished the tale, Gamenta went on to relate the events surrounding the earning of his new name, and Lovernios felt puffed up with pride. As he looked round at the faces nearest him, he knew that from this day on they'd treat him with even greater respect. Far from finished, Gamenta told his audience of the requirements of the gods and how one day Lovernios would become the Supreme Sacrifice, possibly a sacrifice that would save them, save the land.

The young boys were awestruck and left the fireside that night sensing the supernatural powers of the gods as never before, and rather than pitying Lovernios or even envying him, they marvelled that the gods had chosen so wisely. They'd already seen the strength and wisdom Lovernios displayed and knew he'd make a fitting sacrifice. They all prayed earnestly that they would be there to witness the event.

Vitaicus decided it was time to obtain a reliable informant to keep him in touch with the affairs of Rome. He sent his trusted servant Flauston in search of the right man. Flauston as always proved himself and returned two days later with a Roman by the name of Marcus.

He was a trader who spent most of his time in Britain living in the land of the Trinovantes. He had a house on the River Thames where he traded on a large scale with merchants from Gaul, Belgae and Rome, and it was these connections that made him such a reliable and valuable source of information He had brothers, uncles and cousins in high places and seemed to know more of what went on with the Emperor than some of the madman's own senators did.

Vitaicus was delighted with the merchant and offered him the pick of his stores in exchange for worthy information. What he told Vitaicus and Obetach on their first encounter amused the king, but made him nervous at the same time.

Emperor Caligula Gauis was insane, and an insane man was a dangerous man in Vitaicus' opinion. Caligula had fallen in love with his horse, Inciatatus, and was feeding the animal out of gold dishes from his own table and kept it in a marble and ivory stable. He declared that the sight of bald headed men filled him with anger and they were to be arrested and thrown to the lions. His uncle Claudius was bald but escaped the wrath of his nephew by pretending to be a half-witted idiot!

Added to this peculiar behaviour Caligula had a new policy of making his senators prostrate themselves before him, justifying this practice as being his divine right. This was not a good sign! He was turning himself into a god and when Obetach reported this to other Druids over the following days, they were angry and afraid.

There'd been no new threat from the Romans, no further news of the Druids in Gaul being pursued or wiped out, although it would appear that this was largely due to family trouble within the Emperor's household.

It was rumoured that Caligula had planned an invasion of Britain, but his late sister Drusilla's widower was involved in some conspiracy on the Rhine, and this kept Caligula on his toes, not sure what his brother-in-law was up to, but desperately trying to find out. Once that issue was resolved though, and with Caligula's latest declaration of having divine rights, would he not also try to stamp out all priests as his predecessors had done and would he not further upset the already angry gods. Surely they'd all suffer for this blasphemy, Vitaicus fretted.

Not only was Caligula angering the gods, he was also antagonising the Greeks! He'd recently built a bridge of ships that stretched across the entire width of Baiae's Bay, his most spectacular achievement yet, but he dared to ride over the bay wearing the breastplate of

Alexander the Great. He rode the seas like a god and in the style of the Great Alexander he planned his next military adventure.

"The absolute audacity of the man!" Obetach exclaimed as Marcus continued with his report. Caligula had also seen fit to execute anyone he saw as a threat to himself and began with Tiberius Gemellus, grandson of the late Emperor Tiberius who'd been too young at the death of Tiberius' to succeed him.

Caligula, who was twenty-five, had been named Emperor instead, but he now believed Gemellus and every other member of the Claudian family to be a threat to his throne and had them executed. He was living a life of luxury, exhausting the vast treasury left to him by Tiberius for his own use, although he did continue to arrange shows for his people.

A large portion of the treasury was being used to keep his army in a state of preparedness, and this worried Vitaicus more than any of the other news he received from the continent. There were no wars taking place, yet Caligula saw fit to amuse his people while preparing his military force!

It wasn't long before the reason for his behaviour became apparent. Marcus informed Vitaicus one freezing cold winter's day that there was much military activity beside the River Rhine in Belgic Gaul, along the border of Germany. Caligula began an expedition into the area, announcing that he needed to strengthen the frontier, which was always under threat from the Germans. However within weeks Vitaicus heard that the military activity had nothing to do with Caligula's fear of an invasion, but was once again related to the conspiracy that had troubled the Emperor earlier.

Commander Aemilius Lepidus, his brother-in-law and widower of his late sister Drusilla, was dissatisfied with Caligula's leadership and plotted to assassinate him. Lentulus Gaetulicus, Commander of the Upper Rhine, promised to support Lepidus in a bid to overthrow Caligula, but the Emperor received word in time and moved in with his garrisons who were prepared and waiting for just such an event. They executed the two men without question, and then set about disciplining the army.

This unrest forced Caligula to remain in Gaul for the winter months and into the following summer. At the same time he was forced to keep his Rhine Legions in place and at the ready to put a stop to German border forays.

The news calmed Vitaicus and Obetach, as they knew that Caligula could only fight one enemy at a time and while occupied with internal unrest and trouble from the Germans, he'd wouldn't be worrying about the Druids, either here or in Gaul, although according to Marcus, Caligula was still preparing a great invasion of Britain.

As the months went by and nothing materialised, Vitaicus grew frustrated with the merchants and traders who were bringing Marcus such scrappy bits of information, often unfounded, mostly outdated, and all of it unreliable.

A long while after Vitaicus first started to spend time with Ashannon in her home the queen heard of the arrangement. To the king's surprise she left her chamber for the first time in months and when he met her walking towards the kitchens, she smiled at him.

Over the following weeks he received regular reports from Flauston and even Omilia with regard to the queen. She appeared to be feeling more herself and was even taking to walking in the gardens again, provided there were always servants with her. She played with the children and was eating better than before. When the king questioned Omilia, she told him shyly she believed the queen was relieved he was visiting Ashannon, as it meant that the king was unlikely to want the queen, and she was therefore unlikely to fall pregnant again, her greatest fear.

And so it was that life in the castle returned to being much as it had been before Lovernios left. Even Pren was brighter and happier as he secretly learned to read and write and was beginning to compose odes and record his deepest thoughts to read to his brother when he next saw him.

Apart from teaching him literacy, his tutor, a Greek merchant was also teaching Pren how to play various musical instruments. Pren was gifted in music and had a sweet voice and the hours spent tutoring him were the finest Xavista could remember in all of his seventy-six winters. In return for these secret lessons, Flauston promised Xavista as much food and mead as the man could eat and drink after each lesson, and although he drank greedily, it was never so much that the king noticed the drop in his stores.

The arrangement suited all parties well, and Xavista chose to settle in the king's hamlet and leave his trading days behind. He decided it would be a pleasant way to spend his declining years, and Pren was able to spend as much time as he liked in the little grass hut that Xavista built at the furthest corner of the servant's quarters.

Obetach hurried into the king's workroom with strange information from Gaul. The king was irritated by the interruption, but keen to hear what the priest had to say. He wasn't willing to believe the news, but Obetach assured him that Marcus had sent a merchant directly to see the king, as he was one of the more reliable informants who'd left the shores of Gaul just a few nights earlier. The merchant claimed that after Caligula had managed to discipline his troops and still the Germans, securing the frontier, all was ready for his planned invasion of Britain.

He commanded his troops to march to the Channel where they'd been given a strange order. The king refused to believe what Obetach told him next and asked the priest to bring the merchant to him at once.

Obetach went in search of Flauston who in turn sent for the merchant. He was resting in the courtyard, enjoying the hospitality of the king and left the plentiful fare reluctantly.

"Yes, my Lord?" he said patiently when the king questioned him on the same point for the third time. "I saw them with my own eyes. The entire garrison was on the beach and under orders to collect musculi – seashells I believe you call them. They were there many days collecting them by the sack full, but then my boat was ready to leave and as I was in hiding, I was anxious to get off the beach and away. I didn't wait to see them go, but they were waiting for the order to embark. They'll be here shortly with their musculi, although I've no idea what Emperor Caligula intends to do with them."

Vitaicus dismissed the man promising him some fine hides for the information. He and Obetach agreed they needed to have lookouts sent to the coast immediately and that he should warn his neighbours, the Trinovantes, as Caligula was likely to land somewhere along the coast of either his land or theirs.

Vitaicus was unable to sit still, work or sleep and after spending the morning aimlessly pacing through the castle, he called for his horse to be made ready, and he and Obetach left for the coast.

They rode hard through hamlets and across farmlands, barely

greeting people as they headed for Rutu Piae, the most likely landing point of Caligula, and the place where Caesar had twice landed. Here they slowed down a little and accepted the hospitality of the people, resting for a night, then continuing at dawn until they reached the coast.

They were greeted with good news. The Trinovantes had also heard of the assembled garrisons from traders who'd actually seen them, and Vitaicus was able to speak to a man as he stepped out of his boat, having left from the beach where the troops gathered. The huge garrison had apparently refused to embark. Nothing their generals said to them or threatened them with made any difference.

The merchant wasn't sure if it was the storms that came up each evening that made them afraid, or stories told to them by various merchants of the treacherous seas, perhaps even tales retold of Caesar's unsuccessful campaigns to Britain, but whatever it was, the troops wouldn't embark.

They were not going to Britain. Having already spent two years away from Italy, afraid of what was taking place in Rome in his absence, Caligula knew he wasn't able to wait for the men to gather up sufficient courage to board ship and undertake the campaign, so instead he issued a statement formally announcing that he'd annexed Britain, and that was the message he was taking back to Rome!

The seashells were to go with him as a sign of victory. Without having laid eyes on the land, without having set foot on the beaches, he was going to let Rome believe that he had been and conquered the country that not even the mighty Caesar could conquer.

Vitaicus was stunned as were all those who heard the news, but it was with great relief and some amusement that he returned home, first to Ashannon, and then to visit and talk to his wife whose company he sorely missed.

No sooner had he arrived than a messenger came bearing news from Marcus who'd just returned from Rome. Vitaicus could hardly believe what he was hearing.

He told Vitaicus that the earlier information regarding the gathering of seashells had been incorrect, that merchant either misheard, misunderstood or perhaps even lied. Musculi, while meaning seashells, also meant engineering equipment.

Although the fact still remained that the garrison refused to embark and Caligula did announce that he'd annexed Britain, he didn't take seashells back as a trophy.

Perhaps the merchants of Gaul would have the Emperor seem more of an idiot than he was, perhaps they simply wished to frighten the Celts, whatever, the latest news did appear trustworthy coming from Marcus himself, and certainly more believable, although with a madman like Caligula, who would ever know?

Unable to concentrate further on the business of the day, Vitaicus debated leaving the castle and going to Ashannon, but after some indecision, went instead to sit with his unhappy and almost unreachable wife, Trasand.

Chapter 8

AD 41
Winter

Each lesson with Xavista was more exciting than the last, and Pren couldn't wait for the stolen hours with the man he was coming to respect more and more, despite the fact that he was a Greek and so foreign to the boy.

After the day's reading and writing lesson, they'd spend time playing musical instruments and singing, or talking, and Pren learnt many new things from the elderly man.

Today Xavista was telling Pren about the Roman use of money, a concept the boy couldn't quite grasp.

"Imagine," Xavista said patiently, "that you've five hunting dogs you wish to sell to me. I've gold that I wish to exchange for the hunting dogs. I take that gold and melt it down into round discs, this size."

He picked up a stone and showed it to the fascinated boy. "Then when it's flattened into a disc, like a small bannock bread, each disc – which we call a coin – is worth something because it's made from gold."

"Yes, I understand so far," Pren offered.

"Well now, we decide that I must give you ten gold coins for each hunting dog, and you're satisfied. But the next day you want to buy a cow. As a cow is not as valuable as a good hunting dog, you can go to the market and offer the merchant five pieces of gold for the cow, half the value of a hunting dog. The merchant can then take his five pieces of gold, and with one of them, he can go to the hamlet down the way and get vegetables for himself for a week, as vegetables are less valuable than the cow. So the coin has a value. In Rome, the emperor usually has an image of his head placed on the front of the gold coin, and sometimes the image of someone else on the back of it."

"Why don't we use that system here?" asked Pren. "It's so much easier to carry around gold coins rather than dogs or cows." Xavista laughed.

"You're quite right, my young friend, and there are some kings in Britain who have made their own coins. Cunobelinus, the king of the Catuvellauni, who was friends with Emperor Augustus and Emperor Tiberius made use of coins, and even placed his own image on the front of them. However his coins are of silver, not gold. He called himself Rex Brittonum on the back of them, which means 'King of Britain' in Latin!"

Pren left his tutor that day with his mind reeling over all that he'd learnt.

Marcus rushed into the king's workroom unannounced and breathless. Vitaicus was furious and stood up ready to admonish the man but Marcus blurted out his news before the king could speak.

"Caligula is dead."

Vitaicus sat down heavily.

"Tell me," he said, his voice echoing his shock.

"We Romans are as fickle and untrustworthy as we were in Caesars day," Marcus chuckled, "for its Romans who've murdered our Emperor. A Tribune of Caligula's own Praetorian Guard, a man by the name of Cassius Chaerea, who was escorting the Emperor along a deserted passage, unsheathed his dagger and murdered him."

Finally the epileptic madman was dead, sent to his gods on the 24th day of the Roman month of January.

"The remainder of the guard left him to go in search of Caligula's wife, Caesonia, and their child, who they murdered too. A Centurion stabbed Caesonia repeatedly before stabbing her daughter, and then they knocked the child's brains out against a wall. On their return they found Caligula's uncle, Claudius, who himself appears dim-witted," Marcus continued.

"He was shaking with fright and hiding in the palace. Although lame and a man who stutters, they carried him off to the army and proclaimed him the new ruler of Rome."

Neither Vitaicus nor anyone else in Britain was sorry to hear of the demise of Caligula. He'd wanted to conquer Britain so badly, and was sure to have done so at some stage, and in his madness would have been capable of anything.

As Vitaicus mused over the news he was exceedingly grateful for the loyalty of his people and the protection of his priests and the gods. The concern facing Britain was what Claudius would be like, and whether he too would have designs on Britain. With the very next merchant boat came word that Claudius had been accepted by the citizens of Italy as leader in place of Caligula, and that he wasn't as mad as his nephew had imagined him to be.

He immediately rewarded the soldiers who'd acclaimed him as Emperor, and then executed those who'd murdered Caligula, in order to let not only Rome but also the entire world know that Emperors should not be assassinated!

It was a case of wait and see, and life in Britain returned to a semblance of normality with nothing more than occasional warring taking place amongst the Celts, nothing out of the ordinary at all.

Chapter 9

AD 41
Spring

Life in the forest was far from normal for the novices as in a few months time the first of four degrees were due to be conferred on those who merited it.

The young priests and priestesses had become used to the hardships of living with the elements and moved from forest glades to rocky cairns and caves as the weather went through its cycles during the three years they'd been with the Order. Almost the entire time had been spent learning dancing, poetry and music and the novices were able to sing and chant at the various festivals and ceremonies.

Most were able to play the lyre proficiently while some were gifted in composing songs and chants. They'd learned how to please and appease the gods with their voices, and also how to anger them, and their fear of them grew as they learned of the many and varied deities.

As winter approached and the time for their first graduation grew closer, the novices became more nervous and slept less as they practised until they were word perfect in the verses they'd learned thus far.

Summer was spent studying harder than ever before, and autumn was greeted with relief and excitement as the end to their current syllabus was finally in sight.

The ceremony to confer their first degree upon them was a simple one, as no parents would be present, in fact they'd not even know whether their children had been given the honour. Although Obetach knew that Lovernios had excelled during his first three years he wouldn't tell the king this, and the king wouldn't ask.

Throughout the morning Druids assembled with their novices in a large open area in the extreme north of the land of Canti, at a secluded spot along the River Thames near the hamlet of Londinium. Before the ceremony began the priests sprinkled themselves with dew that they'd collected earlier that day. For the first time those who were receiving their degree were part of this ritual too and in future they'd be allowed to gather and sprinkle themselves with dew before ceremonies, their first honour as novice priests and priestesses.

As the weather had been dry for some days, they wore their un-tanned leather skin sandals, much to the relief of Lovernios who found the wooden shoes they wore in wet weather to be hard and uncomfortable for long marches.

For this special ceremony each graduate was given a cap made for the novice by his own priest out of rushes gathered from the riverbank. The rushes were skilfully woven together and tied into a knot at the top. The ends were twisted into a band at the bottom, and hung down onto their necks. Apart from being a sign of graduation, these caps would offer some warmth to their heads during future winters in the forests. The novices were also given new robes of green, signifying nature, which they were to be at one with as they moved into the Vate period.

Lovernios was delighted to see Obetach for the first time in three years, but the priest showed him no special recognition and began the ceremony as the setting sun touched the horizon. Only when those who'd not graduated were led away to be taken back to their families, did Obetach came to where Lovernios stood with Mardial and Delinius.

"You've done well Lovernios, the gods are pleased with you, as am I."

Lovernios proved to be fairly musical and had mastered the lyre well, though not as brilliantly as Delinius who was awarded the highest honour for musical instruments from among all the novices.

Mardial had a beautiful voice and sang and chanted in a way that pleased priests and gods alike, but was unable to compose verse. He'd learned all that was required of him with difficulty, and although he received his degree, he would need to work hard in the future years to remember his verses and learn still more.

Lovernios sang in a deep gruff voice that was best suited to war chants, and when he sang in front of the girls they giggled behind their hands. His voice was broken and cracked and often squeaked and he avoided singing as much as possible.

When Gamenta conferred his degree upon Lovernios that evening he stated that the young priest was receiving high honour for having mastered all that was required of him, and having excelled in the art of composition. His chants calling the gods to be present in times of peril or war were to be used throughout the land.

Lovernios bowed low as Obetach placed his hand on his shoulder. He didn't know how to react in the presence of Obetach in this new role. He desperately wanted to ask after his family, especially Pren, but knew that the priest wouldn't answer him. He looked into the deep fathomless eyes on the once so familiar face, now that of a stranger, and felt an immense sadness.

Obetach sensed the change in the boy and felt the same sombre mood take hold of him. An electrical charge seemed to pass from his outstretched hand into the body of Lovernios and they both shivered.

Obetach turned and left, praying softly to Esus for the protection of their charge who was today a Bard, but launching into the life of a novice Vate.

As the year progressed and headed towards winter once more, merchants from Gaul brought more worrying rumours from Rome. Claudius had decided to pursue previous plans to annex Britain. It appeared that no one believed Caligula when he said he'd already taken the Island and once he'd been murdered his troops would no doubt have admitted that they'd never gone across the sea.

Britain waited for a fresh onslaught from the enemy, however Claudius first needed to address a problem in Mauretania where a rebellion had broken out. He sent over two of his best generals, Suetonius Paulinus and Hosidius Geta to restore order and then announced that he was going to "fulfil a civilizing mission of suppressing Druidism with its human sacrifices and other savage rites."

In order to do so in Gaul he needed to do so in Britain first, as it was the foremost stronghold of Druidism. In his opinion Gaul would never be fully romanised if Britain remained independent.

Vitaicus and Obetach discussed this troubling news at length.

"Rome is determined to rid the world of Druids, but why?"

Vitaicus looked intently at Obetach.

"Do you think they are afraid of the power of priests, or of their gods? Maybe they believe their own gods to be inferior to those of the Druids?" Obetach nodded.

"Ever since Caesar it has been their mission to wipe out the priests, and although they maintained it was because of human sacrifices, and general savagery, what is more savage than feeding men to lions for sport, or constantly murdering their own leaders?" he answered the king.

The two puzzled over these questions night after night, deciding rightly that Claudius was after their wealth as much as he was after the Druids, and that he wanted the fame and glory that would be afforded him if he succeeded in doing what the Roman world wanted – conquer and annex Britain. Inside sources reported that he desired to safeguard Roman traders and to exploit Britain's wealth, but when Vitaicus heard what Claudius believed he'd gain from their resources, he realised it was greatly exaggerated.

Although Britain did indeed have the metal, timber, cattle and slaves that the Romans desired, the quantities that Claudius believed he would find in Britain were outrageous. For the remainder of the year word continued to arrive regularly of his vast preparations, which were only completed months later.

At the same time Vitaicus also worried about his son Lovernios, his household and his personal wealth, but didn't know quite what to do. All his life and that of his fathers they'd lived with the threat of the Romans, but that threat was becoming more real, and the likelihood of the Romans taking Britain by force seemed more probable with each passing year.

Chapter 10

AD 42

Spring

As the graduates entered into a new six-year term and began their studies towards becoming Vates, most of them found it a far more interesting time than the Bard period, although the learning became more intense.

These were the years during which they'd learn to divine the will of the gods, and to do this they needed to know everything relating to ceremonies and rituals in order to carry them out in their proper fashion. Mardial and Delinius found the studies confusing and relied heavily on Lovernios who had spent much of his early life in the presence of Obetach and Gamenta, and already knew a great deal of what they learnt.

Lovernios hoped they'd no longer be made to chant and dance around the fire at night, as his legs and back continued to ache despite the years of conditioning, but it seemed they were still Bards, even though they were Vates in training, and the dancing continued.

Each night as Lovernios lay trying to sleep, shifting his aching body to get comfortable, he thought of Pren and of how he missed his brother. He wondered how much he'd grown, aware that he himself was a head taller than he'd been when he left home. He also imagined how Pren sounded, his own voice having broken and finally settled. To his relief he could sing properly now, in one pitch, without the girls laughing at him.

The priests spent more time learning with the priestesses since they graduated, and Lovernios and his companions didn't mind as much as they'd done in the beginning. One of their more fascinating lessons related to the Ogam rod, which they'd only just begun learning about when one was needed urgently by the priests.

The day started out normally, although they'd been slightly hurried as they were meeting with the other novices for the next few weeks for lessons on the Ogam. They'd marched to the riverbank where these sessions were taking place and it was midday by the time they were assembled and allowed to eat and rest before the lesson began.

The purpose of the Ogam was divination. It was a rod of the yew tree into which Ogam words were carved. These were the only words that the Druids recorded, and they were written in the form of a poem. Each Ogam had a different theme for its poem and they were only held by senior Druids. Using the superior knowledge of the Druid and the sacred powers of the Ogam a priest was able to divine where something was, whether it was water underground, an evil spirit lurking in the mists, or a lost item. The novices listened attentively, each longing for the day they could have their own Ogam, with their own words carved into it.

It was late afternoon before Alana, one of the senior priestesses, discovered that her golden sickle was missing. The teaching was over and Gamenta was about to dismiss the school when she hurried across to him looking distressed and flushed. Gamenta asked everyone to search for the missing sickle which was not only valuable for its gold content, but without which Alana couldn't perform her priestly duties and continue to teach her three charges.

The search continued until the light was close to fading and Gamenta realised that they wouldn't find the sickle in the dark. He called six priests and six priestesses, including Alana to form a circle and placed his Ogam rod on the floor in the middle. They began to dance around the rod, chanting words they knew well and used often. The words they chanted were not those inscribed on Gamenta's Ogam, which he couldn't read, but knew by heart.

His Ogam told how Obetach had found him when he was little, after his parents had starved to death in their small hovel. Obetach had taken in the thin and half starved waif and looked after him until he was old enough to enter the Druidic Order. It told how the gods had chosen Gamenta to take care of Dylan, and how Dylan had saved his life and become Lovernios. Gamenta's own name, given to him by Obetach, meant "the one who was found."

The chant that accompanied the dance was one that all priests used, it was a plea to the gods and the Ogam itself.

As the novices watched and listened they whispered the words themselves, learning them as it was repeated over and over again.

"From north to south
From east to west
From this world to the Otherworld
Nothing is lost
All things are found
Some in the hands of gods of good
And others in hands of evil
Oh sacred Ogam-guard of all things lost
Lead me to the golden sickle."

The twelve Druids were soon in a state of trance, and Gamenta broke the circle and reached in for his Ogam. There was silence as everyone watched and waited, hardly daring to breathe. As he picked the rod up it began to shake violently and took both hands to control. Gamenta walked forward, and the priests and priestesses moved aside, and then followed him. Silently the rest of the assembly got to their feet and joined the procession.

The rod quivered and wavered but Gamenta never broke his stride, climbing over rocks and broken branches, he walked in a straight line to the edge of the river. There he turned left and continued along the riverbank, his bare feet digging deeply into the mud. Suddenly the rod stopped shaking and Gamenta halted. Behind him the long procession stopped too.

Without looking round, Gamenta reached into the shallow water and found a rock. Underneath the rock, just below the surface of the muddy water lay the precious sickle. As he lifted it into the air, the crowd erupted in a shout of victory and praise to the Ogam and the gods who controlled it.

The children couldn't wait for the long day to end so they could eat and sit round their respective fires discussing the day's events, however Gamenta called for silence. He told them to sit where they were, and then asked for the person who'd hidden the sickle to come forward. Three times he asked, and three times he was greeted by absolute stillness. Then to everyone's dismay, he held up his Ogam rod, which had already displayed its enormous powers, and began to chant once again, however this time the last line went "Lead me to the culprit."

Whether it was the boy's fear that gave him away, or the power of the Ogam, was a topic that was debated for many an evening, however it took only a few strides into the crowd before Gamenta stopped before a quivering novice, pulled him to his feet and asked him if he'd hidden the sickle. The boy acknowledged that it was he and tried to explain that he'd wanted to see the powers of the Ogam at work, but Gamenta told him to be quiet.

Before he was led away, Gamenta explained to the rest of the novices that he was to be taken to a cave where he'd be left for three nights, alone, lest he contaminate anyone else with his wickedness, but guarded from a distance, so that he couldn't escape. On the third night, at midnight, he'd be sacrificed to the gods to appease them, but he'd never reach the Otherworld. He would wander in outer places for all eternity.

It was a sombre assembly that left for their sleeping places that night. Already dark by the time they filed out, they were exhausted and drained. As Lovernios fell into step behind Gamenta, he noticed Alana waiting with her three charges. They were pretty girls, two with short dark hair, one with long hair the colour of the missing sickle. It glimmered in the moonlight and Lovernios smiled for the first time since Gamenta had made his dreadful pronouncement.

By the end of their first year as novice Vates, the students could recite the many rules for ceremonies and feasts, festivals and other rituals. Mardial and Delinius still found it somewhat confusing, while Lovernios recited his verses with ease each morning to an attentive Gamenta.

They'd been taught which cloaks to wear at ceremonies, and how to wash themselves in dew before approaching all sacred places in clean bare feet as a token of humility and reverence to the gods. They understood the many ceremonies, dances and chants, and were able to assist in officiating at them.

Once they'd mastered these important rules, they'd learnt more about divination. They understood that if there were poor crops it was due to having bad rulers, and as priests they had the authority to remove those rulers they believed responsible for angering the gods. They'd learnt that the gods preferred the number three, and often operated in three's themselves. Most situations in life had three strands to them, and they were taught to look out for this phenomenon in everything.

During the Beltain Festival the three strands were the Divine Victim, the Devoted One and the Supreme Sacrifice. They were taught how the Divine Victim or the Chosen One's blood and flesh would fertilise the land as his body was crushed into the symbolic embrace of mother earth. They knew that if they chose the wrong sacrifice or victim at this important agricultural ceremony, they'd anger the gods and there would be no young livestock the following season.

They were taught how to watch the course of the wandering stars and predict the future by them. Much of what they learned had been passed down to the Druids from Idris, the Great Astronomer who pursued his studies of the science from the top of the highest mountain in Northern Wales, called Cader Idris.

Once they knew how to conduct ceremonies and read the signs in the stars, they studied the moon. They were taught that one should only kill hogs when the moon was on the increase so that bacon would taste better. They knew to shear sheep only during the first half of the moon, but to fell timber from full moon onwards. Fuel, coppice and frith were to be felled during the first quarter of the moon and peat should be dug for fuel only in the wane, otherwise it would be too moist and not burn sufficiently.

It was unwise to marry or slaughter cattle in the wane of the moon and when the moon was encircled by a halo, or covered in a mist, it would rain but when it was sharply outlined, one would expect windy weather. As the weather was at the new moon, so it would continue during the entire month.

These things fascinated Lovernios, and night after night he longed for Pren so he could share this exciting knowledge with him, but he had a further two years to wait before he'd see his family again.

Chapter 11

AD 42
Autumn

It took Claudius months to still the rebellion in Mauretania and regain control, but the Emperor did eventually succeed and added that country to his growing list of new Roman Provinces.

During this time the leaders of Britain waited uneasily for his next move until inevitably, Marcus arrived one cold afternoon and announce that Mauretania was firmly under Roman control and that Claudius had called upon his commander, Aulus Plautius Silvanus to meet him at the coast to make his final preparations for his invasion of Britain.

Under the competent general he placed three Rhine Legions, and his Ninth Legion Hispana from Pannonia. Auxiliaries and detachments from various other legions brought his expedition up to a total of fifty thousand soldiers.

They assembled and waited the final word from Claudius, and for the weather to allow them a safe crossing, and as they waited so did the whole of Britain, not knowing they'd wait until the winter of the following year.

Three months after Claudius' troops were assembled, tensions were mounting. Marcus mentioned to the king in passing that Claudius was on a mission to rule the world. His latest conquest, while waiting for the weather to favour his crossing to Britain, was that of Lycia, which he'd recently annexed. He'd already added over twenty regions to the Roman Empire during his reign, and desperately wanted Britain to be numbered among his conquests. These military achievements earned him the title he coveted – Extender of the Empire.

The mood was dark throughout Britain that spring. Claudius had been portrayed as a silly man without military training, which drove him to show that he could do what neither Caesar, Tiberius nor Caligula was able. His decision to invade Britain was motivated by his desperation to prove that he was a good general and he was provided with the excuse he needed by Caratacus.

Not long after Caligula was murdered and Claudius became Emperor, the British King Cunobelinus had died and his realm fell into the hands of two of his sons, both aggressive men, Caratacus and Togodumnus. Caratacus demanded that Claudius return a rebel leader named Verica who had been driven from Britain during an internal coup. As a Pro-Roman he fled to Italy.

When Claudius ignored Caratacus he raided the coast of Gaul. This affront made Claudius even more determined to conquer Britain, defeat Caratacus and repay him for the insult. All of Britain seemed to be turning hostile, and valuable traffic between it and the Roman Empire was being threatened.

Vitaicus fretted as word arrived from Gaul on a regular basis. Claudius' troops were reportedly still waiting, and just as Vitaicus began to disbelieve all rumours, they came – four Roman Legions, fifty thousand soldiers, under the leadership of the acclaimed Silvanus. They landed in Canti at Rutu Piae and marched rapidly from the coast to the River Medway.

Vitaicus reacted immediately and sent his warriors to the opposite bank of the river, along with warriors from the neighbouring Catuvellauni under their new leader, the now infamous Caratacus.

Even though the Celts were waiting for them, a detachment of Roman soldiers caught them by surprise as they swam across the river. A fierce fight ensued and Vitaicus' warriors were defeated before the king arrived to join them.

Caratacus fled, taking with him the few warriors of the Catuvellauni that were left alive. There was only one place for him to take refuge, and that was in the mountains of the Silures and the Ordovices, where he could hide in the hills and round up more support.

When Vitaicus first heard of the dreadful defeat he was devastated and wished to confront Claudius himself, but the Emperor was still safely in Gaul. However, as soon as he received word of the Roman victory, Claudius left for Britain and moved swiftly to the River Thames where Plautius waited for him. He'd brought with him reinforcements, which included his Elephant Corps.

Vitaicus was astonished by the fear and trepidation caused by this animal. They were extremely useful for carrying baggage and the many strange fighting implements that the Romans used, but as they'd never been seen in Britain before, the Celts were terrified of the huge creatures. Try as he might Vitaicus couldn't imagine his warriors being afraid of any animal.

As he listened to Marcus describing these enormous and amazing beasts, part of him wanted to go and see them for himself, while the leader in him knew it didn't make sense. He and his warriors needed to prepare for further fighting as devastating news of the submission of the fiery Catuvellauni continued to reach him daily.

Claudius and his army marched south eastwards towards Camulodunum, fighting several battles as they went. The Atrebates, who'd befriended the Romans in Caesar's day, were northeast of where the legions fought, but it seemed as if the constant threat of the Romans and the experiences of their ancestors had worn the people down, and sixteen tribes including the Atrebates surrendered to Claudius without any resistance at all.

Many of the people living in the south were traders who'd come from Belgae and Gaul and settled in Britain. Seeing the wealth of the country they became greedy and realised that Roman occupation of the land was their opportunity not only to stay in Britain but also to exploit its resources.

Vitaicus mused over the poor resistance of his people to fight the invaders, which made the warrior and the Celt in him black with anger. Many of the chieftains had already become romanised, they enjoyed the luxuries that came to them from Italy, and at the same time bitterly resented the domination of the Catuvellauni.

While Vitaicus had little respect for the Catuvellauni and resented their growing hold of Britain, he thought of those chieftains who'd become 'Romanised' as traitors, and would gladly have fought them too.

The Romans continued to march, fight and capture, taking for themselves the prize of Camulodunum, the stronghold of chief Caratacus. Years earlier Cunobelinus had taken over the territory of the Trinovantes, and transferred the centre of his kingdom to Camulodunum, which gave him command of the lucrative route to the Rhine. He'd set up a mint in Camulodunum and poured out enormous quantities of coinage, a treasure the Romans were keen to get their hands on.

In Londinium, Cunobelinus erected the first bridge across the river Thames, using timber. The area around Londinium was marshy and no one had attempted to erect a bridge before, but Cunobelinus saw a stretch of hard ground that afforded a good bridgehead, which meant that roads from the safe landing ports in Canti could connect and spread out across the rest of the country. As traders from Gaul and Belgae used the estuary of the Thames, the bridge gave them access too. The bridge with the port close by became the starting point of the town of Londinium.

Cunobelinus had encouraged Roman traders and craftsman to colonize the towns of Britain and to teach the leading tribesmen Latin. He had the power to cut off the supply of any other tribe at will, and his authority and influence in Britain continued to expand. Vitaicus and many of the other rulers had been as fearful of the domination of Cunobelinus and the Catuvellauni as they were of the Romans, but now with the king dead, the Catuvellauni subjugated and Caratacus in hiding, the remainder of Britain was not sure what to think.

Surprisingly, after sixteen days Claudius left Britain taking many prisoners with him but leaving his Legions behind to continue with the annexure of the island. Before he went he announced that he was appointing Aulus Plautius Silvanis as the first Governor of his new Roman Province – Britannia.

It was almost over, Britain was officially Roman, although brave warriors like Caratacus continued to fight.

Claudius returned triumphantly to Rome and while he celebrated, Aulus Plautius, who'd strategically based himself in Londinium, planned his first move as Governor. He chose to strike the hillforts in the northwest of Britain himself, while sending the Second Augusta Legion under General Vespasian to reduce the Durotriges in the southwest.

Although young, Vespasian was handsome and intelligent, coolly ambitious and ruthless, working tirelessly towards his future when he would eventually become an Emperor of Rome. The Durotriges held and controlled the river near Maiden Castle, and were a powerful tribe.

Plautius recognised them as a true threat to Roman success.

Chapter 12

AD 43
Summer

Sketchy bits of information reached the Druids and with each piece of news, they found it increasingly difficult to keep from their novices the events taking place. They desperately needed to spend time appealing to the gods, and for a while each day lessons were suspended while they chanted and prayed.

The young priests and priestesses were concerned about their families, and knowing how stubborn his father was, Lovernios worried more than the others. The fact that trade was at a standstill meant that Vitaicus' wealth would diminish, but that was not as grave as the fact that the Romans were on their soil and many kingdoms had given themselves over to Claudius without a fight.

The warrior in Lovernios reared up and he wanted to go to his father, fight by his side and drive off the enemy, and then fight against those who'd turned traitor and joined the Romans. He lay awake at night with his young blood boiling in his veins, and his frustration at being able to do nothing grew daily.

Vespasian, with his Second Legion, moved swiftly along the southern coast of Britain and set up camp as they prepared to take the Durotriges. His soldiers busied themselves with digging in and preparing for battle with their huge wheeled catapults and large rocks.

This was a method of fighting not seen before by the Celts and they watched from their forts in alarm as each catapult was wheeled into place. Vespasian called his servant to take down a letter to be delivered to Governor Plautius at first light the following day.

"The first fort we have encountered belonging to the Durotriges is beside the sea," he dictated. "There is a shallow harbour behind it, which the hill protects from the sea. The fort had two walls. As our reports suggested, the warriors of the tribe are brave but undisciplined. The gate of the fort was breached and the place taken."

So arrogant was he that he sent the letter before the battle had even begun.

After successfully conquering the Durotriges, capturing forty-three forts in all, Vespasian headed for and conquered the Ilse of Vectis, while his Ninth Legion marched northwards. The Fourteenth and Twentieth Legions moved northwest, heading towards the mountains.

The news of the marching and victorious army scared the Druids, as many tribes simply gave up with the natural hostility between them aiding the Romans as they continued to take control of their new Province, with little or no resistance.

The Festival of Lughnasa dedicated to the god Lugos was to be the first festival in which Lovernios and the other novices would play a significant role. Lugos was the God of Light and the festival was a time of celebration for the harvest.

This had always been one of the highlights of his life, but this year, far away from home without his family and friends, or the farmers of his father's kingdom to bring their first fruits, Lovernios was lonelier than he'd been since his early weeks away from home and his longing for Pren and his father increased. Not knowing what was taking place at the castle gnawed at him, and he thought often of the boy who'd hidden the golden sickle and been sacrificed to the gods three days later.

His parents had no idea he was dead. They'd arrive in two year's time to see their son, and learn that he'd been dead almost three years. Everything seemed unfair, and Lovernios often wondered what he'd do if he found that one of his family members had died with the arrival of the Romans and the ongoing unrest. He prayed desperately that the gods would keep them on this earth, at least until he saw them again, and when discussing these awful thoughts with Delinius and Mardial he was relieved to hear that they felt the same.

Arrangements for the Festival were going well at the castle, despite the sombre mood, and everyone was excited including Trasand. She'd been feeling much better, stronger for eating and sleeping, brighter for spending time with her children, secure with

Vitaicus seeing Ashannon and so it was much to Vitaicus' surprise that she came to his chamber the night before the Festival to lie with him.

They talked for hours, holding each other lightly, while they discussed the children and Lovernios in particular. They both missed him, although Vitaicus more so than Trasand. He felt a constant ache that not even Ashannon with all her skill could dull for him.

As the new day approached and the sky began to grow pink, Trasand indicated that she had need of her husband, regardless of the consequences. As she didn't fall pregnant on that occasion, she took to coming to Vitaicus more frequently, until he had little need of Ashannon.

There was no feast or celebration for the birth anniversary of Lovernios, however Gamenta assembled the entire Druidic school on the day, and after the usual lessons he allowed everyone to eat and rest while he went through the ritual telling of the birth story and naming of Lovernios, this time in the presence of the priestesses.

Today Lovernios paid little attention to the boys and their obvious admiration, he was watching the girls' reaction. As his eyes scanned the crowd, sensing the priestesses' distress at the gory details of his birth, watching their fascination at his first naming ceremony, feeling proud as he always did when Gamenta related the story of the fox, Lovernios noticed the golden haired girl with the priestess Alana. She sat spell bound, not moving, but also not showing the emotion the other girls did.

When Gamenta began to explain how Lovernios had been called to be a Supreme Sacrifice, she smiled, a smile so glorious that Lovernios felt his heart lurch. He couldn't fathom the meaning of it, but she seemed immensely satisfied with the news.

As they gathered up their cloaks and food provisions later that afternoon Lovernios tried desperately to see her again, but it seemed as if she and the other priestesses had been spirited away. He was dismayed at the disappointment he felt as he followed Gamenta back to their cave, his mood as dark and cold as the evening.

Despite the trouble in the land caused by the Romans, and the fact that the gods seemed to have deserted the people or perhaps were punishing them, the Goddess Brigid was obviously happy with the king and queen once more.

Not long after the Festival of Beltain, as summer approached and Trasand noticed new life around her, she became aware that she was pregnant, but felt well and healthy and was determined to keep the baby that way too.

She gave all thanks to the Goddess, and began taking greater care of herself. This was her seventh pregnancy, and having lost several babies, she was not about to risk another and decided to spend time each day speaking to the gods, seeking their favour.

Obetach was constantly busy with Vitaicus and so it was to Pren that she turned. Pren was delighted. Although still young and learning himself, his knowledge was vast and Trasand was amazed. They set aside time at noon each day to offer prayers and ask the gods to be with the child growing within her, as they watched the changes taking place in her body each month.

Lovernios was becoming aware of changes in his own body too, but was more surprised to see those taking place in the bodies of the girls. Early one morning they met for a lesson and the young priestesses walked to where the priests were already waiting. The sun shining from behind showed the outline of their figures through the thin material of their pale green robes.

Lovernios noticed that most of them had shape under their garments, and many of them were showing signs of enlarged breasts. To his amazement he noticed pink nipples on two of the girls as they passed him by, and he felt the strangest sensation taking place in his own body.

With flushed cheeks he fled in embarrassment and went in search of Mardial. In his haste he bumped straight into a priestess. It was the golden haired girl under the charge of the priestess Alana.

"Lovernios!" she said as he steadied himself and held out his hand to prevent her from falling.

"You know my name?" he stammered, while trying to regain some dignity.

"Everyone knows your name silly." She laughed and turned from him.

For a moment he wasn't sure what to do, then she disappeared into the throng of priestesses he called after her, "but I don't know yours?"

She turned to him and smiled and he felt the same constriction in his body that he'd felt at the sight of the priestesses' breasts.

"Maeve, my name is Maeve," she called and then was gone.

Gamenta was calling for order and Lovernios only just found Mardial and Delinius in time, moments later he would have been disciplined by the priest.

His mind wandered the entire day and that night he had to ask his companions what they'd learned so that he too would be able to recite the lesson the following morning.

Chapter 13

AD 44
Winter

Vitaicus was in a state over the impending birth of his child and paid little attention to the news of Rome that reached him almost daily.

Never sure what information was reliable, he put Flauston in charge of verifying everything they heard, while he attended to a final hurried barter session with the latest merchant to visit him. The man waited patiently for the king to bring his mind back to the business at hand but Vitaicus was distracted and anxious to return to the queen who was in labour.

As he walked into the room, Obetach smiled broadly at him.

"Today is an auspicious day, my Lord, and according to Sebilus the birth of your child is imminent."

"Thank you Obetach, and thanks be to the gods," he said gratefully as Obetach left to offer a sacrifice to them.

Vitaicus sat on the edge of the bed and watched his wife's pain as her labour continued through the morning and into the afternoon.

Just before sunset, Sebilus asked him to leave, and he retired to his trophy room where he drank and brooded. It was getting dark and Flauston was lighting the lamps when Omilia entered the room to tell him that the baby had been delivered. Without waiting to hear what else she had to say, Vitaicus rushed past her and made his way to his wife, holding his breath as he went.

Trasand was sitting up in bed. She was pale and her wet hair clung to her face where she'd been sweating. Tears had run down her cheeks leaving streaks in the colouring she'd applied that morning but she was smiling and holding tightly to her chest, her newest baby.

Vitaicus' immediate impression was of a robust pink child with a mop of dark hair. At first glance the king saw himself, and he knew without doubt that this was a son, his very image. Vitaicus and Trasand clung to each other, the baby between them, and gave thanks to all the gods. They named this beautiful healthy child Tylad.

A few days after the birth of his son Vitaicus was forced to turn his attention to the Roman problem. The few remaining tribal chiefs faced a tough decision, resist the Romans and face defeat followed by military occupation, or join their cause and become clients of the Empire. Even Vitaicus had to agree that the Romans were usually very generous, and a large number of new chiefs emerged as independent client kings of great wealth.

The Empire had a wise policy of enriching these clients, building them sumptuous villas and educating their children as Roman gentlemen. As the power of the Empire grew and the Celts became more Romanised, particularly in the south, the Druids moved to more distant refuges, and Obetach was frequently forced to take long trips to oversee the safety of those in training.

Many Druids, particularly the older ones and those not attached to royal households, made their way to the relative safety of the Druidic haven on Mona. Despite all of this Vitaicus stubbornly resisted, he wouldn't give in to the Empire. He admired men like Caratacus who continued his fight against the legions from his position in the mountains.

Almost the entire south of Britain was under Roman control, from south of Glevum to as far as Camulodunum. Legions were stationed at Isca Silurum, Viroconium, Deva and Lindum where they defended the borders of the fast growing Roman Province against those lands that hadn't yet been subdued.

It was a frustrating and frightening time and Vitaicus often reminded Trasand of the day they'd spent picnicking in the forest so many years previously, when Lovernios and Pren were tiny boys learning to walk. On that day he'd told her why he was so anxious every time he heard mention of the Romans and now his fears had become reality and he was clinging to his kingdom for all he was worth.

Although he'd never been afraid of war, the way the Romans fought was something new to the warriors of Britain, and Vitaicus shuddered when he heard tales of their victorious battles.

The legions would form a human wall, shield to shield, ranked closely together with the back row of soldiers holding their shields up high, the forward rows and those on the flanks holding their shields lower down. In this way they formed a solid wall they called a 'Testudo' or 'Tortoise'.

Unused to the shield, but understanding the merit of it, Vitaicus wondered why the Celts never used them in war but only as a protection for their sons when they were learning to duel. The Romans also used a short, heavy bolt-like spear called a Pila, which was useful for close infighting.

Vitaicus imagined how difficult it must be to penetrate their 'tortoise' and felt certain that his warriors, brave and mighty though they were, would not fare well against Claudius' Legions.

It was impossible to keep news of the Roman domination of Britain from the novices as the Celts submitted and the Druids were forced deeper into the forests in fear of their lives. They split into smaller groups and moved further northwards as the legions progressed into the land and the further they got from home the more they longed for their families.

Mardial and Delinius were as upset as Lovernios, and they lay talking late into the night. Gamenta allowed them to voice their concerns, often joining in as they debated the prospects of Britain under Roman rule, and their own uncertain futures.

One compensation to their new living arrangement was that Lovernios saw much more of Maeve. They'd moved to a forest in the land of the Iceni where they stayed in an open grove deep in the wood along with four other priests and their novices. Within calling distance were four priestesses with their novices, in a similar open grove.

One of the priestesses was Maeve. Lessons were shared and Lovernios and Maeve often sat side by side as they continued to learn the ways of the gods despite the situation outside the forest.

Chapter 14

AD 44
Spring

Pren had noticed for some time that he attracted bees and his fascination with them grew as he spent hours watching and studying them. He waited impatiently for Obetach to return from the forest to discuss them. By the time he saw the priest a few weeks later, Pren had established a bee colony near the river that he watched over daily.

It started out simply enough one early spring afternoon. He'd been ambling along the riverbank communing with the gods when he noticed bees following him. Unafraid of these sacred creatures he began to whistle and within moments other bees joined the swarm. By the time he reached the oak tree where he was headed, the swarm was the biggest he'd ever seen.

He hollowed out a section in the large bowl of the brittle old tree using his sword. While he worked he whistled and the bees hummed about him in the field of wild flowers, darting from blossom to blossom, flying off and coming back, but never leaving him altogether. Over the next few days he went to the tree as often as possible and before long he'd hollowed out a hole large enough for a small animal to creep into. The following day he found to his amazement that the bees had made it their home and were already hard at work producing honey.

The hours Pren spent at the beehive watching them work, talking to and listening to them, were magical ones, and the gods began to speak to him through them. He knew from the bees the day Obetach would return, and was standing at the entrance to the courtyard waiting when he saw the Priest approach along the dusty roadway.

Obetach was fascinated by Pren's story and immediately went with him to see the beehive. He was satisfied that the gods had chosen Pren and were speaking to him through the sacred creatures. When the honeycombs were large and dripping with sweet nectar some weeks later, the bees allowed Pren to reach in among them and take as much as he cared to, and each day he took fresh honey to the royal kitchens, a delicacy the youngest members of the family relished.

Little Tylad was growing swiftly, and like Lovernios as a baby he had a strong and sturdy body. Vitaicus delighted in him and spent many pleasurable hours watching Trasand with the baby, feeding, bathing and singing to him.

Life in the castle was almost as it had been years before. Trasand, although thin and quiet, was happier. Pren was seldom seen and didn't play with the other children much, and Lovernios was missed by all, but there was a sense of peace and normality.

Only within Vitaicus was there turmoil. He worried about the Roman problem, he fretted over Lovernios. He desired Ashannon greatly, so that his loins ached at the thought of her, but hated himself when he was with her because then his desire was for Trasand, and as he lay with Ashannon he imagined she was his wife.

However when he was with Ashannon, he could be himself and vent his frustration, anger and disappointments on the willing young body that lay submissively beneath him. Often when he returned to the castle he'd take Trasand and lie with her and make love to her gently, his emotions already spent. He knew he was courting danger but he couldn't help himself.

Sebilus glared at him whenever she saw him, which thankfully was seldom. Omilia avoided him as much as possible, and even young Pren shook his head at the king as he left Trasand's chamber.

One evening, unable to stop himself, Pren almost attacked the king shouting, "leave her be, leave her be." Sobbing hysterically he fled in search of Obetach.

"The queen is going to die," he blubbered, "the bees have told me. He has to leave her, he has to!"

Obetach held the shaking boy and allowed himself to go into a trance, where he too saw that the queen's death was imminent. He shook his head miserably, knowing he was powerless to stop the king or the gods. He sat and rocked the boy in his lap until he fell asleep.

Throughout spring the novices learnt about the stars, watching their movement and learning how to inform the people of their findings. Through the moon and the stars they would discern auspicious or inauspicious days, foretell the will of the gods, and warn of impending wars, famine or floods. Lovernios wished more than ever that Pren could be with them. Knowing his brother's love and passion for the stars he would have enjoyed and excelled at everything they learnt.

As he lay trying to sleep, his aching body uncomfortable in the hollow he'd prepared for himself, he clutched at the star pendant Pren had given him and thought of home. It wouldn't be long and he'd be allowed to see his family, and it was with that happy thought that he finally went to sleep.

It seemed he'd just closed his eyes when he was shaken awake.

"Hurry," Gamenta said, "we're going on a journey and must leave early."

The sleepy priests rubbed their eyes, and shook themselves awake. They didn't go through the recital of their verses which was a rare treat for them all and their excitement became tangible as they realised this was to be a different kind of journey to the many they'd taken over the years visiting different forests, glades, caves and rivers, where they met with other novices and had lessons.

Lovernios' uppermost thought was whether the priestesses would be going too, but he dare not ask Gamenta or even his friends. No one else seemed to show any interest in the girls but Lovernios found himself thinking of Maeve constantly, and his heart beat faster each time he saw her.

Before they left their grove Gamenta came to them. "Gather all your possessions," he said mysteriously, "we won't be returning for several weeks." Lovernios was immediately disappointed but no sooner had they begun to march, than he heard the sweet voices of the priestesses singing behind them. They sang one of the poems they'd learned as a chant dedicated to the Order of the Druids by a famous priest called Taliesin. Their voices rose and fell with passion as they sang out,

"Profound is the all-sufficient source
Which fully supplied me, the sacred circle,
In every evening festival,
When the calm dew descends,

With the blessing of wheat and the suavity of bees,
And incense, and myrrh, and aloes, from beyond the sea;
And the gold pipes communicating,
And glad precious silver, and the ruddy gem;
And berries, and the ocean wave;
And cresses, – the virtue watered by the gushing spring,
And a joint multitude of the herbs of the gentle flood,
And, borne by the effusive moon, placid, cheerful Vervain,
And stars of intelligence diffused around the moon,
And the wide spread aspect of the pure element;
And below in the moving atmosphere,
The moisture, and the falling drops;
And the increase which succeeds;
And the vessel of glass in the hand of the Pilgrim,
And the strong youth with the rosin of pine,
And the exalted one free from guile,
With the healing herbs where no delusion is,
And Bards with flower meet
For a sovereign is the Druidic lore."

Lovernios made every excuse to slow their progress. Gamenta walked ahead and joined the senior Druids and left Mardial, Delinius and Lovernios to come on at their own pace with the other novices.

At first Lovernios said he had a stone in his sandal and made a great show of sitting before taking it out. Then he said he needed to stop to drink and deliberately dropped his knapsack so the contents spilled on the ground. Mardial and Delinius were becoming impatient. The three of them had always been upfront, leading the way, now they were trailing behind.

They were about to leave Lovernios to come on alone when the priestesses caught up, and the boys became distracted. Lovernios repacked his possessions in time for Maeve and her friends to draw alongside them and the rest of the day was spent marching together. Even Mardial and Delinius enjoyed the female company for the first time.

For Lovernios it was one of the greatest days of his life, the longest time he'd spent with Maeve and the most intriguing too. She had such an inquiring mind that he was exhausted by the time they stopped for lunch. She pointed out trees and shrubs he'd never looked at before, and explained their uses. She noticed little creatures that he missed and gave him their names. She talked of life with the priestesses and the hardships of the forest without complaint.

It was only after they'd eaten and rested that they learned where they were going. They were being taken to Salisbury Plain one hundred and twenty miles southwest of where they'd been staying, to visit Stonehenge, an ancient temple built by Sun Worshipers generations before. Gamenta explained that the incomplete temple had been abandoned for a long time, but was revered by all stargazers throughout Britain and Gaul.

Their previous excitement turned to awe. They'd heard of this holy place, now they were to see it. The chatter during the afternoon was very different, and the six youngsters lagged behind the other novices talking of stars and sharing their limited knowledge.

It took six full days to reach Salisbury Plain and Stonehenge, but the long hard walk hadn't dampened their enthusiasm. The youngsters were overwhelmed by the place and fell quiet as they entered this holiest of holy shrines. They stood stunned and overshadowed by the thirty tall stones standing upright, forming a circle in front of them.

These stones, they were told by Alana, were called Sarsens. Each Sarsen had smaller stones laid across their tops, and the novices couldn't imagine how anyone had managed to get them there. Inside the circle was a group of three stones, one lying horizontally and two standing upright, which they learnt were the Trilithons. Beside the huge stone known as the Altar Stone, was an arrangement of smaller ones in the shape of a horseshoe.

They spent two weeks at this holy and magical place learning about their ancestors, the stars and the moon. Alana took most of the lessons while they were there and taught them that seeing the moon over the right shoulder was lucky, while to see it over the left was extremely unlucky. They were shown how to approach the evening so that they'd always see the moon from the right shoulder. They discovered the secret behind the stone pillars, and listened with fascination as the older priests taught them still more about the gods and the life of a Druid.

During the first night while everyone slept, Maeve and Lovernios lay awake, thinking of each other, wondering if they both felt the same confusing emotions.

Before daylight, they were wakened ready for their first glance of the sun rising over these megaliths. Lovernios managed to stand next to Maeve, and as other novices joined them they moved closer together and their bodies touched. Lovernios felt Maeve shiver and hoped she'd felt the same shock course through her body as he. Later that day when they had a brief chance to talk, they agreed to meet at midnight behind the stone they'd been standing beside when they touched.

Once he'd recovered from the initial excitement of the planned meeting, Lovernios began to feel afraid. What would they say to each other? What if someone saw them? What would the priests do with them? By the time midnight approached he'd worked himself into a state, and for the first time in a long while he felt like the young boy he still was. He wasn't sure he should go to meet Maeve and was convinced she wouldn't be there, but if he didn't go and she did, well, she'd surely never speak to him again. Finally, as he judged the moon to be at its zenith, he slung his fox cloak over his shoulders and crept away from his sleeping friends.

Maeve had been waiting for a long time and had grown cold. As soon as he saw the raised flesh on her arms he wrapped his cloak round her and held her tightly. As he felt her slender body against his, he knew he never wanted to let her go, but she pulled away, took his hand and led him further from the sleeping Druids.

They sat side by side under the moonlight and talked for hours, sharing their innermost thoughts and dreams. Just before the first rays of light were about to rouse the Druids they slipped back to their sleeping places, each knowing they'd found their soul mate, that their lives would never be the same again as they experienced the first pangs of what they knew to be love.

As Lovernios lay sleepless waiting to be called by Gamenta he felt a sense of guilt towards Pren, his first soul mate, but consoled himself with the thought that Pren would always be his blood brother, and soul mate of a different sort.

By the time they left Stonehenge, the novices felt they couldn't absorb a single fact more; their minds were so full. They spent their return trip chanting the new things they'd discovered, and added a further hundred verses to their already large store of knowledge.

Lovernios and Maeve were the only two who were sad to leave. Their midnight meetings had to end. On their last night together they held hands, and as they parted Lovernios leaned towards the beautiful girl who stood bathed in moonlight in front of him and kissed her gently on the lips. She responded by taking his head and pulling him towards her so roughly that their teeth clashed, and as they clutched each other, Lovernios felt a tear run down her cheek. Embarrassed, they parted and didn't get the opportunity to speak privately again until they reached the place they called home.

When Gamenta turned off the pathway with Delinius and Mardial following, Lovernios put out his hand and Maeve touched it briefly as she passed.

Chapter 15

AD 44
Autumn

The novices were halfway through their second degree and had already learned a large number of verses, which Lovernios spent less time trying to remember than his companions.

His thoughts fluttered daily between excitement at seeing his family for the first time in six years, to fear at what may have happened to them during that time. He felt such emotion at the thought of Pren that he was seldom able to eat.

He wanted so desperately to see his brother again, yet felt disloyal to Maeve because of his love of Pren, then disloyal to Pren at the thought of his love for Maeve. Although he'd not seen as much of her as he would have liked over the months since they'd returned from Salisbury Plain, each meeting had been special and they'd grown clever at managing to sit together, sometimes even slipping away from the others, then they clung together and drew strength from each other.

When Lovernios thought of the future he knew with certainty it included Maeve, even with the knowledge that he'd one day be taken by the gods.

"After tomorrow's celebrations, the hardest part of your training begins."

Lovernios pulled his mind back to what Gamenta was saying with an effort.

"You'll travel much, and see little of your family, so spend your time with them wisely."

Whispering and murmuring broke out among the novices as they discussed the following day. Gamenta held his hand up for silence.

"There's great trouble in the land," he continued and they listened attentively. "The Romans have already gained a strong foothold, and when you see your kin tomorrow they'll tell you this. Many of them have become Romanised and given over to the Emperor. New chieftains, and client kings have been established. Many have lost everything and thousands have been killed in battles, so for some of you, your family may not be coming. But you are priests and priestesses now, your home is here with the gods."

He let his words sink in before continuing, and there was absolute silence as the horror of what he said sank in.

"The Emperor not only wants our land, he wants to change our people and make them Roman and to wipe out the Druids. Since the time of Caesar we've been chased and persecuted and driven further into the forests, in fear of our lives. They bring great legions to attack us and wipe us out, even though we are defenceless. The past year of fighting has deeply affected the Belgae and the Durotriges, even their mighty fortresses have fallen. The people living in the forestlands in the northern territory of the Dumnonii were too few to resist, and they too have fallen. At present the Romans are in the mountains at the edge of the territory of the Silures and the northern moors of the Ordovices, but the good news is they are finally beginning to meet with resistance."

His audience sat stunned.

"You'll have noticed over the years that you've been here," Gamenta continued, "that fewer new novices are being sent to us. This year there'll be none. After tomorrow's celebrations we'll be moving further northwards to escape their onslaught. Many of our number, especially our older priests have already fled to Mona."

Again Gamenta paused. "For the past fourteen winters there's been one among us chosen by the gods to be a Supreme Sacrifice at a time such as this."

All eyes turned towards Lovernios. As Gamenta went through the story of his birth, Lovernios felt neither the pride nor privilege he'd felt at each previous telling, but an enormous sadness that his new brothers and sisters, the priests and priestesses around him should be persecuted so. While he longed for the day he could be sacrificed to save the land, he was saddened that it was necessary, and at the hands of the Romans.

Although no one ever grew tired of hearing the story, and Gamenta never tired of telling it, on this particular night it was a sombre group that lay down to sleep.

They met their families on the riverbank in a confused and chaotic mass of shouting and excitement. Although the youngsters had learned to behave as priests and priestesses, their parents were still very much Celts and prone to great revelry and celebration. They brought with them a feast for their novice, and before long each family had met up with its child and settled down to eat and drink the afternoon away.

When Lovernios first saw his father he wasn't sure how to react, having last seen him when he was a little boy, he was shy and uncomfortable. He was aware too of how he'd grown, coming up to his father's shoulders where he'd only reached his waistline before.

Vitaicus had no reservations and flung his arms around Lovernios, hoisted him off the ground and spun him round till his gown caught on the branch of a tree and ripped.

They all laughed and Vitaicus put Lovernios down so that he could greet his mother. He was shocked. She was thin and pale and looked much older. When he hugged her he felt her ribs against his own muscular body, and feared that she was deathly ill. He had little time to think on it though as his sister and brothers waited to greet him.

First there was Filethas who'd just turned eleven. She was tall and willowy with soft brown hair and sad eyes, startlingly like Trasand. She greeted Lovernios shyly, noticing how big and handsome he was.

Waiting eagerly behind Filethas was nine-year old Roulst. Lovernios thought he looked no different now than he had as a toddler. He was puny and effeminate and it was plain to see that the king had no time for him, while the queen favoured him as she did her daughter.

Lovernios looked round for Pren, but before spotting him was introduced to Tylad, the youngest addition to the family. He too was amazed at the striking likeness between the little boy and his father. Lovernios was delighted to meet his youngest brother, who was almost a year old and while he held him and inspected him, Vitaicus told him briefly how they'd lost Mellund, Kwethin and the twins. He didn't elaborate on the death of the twins, and Lovernios didn't ask. He was concerned that he hadn't seen Pren.

"Where is.....?" before he could complete his sentence a voice behind him answered.

"Here I am."

Lovernios spun round and gasped. Nearly as tall as himself and only a little thinner stood Pren, the brother who'd once been a full head smaller and much weaker.

Standing next to him, wagging his tail effusively was Sopa. Pren grinned at Lovernios and noted too how the stranger standing before him in a priest's gown had grown, but was pleased that he himself had caught up well. They threw their arms round each other spontaneously and hugged and kissed and laughed, while Sopa tried to jump up between them.

For the next few hours the boys sat side-by-side, knees touching as they ate with the family, and attempted to fit the six-year gap into two short hours.

Vitaicus was finally satisfied that he'd asked his son all he needed to and gave the boys permission to take a walk and be alone together. Trasand lay against a tree and sighed contentedly. Filethas wandered round watching other family reunions. Tylad slept while Vitaicus watched Lovernios and Pren from a distance.

The boys couldn't talk fast enough, with so much to say and ask. They were grateful that they still felt the same way about each other as they'd done so many years earlier. When the visitors were asked to leave before the sun began its descent they both felt a new elation, despite being heart-sore once again. The farewells were brief and formal. For Pren and Lovernios there was a hug and a promise.

"Blood brothers in this life and the next, blood brothers to the end." Lovernios said sadly.

"To the very end," Pren replied as he followed their father to their carriage.

Lovernios saw Maeve standing with Alana, and wished he'd thought to introduce her to his family. However it wasn't until three days later that he was able to talk to her and tell her he was sorry that he hadn't done this. She shrugged her shoulders and continued picking the mushrooms they'd been sent to gather.

After some time of silence Lovernios asked her how she'd enjoyed the visit with her family.

"I don't have any," was her abrupt reply.

Lovernios stared at her, stunned. He'd known her for a long time now and they'd grown close and come to love each other. They'd shared their deepest dreams and secrets, and in their stolen hours they'd become much more than soul mates, they desired each other physically, and yet Lovernios didn't know that she had no family. He stood rooted to the spot.

"You never told me," he stammered, "why, why didn't you tell me?"

"It's not important," she said flatly "the priestesses are my family, they always have been. Alana found me when I was a baby and I've been with her ever since."

Just then Gamenta called for Lovernios to help Mardial move a fallen tree and by the time they'd done so, the priestesses had moved off, making their way back to their grove as the light in the forest began to fade.

Vitaicus returned to his castle to find that Marcus had been waiting for him for two days. Having already added in excess of twenty countries to his Empire, Claudius had turned his attention to Palmyra on the shores of the Black Sea, which he annexed without resistance.

He then seized the eastern client Kingdom of Judaea, a kingdom that had previously been restored to Herod Agrippa by Caligula, but Claudius had no qualms in wresting it back once again. His control of Britain was growing daily, and Vitaicus found the news most disturbing and upsetting, and his earlier mood from the time spent with Lovernios changed instantly to a dark and depressed one.

Before any further learning during their six years of training to be Vates was undertaken, the Druids moved their charges much further north than they'd been before and they resettled in an area near Vernemeton in the land of the Cortiani. For the novices the move was exciting, but for the Druids it was one which filled them with fear, as they knew there were Roman spies and they became fearful for their lives as they travelled. After the first day's march, they chose to move by night only.

For six nights they marched, and on the seventh they arrived at a place that Gamenta and the other priests judged to be suitable. For their safety, the priestesses would be living amongst them, and the following few days were spent setting up shelters.

The arrangement suited Lovernios and Maeve perfectly and

during the following months they spent most of their time together. Gamenta and Alana often discussed them but unknown to the youngsters who were trying so hard not to show their feelings they were delighted with their obvious affection for each other. "Infatuation," Alana chose to call it.

Alana and Gamenta felt the same about each other as Lovernios and Maeve did, although Alana preferred to call theirs love, and Gamenta, delighted to have someone feel affection towards him for the first time in his life, was happy to have her call it what she pleased.

As Druids they were permitted to marry but knew that the time wouldn't be right until they'd finished tutoring their novices, still many years away.

Chapter 16

AD 45
Autumn

The blissful state that Alana and Gamenta shared was marred only by the struggle for survival in the forest and the arduous task of teaching the novices.

For Lovernios even the hard work, the hours of learning, and the constant repetition of verses were a pleasure so long as Maeve was by his side. However even his contented state wasn't permanent but was shattered the day Obetach strode into the grove disrupting one of their lessons.

He was exhausted and clearly upset as he spoke softly to Gamenta. The novices were told they could have some free time, something seldom given and always cherished and they hurried off before Gamenta could change his mind.

Lovernios remained behind, sensing that Obetach had come for him, but fearing what the Druid had to say. Obetach led Lovernios and Gamenta from the grove and they walked some way alongside a stream before Obetach spoke for the first time.

"Sit down Lovernios," he said softly "I have news for you that is very grave indeed."

Lovernios shut his mind down not wanting to try and imagine in those few seconds before Obetach spoke again, what he might say. He squeezed his eyelids tightly together and breathed deeply.

"Ten nights ago, when the moon was waning, the gods warned me that it was to be an inauspicious day once the sun rose. Pren had spent the time before sunrise with his bees and he too felt that evil was about to befall your father's household. We watched and waited and prayed. My priests sacrificed a bull and slew a dog. We watched its convulsions and they too purported an ill omen. By evening we knew it was time, evil would come."

He paused a moment. "Just as it got too dark to see, a merchant came up the roadway into the courtyard in a large carriage drawn by two huge mares. As he pulled his horses to the left around the pool in the centre of the yard, out of the light of the lamps, little Tylad ran out to greet him. No one saw the lad stumble and fall and it was only when the man alighted from his carriage that the boys legs were seen sticking out from under the heavy wheels. His little chest was crushed. He was taken by the gods instantly without knowing he was to die."

Lovernios rocked back and forth on his haunches wailing softly. He had only seen the child once but felt that a part of him had died too. Tylad had so resembled his father and he felt keenly the loss of him. How then would his father be feeling?

"I'm afraid there is more." Obetach said gently. Lovernios looked at him with disbelief. What else?

"The following night, when the funeral pyre was lit and the child's body was atop the flames, your mother the queen, who could bear no more grief, climbed into the fire and left for the Otherworld to be with all the children she had lost."

When Obetach arrived back at the castle several weeks later he was shocked at the appearance of the king. During the first days after the deaths of Tylad and Trasand, he'd been beside himself with grief and stayed in his chamber where he ate little and drank much.

Obetach had been concerned about leaving him, but knew he should be the one to tell Lovernios of the tragedy. On his return the king was much worse. It was obvious that he was neither sleeping, washing nor changing his clothing. He was dishevelled and dirty and his mood matched his appearance.

He ranted and raved and was physically abusive to anyone who came near him. He threw furniture around and smashed dishes against the walls. The castle was in an uproar, the servants fled to their quarters, and only a handful of brave souls remained to take care of the children.

Omilia and Flauston were attempting to reason with the king when Obetach arrived. On seeing his priest, Vitaicus became calmer and agreed to lie down and rest. He slept for a day and a night and when he rose, he ate a huge meal and then called for his generals.

A good fight was what he needed and he commanded them to round up his warriors, they were going out to battle. He didn't know where or against whom, and didn't much care. His generals would know of someone who needed to be taught a lesson. After the dark mood that had prevailed in his kingdom over the past weeks, his people were delighted to throw down their farming implements, take up their weapons and go off to war.

It was only after the king and his men left that Obetach learned what had taken place while he was away. The very night Obetach had gone in search of Lovernios, when he'd felt so unsure of his going, the king had roused himself and called for Flauston to saddle up his horse.

He'd gone with his servant to the home of Ashannon where he'd taken his sword from his cloak and slain his lover in the house he'd built for her. He left her body on the floor where she had fell and then torched the place. A small wooden structure with a straw roof, it had burned swiftly and within moments nothing remained of that part of his life.

As he headed back to the castle he asked Flauston to burn the shed where she kept the livestock he'd given her.

Immediately he'd done the deed Vitaicus felt worse, for now he'd lost not only the woman he loved, but also the one he desired so fiercely. His longing for them both was physical. His heart ached, his chest constricted and he was unable to breath. He had no desire for food and couldn't sleep as his body, accustomed to daily sexual pleasure, rebelled.

He took his frustration, anger, bitterness and his great grief out on anything and everything, anyone and everyone, and Obetach felt a deep sadness for his friend as he listened to Flauston.

Vitaicus and his warriors travelled north for two days when the king decided in an instant that he needed to see Lovernios. He sent his warriors home in high spirits for having been on a mission, and returned to the castle calling loudly for Flauston and Obetach.

"I'm going to visit Lovernios and will be taking Pren with me," he announced.

The two knew there was no arguing with the king in his present state. It was six weeks since the death of Trasand and Tylad and the king hadn't stopped his mourning or ranting since. They were only too pleased to see him planning a trip, but Obetach knew his chances of finding Lovernios were slim. The priests were well hidden far north of Canti and it would take many days to reach the area.

Without someone like Obetach to guide him Vitaicus wouldn't come close to locating his son, and so it didn't surprise Obetach when the king demanded that he accompany them.

"I will have to think on it my Lord," he told Vitaicus and left the king dumfounded at the first person who'd dared cross his path over the past dark month.

Obetach returned a few hours later to where Vitaicus sat idly pushing pieces of their game of Chelta around the board on which they played so often. He barely looked up as Obetach entered.

"I'll take you there," he said softly. The king smiled to himself, but merely nodded at Obetach and asked him to fetch Flauston.

"We leave at dawn. Prepare for the trip and bring Pren to me."

Pren was excited at the prospect of seeing Lovernios again, but felt a sense of foreboding. He spent the night watching the skies for a sign, reading the stars, searching for a word from the gods, but none came.

The trip started out pleasantly. Sopa had been allowed to come and he and Pren travelled together in the king's chariot. The party consisted of four other chariots with Flauston and Obetach in one and servants and slaves with provisions in the remaining three.

Towards the end of the first day they came to a stream where the king said they should set up camp. The evening sky was clear with brilliant stars. The moon was full, and Pren lay on the cool ground and sighed. He wished he could live out here all the time with Lovernios and the other priests.

He listened to his father as he lay daydreaming, and smiled. For the first time in weeks he was in good humour. Being away from the castle and its awful memories, in the fresh air with a belly full of good food and wine, Vitaicus began to tell tales and delight his small audience with outrageous exaggerations of battles fought and won.

The following morning, despite a sore head, the king's light-hearted mood persisted, but Pren still felt ill at ease as he continued to sense that the gods were against the trip. He again spent the day searching for signs but found none, and so when it happened he was unprepared and not even sure that it was the gods speaking until Obetach confirmed his misgivings.

It was just after midday and the sky began to fill with clouds, which darkened quickly. The party looked about for a place to shelter. The winds picked up suddenly and before they'd crossed the open plain they were travelling over the rain came. With thunder and lightning crashing round them and the wind threatening to overturn their chariots, their horses were terrified. The party stumbled and fell as they attempted to push on the few hundred feet to a wooded area. The soft earth quickly turned to mud and it became more difficult to drag the chariots along with slaves pushing and pulling.

They realised too late that they were in a bog, and the first chariot and horses began to sink, followed swiftly by a second one. In the lashing rain, unable to see where they were going, the slaves hadn't noticed the chariot sinking and within minutes they too were sucked down into the treacherous mud. The squeals of the horses and screams of the men were drowned out by the sounds of the storm and within moments it was all over. The remainder of the party retreated and then huddled closely while they waited for the storm to abate.

It was only after the rain had stopped that they realised that Sopa had died too.

Obetach and a distraught Pren whispered together discussing the reason for the anger of the gods. They agreed the trip had been doomed from the start. The gods had been seeking vengeance for the slaying of Ashannon, and now they had it, but what would this fresh disaster do to the state of mind of the king. Much to their amazement the king looked for a safe crossing into the forest and commanded them to proceed.

By the time they reached Vernemeton a few days later Lovernios' party of priests had moved, and realising that their provisions were running low, Vitaicus agreed to return home.

On the way he hunted at leisure and they stopped to fish and swim in the spring waters of the numerous rivers and streams they crossed. With each passing day the king's mood picked up further, but when they re-entered his country and heard that a party of Atrebates had been stealing cattle, he became ecstatic.

By the time they returned to the castle, Vitaicus was planning to take his warriors to battle once again. The old king was back and his people celebrated.

Chapter 17

AD 45

Autumn

For the first time in the fourteen years that Gamenta had been responsible for telling Lovernios of his birth story, reinforcing into his charge the knowledge that he belonged to the gods, Gamenta hadn't the energy to do it.

He'd not been feeling well of late and on this special morning he'd woken with a fever and a cough. Such was the life of the Druid that coughs and colds were a common ailment, but Gamenta felt worse than he'd ever done before and was unable to rise from his straw mat.

He called for his assistant, a Druid with two years of his own training to complete before he graduated for the final time. His name was Prydayn and he was a serious but likeable priest.

Gamenta had never felt threatened by the great intelligence of his junior, nor overshadowed by the youth's extreme good looks, and Prydayn had always been modest and full of praise for his senior, Gamenta.

Once Prydayn saw the state of Gamenta he immediately ordered hot drinks of specially prepared herbs to be brought. Using Samolus and a mixture of plants and leaves, he prayed and chanted over Gamenta, while other priests and priestesses sprinkled him with holy water. After they'd spent the morning ministering to him they wrapped him up in sheepskins and left him to sleep next to a fire.

That evening after the novices had eaten they sat round their own fire talking quietly. Three of the priestesses were preparing a bannock cake as Prydayn had instructed.

They'd spent the afternoon gathering barley and wheat and they cooked the unleavened bread on a metal griddle over the fire. Prydayn knew they had to appease the gods with a human sacrifice in exchange for the healing of Gamenta.

Before the ceremony began Gamenta woke and with laboured breath asked Prydayn to relate the birth story of Lovernios, as this inauspicious day was the fifteenth anniversary of that day.

It was the first time that Lovernios felt no excitement at the ritual and he despaired that Gamenta wasn't well enough to do the recitation, however once Prydayn began the tale which he'd learnt through hearing Gamenta's repeated telling of it, Lovernios began to relax and even enjoy himself.

Prydayn had a deep and melodious voice, a trance inducing voice, and his audience were completely silent and absolutely still throughout the recital. Without using the dramatics that Gamenta did, without any acting or rising of his voice, Prydayn completed the story that had his audience spellbound, as if they'd just heard it for the first time.

Lovernios was filled with awe and humility that he'd been chosen above all others, and as Prydayn ordered the bannock bread to be placed onto the fire, he was certain that this would be the night he'd be chosen by the gods. How fitting that would be, to be the sacrifice that would ensure the good health and restoration of his priest, Gamenta.

The silence continued as the priestesses supervised the cooking of the bannock, and once it was done, they moved out of the way for Prydayn. The priest rubbed his right index finger lightly over the hot griddle ensuring that it was well coated in soot, then he picked the bread up making sure that his finger touched just one small spot. The priests followed him away from the light of the fire and sat in a circle on their haunches.

The warm bread was passed round and once each priest and novice had broken off a small portion they moved back to the light of the fire. Prydayn walked past them, one by one, examining their pieces to see who had drawn the blackened bit. He was the priest the gods had chosen to be sacrificed, to be singled out for this great honour.

No one dared look at the bread he held out to Prydayn, and Prydayn wouldn't reveal who'd been chosen until he'd examined every piece, lest two portions contained a blackened part. Lovernios held his breath, this was surely the moment he'd waited for his entire life, and today would be a fitting day indeed.

When Prydayn had completed his tour, he moved out of the circle of priests and said solemnly,

"The gods have chosen Delinius."

There was a gasp from among the novices as the news shook them. They'd all assumed it would be Lovernios who was himself shocked beyond words. Delinius stood up and Mardial embraced him wordlessly. He moved to where Lovernios sat. Lovernios stood on shaky legs and with tears streaming down his cheeks, he embraced his friend.

"May the gods keep you safely until we meet again. May Gamenta be healed because of your great sacrifice my friend," he managed to say before his voice broke.

After their initial shock each priest came forward to say farewell to Delinius with embraces and words of praise.

The priestesses had their turn too, and tears were shed as the likeable young man said goodbye to the people who'd been his brothers and sisters for seven years. Delinius was taken to Gamenta who lay in his coverings well away from the ceremony beside a fire of his own. He was bathed in sweat and talked deliriously as they approached him.

They knelt on either side of him and Prydayn explained what had taken place. Gamenta was unable to understand or respond, but when Delinius leaned over to embrace and kiss the Druid, Gamenta hugged him weakly before lapsing back into a comatose state.

Prydayn stood and signalled for Delinius to follow him back to the fire. It was necessary to build it up higher, and the younger novices were sent to collect more wood.

Because this sacrifice was different, Delinius had committed no crime and was being offered to the gods as an appeasement of the highest order, he'd be treated differently. A log was brought for him to sit on and while the novices rebuilt the fire, the priests and priestesses chanted and sang and played their lyres and kept Delinius company. He sat staring into the flames, waiting. He'd no regrets about his life in this world, and looked forward eagerly to life in the Otherworld. He was proud to be the Chosen One, the one who would rescue Gamenta from the hands of the evil forces that presently held him captive.

He was a little scared of the long and dangerous journey he was about to take through lakes of fire, and into deep dark caves, but felt certain he'd reach the other side in time, and that at that point Gamenta would be well again.

Without prior warning Prydayn came up behind Delinius as he sat musing, and struck him firmly across the base of his skull with an axe. Delinius fell forward, dead in an instant, with a faint smile on his lips. Lovernios and Mardial were given the honour of lifting him and with the help of Prydayn they threw his body high into the fire. The priests and priestesses danced and chanted until the flames died down and the last of his earthly body was consumed many hours later. Only then did they go to where Gamenta lay, sleeping peacefully.

The following morning Lovernios was up before light, and moved quietly over to where Gamenta lay. Prydayn was already there. When he saw Lovernios he nodded, and at that instant Gamenta sat up and rubbed his swollen eyelids.

"He's arrived!" exclaimed Lovernios. "Delinius has arrived!"

Not knowing what he was talking about Gamenta smiled indulgently and stood up on thin and uncertain legs, ready to begin the new day.

Chapter 18

AD 46
Winter

The priests were forced to move north once again. Ever aware of the presence of the Romans they agreed not to stay long in one place, and were aware the legions were getting closer. They kept their cooking fires lower than usual and seldom built a pyre, in case it was seen by the enemy.

After a few days marching they decided to settle near the Black Lake in the land of the Cornovii, in the heart of the forest where the area was protected by peat bogs, a safe haven for a while. They found an ideal spot along the banks of the River Bolin where there was an abundance of fish and birds for food.

Within a few days they were settled in and ready to begin lessons again, but these were once more interrupted, this time by the arrival of a group of priests who'd travelled from Verulamium near the southern border of the land of the Trinovantes. The area had become a Roman stronghold and the priests fled for their lives, bringing with them all their accumulated wealth.

Gamenta and his senior priests sat with the visitors the entire day, discussing the events of the past months, praying to the gods and divining their will.

The following morning while the frost was still thick on the ground, both parties of priests rose and washed themselves, sprinkling their bodies with the clear, cold dewdrops. They put on fresh gowns and with clean bare feet approached the riverbank. The visiting priests wore their finest golden torcs around their necks, and carried other jewels, goblets, cauldrons inlaid with precious stones, and ornaments of gold and silver. The priestesses sang while the priests under the leadership of Gamenta danced along the riverbank.

The visiting Druids walked into the water and when they were waist deep they flung their offerings as far as they could, pleading with the river gods to accept them and in return bring peace and stability the land.

Once they'd given over the last of their wealth to the gods they left Gamenta and his group continuing on their way towards Mona, and safety.

"Why did they come here?" Lovernios asked Gamenta later that day as they prepared for the evening meal.

"This is a very sacred place," Gamenta answered "and a fitting one in which to offer such magnificent sacrifices to the gods. They've travelled many days out of their way to get here, but I'm sure the gods led them." Lovernios nodded.

"I suppose it's better to leave their treasure in the hands of the gods rather than the hands of the Romans."

Gamenta smiled at Lovernios. "Indeed it is, but they would have given them to the gods even if the Romans weren't a threat, to appease them should there have been a drought or any other trouble."

"Why haven't we given our torcs to them too, we still carry them with us wherever we go?"

"The time will come." Gamenta mused. "It isn't yet, but I fear it will soon be here and then we too will seek to appease the gods with our offerings of wealth."

Lovernios couldn't sleep that night. It seemed his entire life was in turmoil and he once again longed for his family. He grieved over his mothers and the brother and sisters he never knew, as he tossed and turned, his body aching from the hard earth and the constant dancing round fires.

After the second battle against the Atrebates in the past two years, Vitaicus decided to visit King Beditath of the Dumnonii. Their land was rich in minerals and Vitaicus promised himself a trip there to see what this famed place produced.

Now that his responsibilities at home had lessened, he felt no need to rush back there. The children were being cared for and his bed was empty. His warriors, victorious and anxious to take their trophies home, left him and a small party of servants to continue on their journey.

They crossed through the land of the Belgae by night and set up camp just over the border in the land of the Durotriges the following morning. They rested until midday and were about to move on when a rider was seen approaching them. With swords at the ready the men waited, Vitaicus standing out in front.

The rider greeted them and asked permission to dismount. After they'd given him a drink, they sat under a tree and waited for him to speak. He told Vitaicus he was fleeing the land, making his way to the coast where he intended to travel towards the land of the Regni, and ask for a safe place to set up home for himself and his family, who were following him.

He was going ahead as a scout, in search of Roman soldiers. The Romans had already marched into his country and subdued the people, making treaties with some, running others off, killing many. They'd set up an army encampment at Durovaria. Their king had given up his throne, and the Romans ruled the land. The people were expected to pay taxes, and make obeisance to Emperor Claudius.

The rider carried two large sacks of coins that the Durotriges had minted and buried just before the Romans arrived. He was hoping to be able to use them to trade with when he reached the Regni, trusting that they'd take the coins and give him a farm so he could resettle his family in peace. Vitaicus shook his head sadly.

"There are no coins in use among the Regni, they'll not take them for a farm, they're valueless." He said, shaking his head.

"But Sire, they're of pure silver. The value of them is far greater than fifty slaves!"

"How many of these are buried?" Vitaicus asked.

"Many hundreds, wealth far above what we can imagine, just so that the Romans couldn't have it. Without the coins our people cannot pay the taxes they demand. We'll not make them richer, we'd rather see the silver returned to the earth."

"You've spoken wisely," said the king. "Come," he called to his party. "Let's leave this place and return home, there's nothing here for us to see and I've no desire to set eyes on the Roman enemy. We'll not return home depressed by thoughts of the Romans, but triumphant from our battle."

Vitaicus arrived at the castle to hear that Claudius had been triumphant in battle too, having recently annexed Thrace. Although he had no idea where these places were that Claudius was taking control of, he knew that the Emperor was well on his way to fulfilling his dream of ruling the world, and the news upset the king and his kingdom afresh.

Chapter 19

AD 47
Autumn

Gamenta hadn't been well during the past two years, and although not as deathly sick as he'd been when Delinius was sacrificed, he was never the same healthy person as he'd been in his youth.

He was prone to bouts of coughing and fever, quick to catch a chill, and filled with aches to his bones, but he never complained as the priests were forced to move regularly from one end of the country to the other. Their next move however, was one that they all looked forward to with great anticipation. They were going to visit Mona, the island where many hundreds of priests had already fled and the novices talked of this sacred place often, longing for Gamenta to announce their departure.

They were so caught up with excitement they gave little thought to their impending graduation. Although they were being taught more vigorously than before and were made to recite verses until their heads swam, dance until their bodies ached and sing until their voices croaked, they still talked more of Mona than they did of graduating from their six years of training to be Vates. During a brief rest period one midday, Lovernios found Gamenta sitting alone, coughing violently. He took the priest a drink of fresh water.

"Gamenta," Lovernios asked tentatively when the priest stopped coughing, "when will we be leaving for Mona?"

"When the gods permit."

They sat in silence awhile but as Gamenta rose to continue with the day's lessons, he turned to Lovernios as if there had been no pause.

"You'll be graduating first, only then will the gods speak."

The night before the graduation ceremony was one of mixed

feelings for the novices, and they spent it in the forest where their first initiation ceremony had taken place.

They'd been delighted when they were told that they were returning south, and hoped to see their families while they were there. But as it was they returned swiftly and silently, travelling by night and keeping to deep forests and glades, secret places they'd never seen before with paths and passages known only to the most senior Druids.

Obetach had come to lead them and the night he arrived they began their march, arriving six days later, totally exhausted. The priests and priestesses allowed their novices to talk informally after they'd eaten their evening meal, resting while the Vates lit a fire. Once it was burning brightly Gamenta addressed them.

"Tomorrow is an important day in your lives, and one which you'll long remember. Regrettably there are those among you who've not qualified for the second degree, and will not be graduating tomorrow."

Lovernios was relieved to hear that Mardial was to become a Vate and that he too had met the stringent requirements, but his greatest delight was in knowing that Maeve would graduate. They could still be together.

During the long ceremony early the next morning, he tried in vain to see her but the huge cavern in which they'd been initiated nine years previously, was so dark it was almost impossible to see anything. Only the single fire in the centre where the ceremony was carried out offered some light. Each group of novices was brought in and made to stand before Obetach.

Lovernios was pleased to see him again, not having had the chance to get near him on the long march southwards, he had many questions he wanted to ask, but this wasn't the appropriate time. In the dim light he couldn't be sure but he thought the priest had aged alarmingly.

After a lengthy ceremony the novices were led out through the tunnel at the back of the cavern towards the river they'd crossed so many years before, but this time there was no going into the water, no swearing of oaths, just a sad farewell to those who hadn't graduated. They would remain with Obetach and a few other priests until their families were able to fetch them. Some chose to remain Bards and they could return to their families, or stay with the priests, without studying further.

The party rested that night and the following day, and at the first sign of darkness that evening they moved off. Travelling northwards once more, they kept to the deepest forests making their way towards the far northwest coast, where they'd board boats and cross over to the most sacred of all Druidical sanctuaries, the Island of Mona.

To the relief of the novices they weren't expected to learn anything new as they journeyed, and only chanted their verses once a night as they marched, after which they could sing as they went. No speaking was permitted unless they stopped to rest, and then they were allowed to talk.

Lovernios and Mardial cherished these times, as they sat with Maeve and her two closest friends, Couvena and Rynath. The five of them missed Delinius dearly, and spoke of him often. Since his passing into the Otherworld they'd become more aware of life in this world, and held each other and each day more precious than before.

Mardial and Couvena were becoming especially close and he often remarked to Lovernios how slow he'd been in becoming aware of the priestesses, unlike Lovernios who seemed to be ahead by years in everything.

Although the march was long and hard, their rest periods few, their meals scarce, and the nights harsh, the two weeks they travelled were probably among the best of their lives, and their relationships changed subtly each day. A bond grew between the five friends that would see them through the many hardships they still faced in their allotted time on earth.

They arrived at Deva, only to find they were settling into a new temporary home in a forest area many miles from the coast. For those novices who'd never seen the sea there was bitter disappointment as they learned they were to wait there until such time as the gods decreed.

Within a day of arriving lessons began once again in this new phase of their schooling, however all disappointment soon vanished as they delved into the fascinating world of medical mysteries. Left behind them for now were the stars and moon, no longer was chanting and singing a priority. Dancing and playing the lyre fell to the Bards that remained with them, predicting the future to the Vates, as the novices were thrown exclusively into the world of medicine.

They learned the value and properties of herbs such as Selago, something they knew of but only by name. Now they learned that Selago was collected when wearing white clothing only and in bare feet – newly washed – with an offering of bread and ale to be given to the gods. Selago was carried to ward off evil and smoke from burning Selago was good for curing all diseases, especially those of the eyes. Once they'd collected their own Selago they'd always carry some in a pouch with them.

Samolus was gathered with the left hand only and when fasting. It was used as a charm against all illnesses affecting cattle. The gatherer of Samolus must never look behind himself when gathering or the plant would lose its power. This too they would gather for themselves and keep in their pouches.

Vervain was to be gathered at the rise of the Dog Star, and before digging it up they were to walk in a circle around it. It was gathered with the left hand into a clean white cloth and infused with wine then used as an antidote for snakebites.

They learned of Herophilus, a Druid who'd studied anatomy using the bodies of more than seven hundred men, and whose wisdom had been passed down through the Druidical Order over the centuries. In order for the novices to learn the secrets of the body, they caught and dissected insects and snakes, frogs and fish, and when they'd mastered these, they went onto larger prey, birds, rabbits, small game, and each time they dissected a fox, Lovernios felt a sense of destiny.

The priestesses who'd grown up with the sight of animals being slaughtered were as hardened as the priests and thought nothing of the death of the creature, but enjoyed rather the learning experience. They never tired of seeing a heart pumping inside the body of one they'd sliced open, until its life-source emptied onto the ground and it died. They were fascinated by the length of time each animal took to grow cold and for rigor mortis to set in.

The priestesses learned each group of muscles and the name of each bone far more quickly than their male counterparts, and the competition among them became fierce.

Only Maeve showed any emotion at the sight of a beautiful young creature being slain for their learning purposes, and Lovernios noticed that she too shivered each time they cut up a fox. She felt the same disturbing sense of destiny that he did and it confirmed for him that their lives were linked. At these times he once more felt a deep longing for Pren, but as strongly, he felt guilt at his love for Maeve.

While they waited for the gods to sanction their visit to Mona, a new format came into their daily lives. The first five days of each week were spent learning the ways of the Druids while the sixth day was spent reciting the verses they'd already learned in the proceeding nine years, which numbered close to ten thousand.

The seventh day, the day of the sun, was dedicated to the worship of the gods and to divining their will, to praying, singing and dancing. It was a day of renewal for the priests and priestesses as they ended their week, and a day in which the gods looked favourably upon them.

At every opportunity, although few and far between, Lovernios and Maeve spent time together. Sometimes they were with Mardial, Couvena and Rynath, but as often as possible they were alone, and then they drew strength and comfort from each other through physical contact. Just the slightest brush of a hand, the touch of hair to face, the smell of breath on cheek, was enough to satisfy and renew their commitment to each other.

They spent their time together holding hands under their robes and talking of the future, hoping and praying that their visit to Mona would be soon and that the sacred groves there would be the place the gods would reveal to them the appointed day, the hour of their Supreme requirement, the life of their Chosen One – Lovernios.

Gamenta was ill frequently and when Alana wasn't standing in for him with tutoring, she cared for him. He too longed for the day the gods decreed they could leave for the island, praying that he'd be healed in the sacred waters there, but as it was he was ill on the day the gods gave their permission for the party to depart.

They'd just celebrated the anniversary of Lovernios' birth for the seventeenth time and Gamenta announced that as a gift, Lovernios was to receive a horse. Lovernios thought fondly of his Shetland, Luath-Reul, and realised with a start how many years it was since he'd last ridden the pony and that with the passing years and the way he'd grown, the poor creature wouldn't hold his weight and his own legs would drag on the ground if he ever again sat on its back.

Gamenta told the novices that Epona, the Keeper of Horses and Goddess of Fertility, was in the forest north of where they were, across the river Maeresea. It was the seventh day of the week when Gamenta told them this and by the end of the day the excitement among the novices was so great that the priest decided they could all go in search of Epona and the gift for Lovernios.

The party had only just entered the forest two nights later when they saw the horses, a herd of magnificent wild creatures feeding quietly on the lush grasses where they stood. With the patience that comes of years of practice, the Druids waited, inching forward slowly, taking the entire night to reach the horses, who by then were quite used to their presence.

As the sun rose Gamenta began calling for Epona, who answered swiftly. To the delight of the priests she said they could all have horses, and tantalisingly added, "If you can catch them."

She wasn't going to help them this time, but still, she'd given them her permission, now it was up to the skill of the priests to take her up on her offer.

Lovernios was given first choice, and as the priests sat quietly whispering among themselves, the horses continued to eat and move about the glade, warming themselves in the morning sun. The horse that Lovernios chose was a magnificent white beast, larger than the rest and without spot or blemish. Everyone agreed that it was a fitting animal for Lovernios.

By midday the priests and priestesses had moved in among the herd and were slowly mingling with them, imitating their snorting and snuffling noises, each picking out their own and befriending it. For the remainder of the day they wooed their chosen beast.

By nightfall, cold, tired and hungry, they were ready to lie down with the animals and rested contentedly, many of them with their heads lying up against their horses. As the animals stirred the following morning the Druids made their move, and began mounting them.

Wild as they were the hours of patient courting paid off, and all but three horses allowed the priests to sit on them. They sat still and silently that morning as the horses again moved around the lush glade, getting used to the feel of a rider on their backs.

Startled at first by the feel of the Druids as they leaned forward to graze they became jittery, but as the morning wore on the horses seemed to forget they had a weight on their backs and were no longer nervous.

During the afternoon Lovernios slipped off his horse and offered it a sweet apple that he'd kept in his robe for the right moment. Delighted, the horse accepted the gift and nuzzled up to the now familiar smelling priest, hoping for another treat. He stood there accepting the affection the horse was showing him, his face up against that of the beautiful creature.

"You will be called Slydau," he whispered, 'Flowing Breath,' to remind me of this moment when you breathed on me and accepted me."

Lovernios rubbed Slydau's forehead and led the horse away from the rest, towards a nearby pool of water. When he'd drunk sufficiently, Lovernios offered him a second apple and then carefully mounted him again.

The horse munched happily, and at Lovernios' quiet urging started to trot away from the glade to the gentle nudging of the skilled priest, who rode the steed with ease.

The others followed suit, with just the three who'd been unsuccessful in obtaining a mount walking the long journey home. They arrived a day after the others, exhausted and ravenously hungry.

One of them was Gamenta, and the time in the glade waiting without food or drink, the cold of the evenings, and the long march all contributed to another bout of coughing and fever and once again Lovernios feared for the life of his mentor.

Chapter 20

AD 48
Winter

Two mornings later Gamenta was strong enough to speak once more and he announced that it was time to leave for Mona.

It was clear though that he wouldn't be going with them as he was barely able to stand unsupported, and so he remained behind with Alana and her priestesses and the junior Vates and Bards who were left in charge of the horses.

Lovernios was sad to leave Slydau and Gamenta, and prayed fervently that he'd see them both again. Leaving Maeve was harder than he anticipated, for both of them.

They reached the shore where boats waited for them late in the afternoon and were greeted by dismal news. It had been a while since they'd last heard of the Romans and what they were told frightened and shocked them, turning their excitement at going to Mona into reluctance to leave Britain. They departed knowing that they left behind uncertain times, great turmoil, and families that they'd not seen for years, families that may or may not still be alive.

They discussed the latest information as they boarded their boats. Claudius' army had moved further north and occupied Britain as far as the River Severn in the land of the Ordovices and the River Trent in the land of the Cortiani. The new Roman Governors were enjoying high status, with each one commanding his own large group of legions, while still more soldiers landed in Britain every month.

Aulus Silvanus Plautius was congratulated for his commendable work in securing the New Empire and was sent back to Rome where he was afforded the highest honour of a Triumph. His replacement was general Ostorius Scapula and like his predecessor he ruled

Britain with an iron hand.

The Romans began to exploit Britain's mineral resources and took over the wealth of the country. The silver bearing lead of the Mendip Hills in the land of the Durotriges, was mined under state control.

Cartimandua, the Queen of the Brigantes, the largest territory in Britain, entered into a treaty and accepted the position of a client state. The Romans were keeping the Brigantes as allies for good reason. They were using them as protection against attacks from the Forthri and other tribes across the northern border of the country.

A substantial portion of the south, including King Verica's old kingdom, the Regni, was in the hands of the disliked and unstable leader Cogidubnus. Of all the client kings and queens who made treaties with Rome, the Emperor's greatest success was the enduring loyalty of Cogidubnus, who wouldn't come to the aid of any of the Celts who later rose in rebellion against Roman rule. A grateful Claudius awarded him the title 'Rex Et Legatus Augusti in Britannia'.

As Ostorius Scapula took measures to counter raids from those who'd not made treaties with Rome, he forbade the carrying of arms. The Celts who'd voluntarily submitted to Rome didn't expect this to apply to them, but to their dismay, it did.

The Roman frontier was marked by the Fosse Way, which ran straight from just east of Isca Dumnoniorum in the land of the Dumonii to Lindum in the territory of the Cortiani, where the headquarters of the Ninth Legion had been established.

Lovernios and the priests and priestesses travelling with him, watched the receding shores of Britain with heavy hearts. Their country was almost entirely in the hands of the Romans, which meant that the Druids would never be safe there again.

Their spirits lifted as soon as Mona came into view, such a welcome sight it was. The island of two hundred and seventy six miles square and separated from the mainland by the Menai Strait, was on a platform ranging between two hundred and fifty and three hundred feet above sea level, and was surrounded by hills. Although the soil was not very fertile, the wet but mild climate was perfect for the growth of natural forests and glades.

The novices secured their boats and climbed the steep path leading off the beach to the top of the platform, and were amazed to see hundreds of sheep and cattle roaming everywhere. They were sad to leave the holy and magical place several months later. Having left Britain so reluctantly previously, their first sight of Mona allayed their fears and they immediately felt the presence of the gods stronger than ever before.

As soon as they arrived they were taken to meet the Supreme Druid Pantra. For Lovernios the occasion was an overwhelming one, and he and Mardial talked long into the night of the wisdom of the great man, and the blessing of the gods that hovered over him like an unseen mantle.

There was about him a presence, an aura of peace, despite the turmoil, and an impression of destiny – he harboured no fear. Within hours Lovernios and the others felt the same sense of peace and destiny and they slept better that night than they'd done for many years.

The months spent on the island were filled with lessons. The novices continued with their learning each morning, while afternoons were spent calling on the gods for guidance and help. During the evenings they met with the senior Druids already living there. Tragically their number was far fewer than should have been. Many priests had been wiped out before ever reaching the sanctuary, many had died since their arrival, their elderly bodies no longer capable of the hardships and undue stress the Romans had brought to them.

It soon became clear as the meetings continued night after night, that if the Druidical Order were to be saved in Britain, all Druids throughout Britain would need to move to Mona.

Many arguments and debates arose. What would become of the country without Druids to guide it? What would become of each household to which a priest was attached? What would be the policy regarding those priests who might refuse to leave? How long were they to stay on Mona? The senior priests set guidelines until general agreement was reached.

Every Druid must be forced to leave Britain for the good of them all. Any priest refusing to obey the order sanctioned by the Supreme Druid under the guidance of all the gods, would be put to death. Death would be preferable to being left to the Romans, for fear of being captured and tortured, or taken to Rome, there to entertain the people.

The Romans loved entertainment and games and Pantra feared that Claudius would have any captured Druids paraded through his stadiums much the way he'd been parading other priests, men who were called Christians and came from other faraway lands, only to be fed to the lions for the amusement of Claudius and his bloodthirsty people.

Once the policy was agreed on the Druids set about choosing messengers. They wouldn't send any senior Druids back to Britain, and most of the novices were too young and had too much still to learn, but they were equally loath to send those who'd already passed a number of degrees and were almost fully fledged Druids.

Eventually after weeks of indecision, and no specific word from the gods, they chose to send the fittest and strongest of the seventeen to twenty year olds. Priests who were learned enough to miss a few months of training, old enough to have their word respected by those more senior to themselves, and strong enough to ride across the length and breadth of the land carrying the message.

Once the fleeing Druids began to arrive on Mona, a party would sail across the Irish Sea to Tara and meet with the Druids there and appeal to them for help, praying they would be willing to set up a second safe haven in Tara, a place to which the Roman's hadn't yet ventured.

After months of resting on the peaceful island, learning more of the gods and soaking up the wisdom of the great men that surrounded them, there wasn't a priest among the group chosen to go back to Britain who left without some reluctance.

Among them were Lovernios and Mardial, and it was only once they were aboard the boats that Lovernios thought of what awaited him across the sea. He prayed that Gamenta would still be there, that he wouldn't have succumbed to his constant ill health and gone to the gods.

He prayed that his horse, Slydau, would remember him and accept him, but above all he prayed that Maeve would be waiting for him. His love for her had grown during their time apart and he'd thought of her daily. He missed her gay laugh, her enquiring mind and the soft touch and sweet smell of her. As he thought of her he felt familiar stirrings in his body.

His chest grew tight, his heart pounded and he quickly changed his train of thoughts to the gods and the priests left behind, back to safe ground.

Chapter 21

AD 48

Spring

As soon as they landed in Britain there was unexpected excitement. Lovernios hoped they'd be greeted by the priests they'd left behind, but instead they found the beach all but deserted, save for one very old Druid.

He was dancing in circles around a fire he'd made of drift wood, chanting loudly and preparing a 'madman's wisp'. The little wisp of straw that he held clenched in his fist looked innocuous enough, but as the priests moved up the beach towards him and heard the words he used in his chant, they knew he was preparing the most horrid spell.

Using the skills passed down through the ages from the Druid Fullon, he danced and screeched and the priests watching could feel the presence of the gods as their skin crawled and rose with goose flesh. They smelt in the fumes of the fire the terrible odour of burning flesh and hair and knew the gods were working in among the ashes of whatever it was that the old man was burning.

They watched silently as he came to the end of his chant and in a trance, walked away from them, up the beach towards the trees that surrounded this safe landing place. They followed him.

At the edge of the forest, tied to a tree, was a Roman soldier. He was a middle aged man who'd lost his way in the dark after deserting his legion, and in his travels in this unfamiliar territory, had also lost his armour and torn his uniform. Not knowing how to live off the land he was starving and disorientated from exhaustion when the old priest found him.

The Druid immediately tied him up and set about preparing his madman's wisp. He thrust the powerful object into the face of his victim, pronouncing the most horrible incantation as he did, and at once the soldier became insane, howling like a wolf one moment, cowering like a frightened rabbit the next. He hissed like a snake, pulled against his ropes and gnashed his teeth together until they chipped. He spat out the bits and sat slobbering in the dust.

The old man turned and left the soldier, neither looking at his victim or his audience, he disappeared so swiftly it was as if he'd never been there.

Lovernios and the twenty priests who'd been on the boat with him stood bemused, until Mardial spoke.

"What are we to do with him? We can't leave him here in case other soldiers come in search of him, then they'll surely find us!"

Lovernios considered this. He agreed with Mardial although some of the other priests were suggesting that wild animals would eat the victim long before any soldiers found him, and that he was best left to die where he sat.

"No," Lovernios announced, "we'll not leave him here, we'll take him with us, but first we must prepare a drink of forgetfulness to give to him."

Some of the priests nodded, others questioned him further.

"What's the purpose of taking him with us, why not just leave him here?"

"We're short handed, we have no slaves, and we need someone to help us care for our horses, gather food, go with us when we journey with our message. Who better than a tough soldier who has no memory of who he is?"

At that the rest of the priests agreed, some even laughed, but they all marvelled at Lovernios' wisdom.

Mardial took out his pouch and the ingredients needed for the preparation, while two other priests went into the forest in search of a stream. They brought back a cauldron of fresh water for Mardial who'd already begun to grind together poisonous mushrooms, bitter aloe juice, venom from an adder and three leaves each from the various herbs that he carried. Once they were sufficiently ground, he mixed the ingredients into a paste using a little of the water.

They left the soldier who was still hallucinating and ranting incoherently where he sat tied to the tree, and went back to the old priest's fire. Mardial boiled his preparation with the remainder of the water. The priests danced round the fire, calling on the gods as the smelly liquid cooked. They left it to boil for a long time, allowing the poisons from the snake and the mushrooms to weaken, until only their forgetful properties remained. Then they returned to the madman.

As soon as the drink touched the lips of the soldier his madness began to leave him and for a brief instant he remembered who he was and looked round in confusion, but the priests forced him to drink more, and as the fiery liquid burned its way down his throat, forgetfulness came on him, and he no longer knew who or where he was.

The priests left him to rest while they gathered their possessions and put out the fire on the beach. When they untied him some time later he stood up and followed them, not knowing where he was going but not questioning either.

They called him Dlui Fulla – Madman's Wisp, and from the moment they left the beach, Dlui Fulla was an asset to them. Hard working and strong, willing to do anything he was asked and always with a smile, he settled into his new life and began to understand the role he was called to. He developed a sense of humour that kept the priests amused even in their darkest hours.

They were disappointed not to find their party where they'd left them months earlier, but with the gods leading them, they continued to walk north-eastwards and two days later found the priests and the horses.

Gamenta and Lovernios hugged like long lost family, and spent the first hours together catching up on each other's news. Lovernios told Gamenta in great detail of the many meetings they'd had with the Supreme Druid, and the decision of the council to round up all Druids from across the land. Gamenta was relieved to hear of the proclamation.

While Lovernios was away the situation had continued to deteriorate and Gamenta filled him in on the details.

Emperor Claudius was having trouble on the home front, this time it was his wife Messalina who was the cause of his problems. He'd married her for political reasons in a marriage that had been arranged by Caligula. She had already borne him two children, a daughter Octavia, and a son whom he'd named Britannicus in celebration of his conquest of Britain.

She'd recently become bored with her husband. Messalina had always been a cruel and sexually depraved woman, and was becoming more so. Married at a very young age in this prearranged union, to an exceptionally ugly man thirty years her senior, did not help her promiscuous ways.

As a child Claudius had been struck with an attack of paralysis, which left him with a grotesque appearance. He had a palsied head, and slobbered continually. His hands shook and his spindly legs barely supported his huge belly, as a result he was unsteady on his feet.

Claudius was an arrogant man, but he did ignore the lax morals of his wife through many years of her scandalous conduct, perhaps realising that she was justified in some way. However, when she married the Consul Elect, Gaius Silius, in a public ceremony while still married to Claudius, he was furious and not prepared to ignore her latest affront.

Lovernios wondered what Claudius would do about the situation.

Once he'd listened to Gamenta and assured himself that the priest was looking much better, Lovernios went in search of Slydau. It did seem as if the horse remembered him. He certainly remembered the sweet apples that Lovernios brought as a treat, and he was able to mount and ride the horse before the day ended, but even so he wasn't happy when he returned to the grove where Gamenta had set up home for the novices. He'd not seen a single priestess the entire day and he longed desperately to find and speak to Maeve.

He was so lost in thought that it was only when he heard the high-pitched voices of the priestesses chatting around the fire that he looked ahead. They were there, all of them, cooking the evening meal, and when Lovernios saw Maeve his heart leaped. She was standing with her back to him and he ran to her and flung his arms around her, almost knocking her off her feet.

They hugged unashamedly then sat up the entire night talking, and Lovernios felt that he could never leave her again, yet he must. At the first sight of the new day, they clung together, knowing that this brief intimate time was over, not knowing how long their next separation would be. The only thought that cheered Lovernios was the possibility of seeing his family again.

The party of priests was ready to leave. Lovernios said goodbye to

Maeve and she stood bravely waving to him, but with tears in her eyes. Lovernios couldn't bear to look at her. Gamenta called on the gods to go with their messengers before he hugged each of them and said goodbye.

Lovernios was immensely sad to leave Gamenta again and as he and Mardial rode off, he dared not look back, afraid his courage would fail him.

There were thirty priests in the party and they were to travel in threes, a number sanctioned by the gods and likely to bring them the most protection as it was not too big a group to be seen easily, not too small to be vulnerable.

They were to go in different directions, one party travelling northeast through the land of the Brigantes, two southeast to Parisi and the eastern corner of the land of Cortiani. One party would travel southwest to the Cornovii, the Degeangli, and the Ordovices, one to the Silures and the Demetae. A group would work their way southwards to the Dobunni and the Belgae.

Two parties would make their way towards the Trinovantes and one would branch off to the Iceni. Dlui Fulla was to accompany the remaining two parties who would go the furthest south, one to the Atrebates, the southern Belgae, the Durotriges and the Dumnonii.

The last trio made up of Lovernios, Mardial and Kierona were going to the Catuvellauni, the Regni and the Canti. Kierona was the same age as Mardial and Lovernios and was placed with them shortly after Delinius was sacrificed to the gods.

They were to send any Druids they met on ahead of them to the Black Lake and once they themselves had completed their mission they were to return to the rendezvous point. It was hoped they would all return before the Festival of Lughnasa and winter.

Even though they travelled on horseback, moving by night made life difficult for the priests and the going was slow. Lovernios and Mardial were amazed at the change in the country since they'd last travelled through it. Although they stayed in forests as far as possible, many had been destroyed, and farms and agricultural holdings were sprouting up all over in places previously sacred to the priests.

They were shocked to come across Roman roads where once

the Celts had travelled on rough pathways. The roads were made like no others they'd seen before and early one morning they stopped to examine them before disappearing into the glades to rest, where Dlui Fulla explained the Roman method of construction to them.

Once they'd reached the area they were responsible for, they found their task to be an arduous and depressing one. Firstly routing out priests and priestesses from the deep forests was more difficult than they imagined. Not wishing to be found by the legions they were well hidden from their own kind too.

The priests wandered round in circles for days sometimes, after the elusive Druids. Often when they did find them they met with resistance, but for the most part the priests and priestesses were happy to move to the safety of Mona.

The strongest resistance came from the priests still attached to royal households. Some were reluctant to leave their charges, some were loathe to leave the comfort their great wealth afforded them, still others felt they were too old to travel. Many protested that the gods would protect them.

It was a slow and frustrating process as they spent days, even weeks with a priest, convincing him one moment, only to have him change his mind the next. After their first few months of travel with such a slow rate of progress, the three decided they would need to be firmer, and gave each priest far less time to comply with the Proclamation before carrying out the drastic measures called for by the Supreme Druid.

After having made this decision their progress was swift, but they found to their horror that they were forced to sacrifice one in six priests who adamantly refused to leave.

Word quickly spread of the tough measure they were taking and before long the resistance lessened. By the time they reached the land of the Canti, their last stop before they themselves could return northwards, they were sacrificing only one in twenty priests.

Lovernios prayed fervently that Obetach wouldn't be one of the stubborn ones as they approached the kingdom of his father. This thought was uppermost in his mind, more so even than the thought of seeing his family again.

Chapter 22

AD 48
Autumn

Vitaicus knew that priests were on their way with a message from the Supreme Druid but didn't know who the priests were, and so he wasn't in the courtyard to greet the weary travellers, neither was Obetach who was seeking the gods' will for his life. He knew he had to join the priests, or the gods, and he wanted to choose wisely. Knowing he would be leaving Vitaicus forever either way, he avoided the king while he awaited his fate.

Omilia was the first person to spot Lovernios and instead of greeting him she ran screeching into the castle, through the kitchens into the great hallway as the king came to see what the uproar was.

He stood in the courtyard and stared, not daring to believe his eyes. There before him, dusty and tired, but so grown, so tall and handsome, was his beloved son. He gripped Lovernios tightly in an embrace, feeling the hardened muscles beneath his flimsy cloak, amazed at his height, the same now as the king, and sensing the absolute strength of the fully grown man in front of him. Vitaicus held Lovernios at arms length to look at him properly. He was indeed good looking under the dirt of travel, and his piercing eyes held depths of wisdom and knowledge that Vitaicus could only begin to guess at. He shivered slightly as he let go of his son to greet Mardial, Kierona and to his utter amazement a man who was clearly a Roman, Dlui Fulla.

Vitaicus ordered a feast and sent the travellers to Flauston who supervised hot baths and clean robes for them. Later that evening Lovernios saw his brothers and sister for the first time in four years. Filethas, at fifteen, was beautiful and fast becoming a woman, which Lovernios noticed with dismay.

Much as he loved Maeve and constantly watched her body,

noting the changes it had undertaken over the past years, he hadn't expected the same to be taking place where his sister was concerned. He was choked with emotion when she kissed him on his cheeks and afraid to hold her body close to his, for fear he would feel as he did when holding Maeve. He was pleased when Filethas moved on to allow him to greet his brothers.

Roulst hugged Lovernios, summoning up all his thirteen-year-old strength and Lovernios smiled at the puny boy who seemed to have hardly grown at all. Lovernios looked round anxiously for Pren and was shocked to see that the tall, well-built man standing next in line was he. They embraced fondly and Lovernios motioned for Pren to stay beside him. He was delighted to see how strong Pren had grown, how his arm seemed to have healed, and the way his long curly hair was styled to cover his missing eye.

The feast continued through the night and Lovernios and Pren never grew tired of questioning each other, talking together as intimately as they'd done when they were little boys. They were delighted that their relationship hadn't suffered with the years, that they still felt the same bond and both still longed to share their remaining years with each other.

Hesitantly at first, Lovernios told Pren about Maeve. He was shy and concerned that Pren wouldn't understand, even be jealous, but Pren was intrigued and wanted to know more each time Lovernios paused for breath. The night passed swiftly with more food and drink being forced on them than the priests had seen in years, and by morning they collapsed into bed, forgetting their mission, to sleep the deepest sleep of the truly exhausted.

Obetach wasn't present at the feast, which upset Vitaicus enormously, but as the priest stood before him now, the king understood the reason.

"The gods have spoken," Obetach said. "I am still needed here on this earth. They require me to teach and lead their priests. I am to go with Lovernios to Mona. As I'm to leave you and your family, my Lord" he continued softly "and you will be left without priest or priestess, I found no reason to celebrate."

Vitaicus was devastated but knew there was nothing to be said or done. He wished the people of Britain would unite and fight against the Roman enemy and drive them from their land, only then would the priests be safe. But it was already too late.

The farewell a few days later was agonising. Lovernios had no idea when he'd see his family again and as much as the Druidical Order had become his life, he missed his father and Pren dearly. For Vitaicus there was a great sense of foreboding as he watched his son leave with Obetach. He feared he'd never see the priest again. Obetach had been the one constant in his life and now he too was gone.

Vitaicus turned back to his castle and went immediately to his room where he stayed for four days, drinking himself into a stupor, eating little and sleeping through his drunkenness until he began to sober up, then drinking further until the pain eased once more.

Pren turned to the gods for his succour. He spent hours with his bees, talking to them, and stilling his own heart, which seemed wrenched in two. Not only was he sad to say farewell to his brother once again, he was devastated to lose Obetach, who'd taught him so much that he knew almost as much as Lovernios.

As they rode further and further from the castle, Lovernios looked back repeatedly until he could no longer see any familiar sights and then he sighed deeply. He rode alongside Obetach and questioned him until the elderly man was too tired to answer.

Lovernios had been astounded by Pren's understanding of the gods, his wisdom and foresight, his knowledge of medicine, and of the stars and moon. All that he lacked was the twelve thousand verses that Lovernios could repeat by heart. Save for them, Pren was equal to Lovernios and he wished desperately that Pren could have joined them as they journeyed to Mona.

His only comfort was in knowing that Pren was the nearest thing to a priest in his father's kingdom, all matters of the gods now rested on his shoulders. Pren would need to be priest and counsellor, advisor and comfort to their father, the king.

Lovernios' arrival at the Black Lake was hardly noticed in amongst the thousands of Druids who were already assembled there, and it took some time to locate familiar faces. He was relieved to see Gamenta again. Although he looked pale and thin, he was very much alive and anxious to hear all that Lovernios had to tell to him. Gamenta was delighted to see Obetach, as he too had been concerned that the priest wouldn't be willing to leave Vitaicus.

It was only once the priests began to organise parties to begin marching to the coast that they realised how many Druids they'd missed, and how many must have slipped back into the forests on their journey northwards.

At the final count, it was estimated that there were at least a thousand priests roaming the country but without the Supreme Druid to advise them, they agreed to let them be and continued to organise the transportation of those who'd come voluntarily.

Only half the priests were able to cross before the sea became too treacherous with the onset of winter, and the remainder divided into smaller groups and hid until winter passed.

Learning continued and life returned to normal for the novices. Maeve and Lovernios spent an idyllic few months together, talking constantly of their recent time apart, looking forward to their future, and promising that they'd never again be separated.

Chapter 23

AD 49

Spring

Life returned to normal for Vitaicus too. After a few weeks of heavy drinking, he pulled himself together and summoned Flauston.

"We're going to take advantage of the situation in the land," he announced, "and we, like everyone else, are going to get rich!"

With his changing circumstances there was little left for him to do but drink, take women to his bed and increase his already vast wealth, and he did all three with gusto. There was hardly any tribal feuding as those kingdoms not under Roman rule were too busy fighting off the legions, trying desperately to survive, while those already under Roman rule were getting stronger, setting up towns, building roads and prospering.

With no priests to interpret the will of the gods, people went about life in a quiet and ordinary fashion while subtly becoming Romanised, and like Vitaicus, they took advantage of the lull to get rich.

Vitaicus travelled extensively, with Flauston as his economic sounding board and Pren as his spiritual advisor, although he seldom listened to the youngster or paid him due respect simply because he wasn't officially a priest.

Marcus visited the king on one of the rare afternoons that he was home to report that Claudius had ordered both his wife, Messalina, and Silius, the lover she'd married, to be put to death. Although Messalina had repeatedly married other men without divorcing Claudius, it was the rumour that she planned to depose him that made the Emperor act.

He immediately took for himself a new wife, his niece, the second Agrippina. She too was promiscuous, and had been married twice before her union with Emperor Claudius in what was an incestuous marriage under Roman law. Shortly after their wedding, in a show of her own strength and power, Agrippina convinced Claudius to name a new Roman colony in their honour. It was founded on the site of the fortress of the First & Twentieth Legions on the southern bank of the Rhine in a township known as Oppidum Ubiorum. At her persuasion, Claudius named it Colonia Claudia Ara Agrippinensis.

With things going so well in his new Province of Britannia, Claudius turned his attention to Ituraea, growing his Empire even further. He wouldn't be satisfied until he indeed ruled the world.

Vitaicus and Flauston spent hours discussing Rome over the excellent flagons of wine that filled his stores to overflowing. Neither of them could understand how the Romans could accuse the Celts or the Druids of barbarianism when they conducted their own affairs the way they did, murdering Emperors and their wives at a whim, incestuous relationships and marriages, changing the name of a colony at the will of a woman, all the while conquering the world so that it too could be ruled in such a barbaric fashion!

At the Black Lake the transfer of Druids to Mona was going slowly. The bad weather finally improved and boats were ready to leave once again. The Druids were being hurried to the coast. The senior priests were to leave first, and this task took a number of weeks. Assembling the elderly men and getting them into boats was difficult enough and often once they were in and settled a storm would blow up and they would be forced to disembark.

Obetach was one of the last seniors to depart from Britain, leaving the country in the hands of juniors and complete novices. Gamenta and Lovernios were at the beach to bid the priest farewell. Fully expecting to see him soon, they nevertheless spent a long time with him, calling on the gods to protect him. It was an inauspicious day and they felt ill at ease, however too much time had already been lost and none of the other priests were prepared to postpone the trip.

Gamenta and Lovernios stood at the water's edge until the boat was out of sight, after which they lit a fire and began to dance and chant around it, begging the gods to be merciful.

It was not until the following morning when the empty boat returned that they left their vigil to greet the boatman. The priests had arrived safely and all was well on the island, however the

Supreme Druid Pantra had declared it impossible to bring over all the Druids remaining in Britain as Mona could barely sustain those already there.

He further declared Britain too vulnerable to leave totally unprotected. Therefore only the youngest novices would go to Mona at this stage to continue training under the senior priests. The remainder would stay in Britain for the time being. They were instructed to spread out and go into hiding in the forests, but to remain in areas nearby the beach, around the Black Lake and in the forests north of the River Maeresea, to ensure that it would be easy to move them to the boats should urgent transfer to Mona become necessary.

Gamenta and Lovernios realised that they wouldn't be seeing Obetach as soon as they'd anticipated and were concerned that the inauspiciousness of the day that he left meant that they wouldn't see him again at all. They immediately prepared to leave for the area they'd previously occupied near the Black Lake, taking with them the same group as before.

Once again their studies resumed as they proceeded through summer and headed towards yet another uncertain winter, a winter that affected Gamenta's health severely and left him weaker than before.

The priests continued to celebrate the various festivals calling on the gods to bless them and the country in those uncertain times, but they were celebrated with a minimum of fuss, noise or fire. As the Druids were no longer among the people, their festivals too were small, subdued affairs without any spiritual connotations, performed purely out of habit.

The novices were confused and unsure of themselves as the gods no longer looked on them with favour and they longed for the wisdom of the more senior Druids, as they enjoyed the last of summer and dreaded the hardship ahead the arrival of Autumn signalled.

After the Festival of Samain, Lovernios and Maeve sat talking. This was a fire festival dedicated to the gods in times of danger and uncertainty and they fervently prayed that the gods would hear their plea even though the priests had been too afraid to light any meaningful sized fires.

It was the prayer of the Druids that the people of the country would rise up against Rome which was fast destroying them and that the gods would destroy the legions in some spectacular fashion, perhaps with fire, or a flood, anything that would stop their ever growing hold over the country. The longer the Romans remained the more the people accepted them, and as Britain became romanised, so the people forgot their gods. As the Celts stopped caring it seemed as if the gods no longer cared either. The Druids were disappointed and terrified.

At the festival, Lovernios had thrown himself at the mercy of the gods, begging them to take him as the Supreme Sacrifice so that the country could be saved, but they either didn't hear him, or didn't want him yet.

Although bitterly disappointed Lovernios and Maeve were happy that they could continue to be together for a while longer. The nineteenth anniversary of his birth had passed without event, and he'd felt sure that if the gods hadn't called for him then, they'd do so now at this festival dedicated to them.

Lovernios sighed and hugged Maeve to him. They needed to get back to the meagre fire to warm themselves and rose reluctantly. All time spent together was precious and served to strengthen their bond further and they walked hand in hand to where the others sat huddled round the small fire, warming their frozen limbs before moving off to their sleeping mats, where they'd spend yet another cold night exposed to the elements.

Lovernios looked fondly across at Gamenta and wondered how many more winters the frail priest could survive.

Chapter 24

AD 50

Spring

Gamenta did survive the winter and kept his charges studying throughout the short, cold days, despite being weak and ill most of the time. As spring approached his health improved and a twinkle returned to his eye. When Gamenta smiled the way he did now, standing before his charges, they knew something was up, something good.

"We're going to Tara," he announced. "The Supreme Druid Pantra has sent word that half of the Druids left in Britain can move across to Tara during the spring months, the remainder will stay in Britain a while longer. We've been chosen to go. We move to the coast immediately."

The news excited them all. After months of uncertainty, trying to continue as normal when life was far from normal, something was happening. They discussed Tara at length during the march, as none of them had been there before and they wondered what that magical place would really be like. The difficult journey was made easier by their excitement and they soon found themselves on the beach, waiting for boats.

The trip across the Irish Sea to Tara was dangerous, and some of their enthusiasm dwindled before they boarded the small and rickety boats that would carry them such a long and treacherous way. Each boat left to the sound of much chanting and praying and when the turn came for Gamenta's party to board, Lovernios clutched tightly to Maeve as they waded into the cold water and climbed aboard. The journey was awful and most of them experienced seasickness the entire way.

Gamenta suffered the most, and his constant bouts of vomiting brought on attacks of coughing that were uncontrollable. By the time they reached the shores of Ireland, the priest lay unconscious in the bottom of the boat, being tended to by an extremely concerned Alana.

Before they could move inland, they needed to set up a temporary camp and tend to Gamenta. They stayed on the beach for a week as the ailing priest slowly regained some strength and was able to stand on shaky legs. The younger and stronger priests made a litter to carry him, and on the eighth day they moved off the beach and headed towards Tara, the seat of Royalty in Ireland.

It was indeed a magical place, and as spring passed into summer and the island gave forth its bounty of fruit and vegetables Gamenta became stronger still. They met with Druids from Ireland and spent many days conferring together deciding the best course of action for the good of Britain and of the Druidical Order. After a number of weeks of waiting, Pantra, and his senior advisors, which now included Obetach, arrived to join in the discussions.

It was during one of these long but pleasant days of debate that Lovernios learned that his family were originally descended from the Island. His great-great grandfather had come from a royal household not very far from where they sat. He'd married a young girl who'd sailed to Tara from Britain after her family had been wiped out in a tribal feud. A few years after her marriage she'd implored her husband to leave Ireland and return with her to Britain to reclaim her rightful land.

The king had done so and they'd travelled to the south of Britain, to the land of Canti. He'd taken with him his entire household and left his kingdom to his only son. Using some of his enormous wealth he'd traded with the tribe who'd taken over the land and they'd gladly taken his gold and precious stones and left. The land that was once owned by his wife's father now belonged to him.

As Lovernios listened to the Druid sitting opposite him, he looked around at the Druids from Ireland and could see that he resembled them. He did indeed seem to share the same blood as these friendly priests with their soft lilting voices.

Maeve too looked at the priests and then back at Lovernios. He was a good looking young man, most striking with his large head and deep-set eyes that were so similar to the older men. He had a bulging brow and Maeve thought fondly that this was where he stored his great knowledge. The colour of his hair had deepened as he'd grown older and was a dark red.

His full beard shone in the sunlight and a few lighter strands gleamed like gold in amongst the amber. Not as tall as some of the British Druids he was only five and a half foot, but he was a robust and healthy man, well built and muscular. As he smiled at Maeve her heart melted. He was without a doubt the most appealing male she'd ever laid her eyes on.

News of what was taking place in Britain filtered through to Tara, and by mid summer the senior Druids knew they had to make a decision. It seemed vital to have priests in Britain calling on the gods to stop the onslaught against the Druids, despite the obvious peril. Tara would always be open to them should they need to escape, and Mona would continue to be the safe haven of the elderly and more senior priests of Britain.

In the case of the younger priests and novices, it was agreed that the best place for them to continue their training was in their own country, hidden as they'd been previously in the north, where they could flee quickly if necessary.

As they were about to leave Tara, the priests who'd told Lovernios of his ancestors approached him with a gift. A craftsman had fashioned a statue of Lovernios, which the priests presented to him as a keepsake, a memory of his trip to Tara and a reminder of his roots, his Irish blood. A proud people, they wanted Lovernios to know that a part of him belonged to this island.

It was a wonderful work of art, painstakingly crafted out of grey marble. Lovernios was delighted with the large and heavy gift, but shocked at the sight of the actual face. It didn't resemble him in the least but he took the statue graciously and he and Maeve left the island laughing happily, their earlier mixed feelings dispelled. They looked forward to returning home with the eagerness and excitement of youth.

After her small victory in having Claudius rename a colony after her, Agrippina became more brazen still and convinced her husband to adopt her son from her first marriage. He was L Domitius Ahenobarbus, and his adoption ensured that Claudius gave him priority over his own son Britannicus. Ahenobarbus' name was changed to Nero and Claudius began to train him for succession, ignoring Britannicus.

On hearing this news Lovernios wondered how he would have felt had his father treated him in the same manner, and he knew in his heart he wouldn't have stood for it.

He waited with interest to hear what the reaction of Britannicus would be.

Chapter 25

AD 51
Spring

The new year brought about astonishing events in Britain, and as Gamenta and the novices continued to travel round the northern districts, visiting with the Druids they found in hiding, rumours continued to reach them of the various developments taking place.

Camulodunum was expanding rapidly and was given the status of Colonia, becoming the first city in Britain to obtain this status. It was the centre of administration of the Romans and also the centre for official "Caesar-worship".

Londinium was already larger in size and was rapidly becoming a great and busy port. It was being built with the view to it becoming the seat of the Imperial Procurator.

In southern Wales Caratacus was gaining fresh support, and enticed the warriors of the kingdom of the Silures to join him. They marched northwards to meet the Ordovices. Caratacus was counting on the Brigantes joining forces with him as they marched towards the Romans, but before he met up with them he was decisively beaten in a surprise attack in the mountains of the Snowdon Massif. He fled further northward, this time into Brigantia, but Cartimandua, Queen of the Brigantes, was in league with Rome, and finding himself trapped Caratacus voluntarily gave himself up to her to save his warriors from further slaughter.

The queen wasted no time in handing the fugitive over to his enemy and he was taken back to Italy in chains. At a celebrated interview with Claudius, Caratacus so impressed the Emperor with his defiant courage that he was spared his life, however he spent two dreadful years in a cage before being dragged through the streets of Rome, after which he was publicly strangled, a bitter and tragic end to one of the bravest fighters in the British cause against Rome.

Shortly after her victory over Caratacus, Cartimandua divorced her husband Venutius, who commanded wide territories to the north, and was anti-roman. Her only hope of survival as queen lay in Roman protection. With this in mind she married her husband's standard-bearer, Vellocatus.

It was a strange situation as Venutius was formerly loyal to Rome like Cartimandua herself, but she discovered that he'd become disenchanted with the Empire and was leading a resistance movement.

As they hid in the northern territories, Gamenta fretted over their proximity to the Brigantes and Queen Cartimandua and the druids felt more insecure than ever.

Vitaicus and Flauston had been shut away together for many hours in the king's workroom. The heat of summer was stifling but they were oblivious to it. A new shipment of wine had recently arrived at the country's fastest growing commercial town, Londinium, but as it had been built by and was ruled by the Romans, it had garrisons guarding it. Vitaicus wanted the wine badly. It was the finest Italy had yet produced according to his sources, but the price would be high.

He and Flauston and been through the storehouses and taken stock. They'd examined the king's hunting dogs and set aside the best of them, now they haggled over what else to offer the wine merchant.

Vitaicus was in favour of bringing the man to the castle to allow him to choose for himself rather than risk the possibility of losing the shipment to another trader. Flauston felt it wise to take with them whatever they decided to trade so the merchant could see and take immediately what they offered. They argued and haggled for many days until Flauston bowed to the king. He could see that nothing would change his stubborn mind and so they called Pren to make ready for the trip.

Carrying little, they were able to leave early in the morning of the following day, and riding rested horses they made excellent progress. Once they'd passed through Vitaicus' land the roadways were vastly improved as Roman influence abounded everywhere. The few major thoroughfares in the land of Canti were paved with wood, such as the one leading up to the castle, but many of these were old, rotten and rickety. Other roadways were cobbled with rough stones, but most were just dirt tracks, hardened by frequent travel.

Once outside his kingdom they came across new Roman highways. Some were still stone cobbled or hardened earthen paths, but they'd been widened by the legions for quick and easy passage. Others were well constructed roads with bridges and proper crossings for the many rivers and course-ways. Before the Romans came, one would either go around a river, often a long way, or find the shallowest and narrowest point to dismount and cross. In rainy periods, one could often not cross a river for days, and be forced to camp and wait until the water subsided. Now the Roman-made crossings enabled travellers to pass over at any time of year.

Vitaicus wouldn't admit that he was impressed but deftly changed the subject each time the roads were mentioned. He'd just managed to skirt around the topic once again when Pren brought his horse to a standstill and held up his hand for silence. Vitaicus and Flauston reined in beside him. They'd heard nothing but strained their eyes to see what had stopped Pren.

He whispered to them, "I feel an evil presence, we must hide and wait."

Impatient to get to Londinium, Vitaicus began to argue, but even Flauston found the courage to overrule the king.

"My Lord," he said, "you know that Pren is wise in the way of the gods. You know that he's the only priest we have. We must listen to him."

The king sighed and dismounted and they led their horses to a tree where they let them feed while he and Flauston rested. Pren crept out of hiding and stealthily made his way through some bushes heading in the direction he felt the trouble to be. He returned after a long while, just as Vitaicus grew impatient. He was about to leave when he spotted Pren who was filthy. It was obvious he'd been crawling along the ground like a snake.

"What is it?" Vitaicus demanded loudly. "Roman soldiers," Pren whispered, "twenty of them, guarding a river crossing up ahead. It's the only way to get across anywhere near here. We need to back track and try and cross further west, at the border of the Regni."

"Never!" shouted Vitaicus "That will take us days, we must cross here and get on our way."

"My Lord," said Pren reasonably, "keep your voice down, please. If they should hear us, they'll come looking for us. If they find us we'll need to explain what we're doing here. We are vulnerable being just three. There have been many instances of soldiers attacking small parties, and besides, with you being a king they may force you into a treaty, or follow you back to your castle and overrun it. We need to think."

Vitaicus looked away ashamed. This young man was displaying maturity and wisdom beyond his years while Vitaicus was behaving like a spoilt child. His acquisition of good wine had been his only thought. They sat in silence for a while before Flauston spoke.

"What of further east, I'm sure there's a safe crossing a little further beyond that hill there. If we skirt round at this point here, perhaps we'll be able to cross."

As Flauston pointed out his intentions, Pren nodded thoughtfully.

"I'll go and see. You wait here, but it'll take me the rest of the afternoon to get there and back."

He said this while looking directly at the king, warning him with his tone not to come looking for Pren before the day was done. Vitaicus assured him that they'd wait, and settled down to sleep in the warm sun.

He lay for some time thinking of his need for the wine, which led him to thinking of the tragedies that had befallen his family and given him such a hunger for the glorious liquid that took away his pain. He thought of his loss of Obetach and even Gamenta, all due to the Romans, and began to blame them for every ill that had ever occurred.

All his life he'd been haunted by the Roman threat and now they even prevented him from getting his wine. His anger boiled as he thought of Hilfuth and Trasand, his wives that he loved so dearly. He thought of his dead children and his son Lovernios, almost a priest, but being hunted by the Romans. If only Obetach were here to advise him, but he too was hunted!

Finally he couldn't bear it and he jumped up and shouted, "We are going to kill them, we are going to kill the Romans."

Grabbing Flauston he dragged the sleepy man to his feet and pulled at the reins of his horse. Realising what the king was planning Flauston tried desperately to stop him, but Vitaicus was not only in a rage, it was almost as if he were in a trance.

Madness had come over him that Flauston couldn't reach through, no matter how he pleaded. He resorted finally to pushing and pulling at his king, but to no avail. Eventually as Vitaicus made to mount his horse, Flauston shut his eyes and slapped the king full in his face.

There was silence, and then Vitaicus asked as if nothing had happened, "do you ride with me, or do I go to kill them alone?"

Knowing that the battle was lost, Flauston mounted his horse and followed the king.

In the true style of a great warrior, victor in many a battle, the king rode in amongst the soldiers screaming, thrashing his sword in a frenzy, striking at each one as he caught them unawares, while Flauston who was never a warrior did his best to match the king's fury.

Flauston managed to mortally wound one man with the lunging of his sword to the jugular, but he took too long to retrieve his weapon and two soldiers came up beside him and pulled him from his horse, thrusting their own swords deep into his heart and stomach.

He died without seeing his king valiantly fighting on, killing four soldiers before the others, bleeding from their wounds, cut the legs from his faithful horse Iorrach who crumpled forward hurling Vitaicus over its head.

Vitaicus landed heavily and was winded, and before he could get to his feet the soldiers fell on him and in their own fury at the surprise attack, an attack that had caused much injury and death, they set on him like wolves on a kill and all but tore him apart. They left him to die in the afternoon sun in a pool of his own blood mingled with that of his servant.

Pren found Vitaicus' mutilated body later that evening. Once the Romans had treated their wounded and buried their dead they tied the king and his servant to Flauston's horse and chased the frightened animal away. Exhausted from dragging the dead weights he didn't get far before he was forced to stop and blow, and then sensing that the danger was passed, he began to graze.

When Pren returned just as the sun was setting with the good news that there was a safe place to cross the river just a few miles upstream, he found the king gone. He felt a great sense of foreboding, but nothing prepared him for the sight of the horse quietly grazing with its gruesome burden tied behind it. Pren knelt beside his father and wept and it was only when he felt the rising sun of the new day warming his back twelve hours later that he rose. He spent most of the morning covering the bodies with rocks to protect them from predators before he rode for home and help.

Three days later, after a fitting funeral had taken place for the king and his faithful servant Flauston, Pren disbanded the royal household. Taking a few servants with him, he went straight from the funeral pyre to the king's vast storehouses and set them alight. He chose to burn Vitaicus' wealth rather than leave it to fall into the hands of the Romans.

The fire was larger than any funeral pyre and the black cloud of smoke and the stench of burning hides and corn hung over the kingdom for days. Gold and silver, precious stones, goblets and cauldrons of great beauty crafted with enamel and precious stones, even weapons of war, burnt together.

Next Pren went to the stables and torched them, after opening the doors and spooking the horses. They fled, many of them not stopping for hours until they were well clear of Vitaicus' land, free to be claimed by whoever found them, but at least it would be the people of Vitaicus' kingdom and not the legions.

After torching the stables Pren went to the sheds where the hunting dogs were kept. They were magnificent animals, highly bred and well trained, the finest in Britain, it was often said.

Pren sat dispiritedly and watched the beautiful dogs. He had no idea what to do with them. If he let them loose they wouldn't run like the horses, but would hunt and kill the chickens and rabbits and other small animals that the king's people kept. Part of their livelihood would be endangered, yet Pren hadn't the heart to kill them.

He sat for a long time, while images of the mutilated bodies of Flauston and his father filled his mind and then he did what he knew he had to. He ordered the servants to torch the sheds with the dogs locked up inside.

Vitaicus' remaining kin, his sisters and their families, were allowed to remain on the king's property. However they'd need to farm to survive the same as the rest of his people as the kingdom of Vitaicus no longer existed. There was nothing here for the Romans to lay hold of. No one to make treaties with, no wealth for them to claim tributes.

When they arrived they'd find a subsistence farming community, nothing more. There'd be no triumph for the Romans at the expense of Vitaicus and that thought alone kept Pren going with his awful task. The servants and slaves were given their freedom and told to take what they could carry from the castle and the gardens and set up their own homes. The livestock was divided up among them according to length of service to the king.

Omilia and Sebilus were allowed to take what they wanted from the queen's personal chamber, but no one was allowed to enter the king's chambers or trophy room.

Roulst was sent to Vitaicus' eldest sister and was adopted into the family.

Within a week the castle was stripped bare. Only the king's private rooms remained intact, painful reminders of the once great man and his magnificent trophies won in many a victorious battle. Pren wandered through the rooms, filling himself with the sense and smell of his adopted father, the once mighty King Vitaicus.

He took a long time to choose a few items to take with him. A cloak each for himself and Lovernios, ones that the king had loved and worn at times of feasting and celebration. He selected two elegantly crafted wooden goblets, one of prancing horses with the customary mystical twirls of tendrils and spirals interlinked, so that the horses appeared to be in a forest where leaves and mist swirled about them. The other slightly smaller goblet depicted a fox and eagle and again the craftsman had linked the two together so that one could not easily tell if the fox were catching the eagle or the eagle hunting the fox.

They were both magnificent works of art, and although the king had used them to hold his wine, Pren hoped they could be used for water, perhaps even holy water, and knew in his heart that Vitaicus would have approved.

With a final glance at the heads of the vanquished, men like Fer Niall, Pren shuddered and left the castle. The servants were waiting to say farewell and carried out their last duty to their king with sadness. They set the castle alight with a hundred torches and then left together, walking through the courtyard, past the central pool around which so many wonderful ceremonies had taken place.

They passed familiar trees and remembered happy days when they'd worked outside in the sun, sitting under these very trees preparing food for feasts. They went through the gateway and down the wooden pathway that led into the kingdom. On the right were the royal gardens, now an empty plot of recently dug earth. On the left the orchids where they'd picked fruit daily, but the trees were bare, the ground poisoned so that they'd wither and die before ever yielding again.

They walked past the forest where they picked wild strawberries and mushrooms, the place where Trasand had been kidnapped so many years before. The hamlet where the servants and slaves lived was over on the left beyond the orchards, and they saw smoke hovering above their burning homes as the wind shifted.

Each person had torched his house so that nothing remained of their past lives. On and on they went, a sad group of homeless people, singing a lament, crying out to the gods who had indeed deserted them and their beloved king – a king no more on this earth, but one they would surely be with again in the Otherworld. They all wished to serve him again in the other life, for he was a great and mighty man and one they loved.

The lament continued throughout that day and the next as the people wandered the land looking for somewhere to start a new life. Only Pren and Filethas knew where they were going.

Filethas was being taken to join the Priestesses of Gallizena who lived on the tiny island of Sena, off the coast of the southwestern tip of Brittany. Until recently just nine priestesses lived on the island, women who possessed great powers of prophecy and healing. Their time was spent ministering to sailors who stopped at the island, curing them of illness and telling their futures.

Because of the frequent visits of sailors, the priestesses were sworn to perpetual virginity and if it seemed that a sailor were about to take a priestess to his bed, the other eight would raise up mighty a storm so that the remainder of the sailors would gather up the offender and leave the island immediately, for fear of their boats being wrecked.

Pren learned that the Priestesses of Gallizena had been taking other young priestesses onto the island since the Roman invasions, and that they were hiding and protecting them there while they continued their training. He prayed to all the gods that they would take Filethas too.

Chapter 26

AD 52
Winter

It was almost a year after Vitaicus died before Pren and Xavista managed to reach Lovernios. A few days after leaving the castle, all the king's servants and slaves found somewhere to set up home, and as Pren said farewell to the last of them, he realised that Xavista was still with him. He invited the old man to accompany him on his journey, wherever it may take them, and without hesitation Xavista agreed.

It took many weeks for them to get Filethas to the coast in the land of the Dumonii, and then find someone willing to take them across the sea to the island of Sena. Enormous superstition and fear surrounded the island and its priestesses, and only hardened sailors were willing to go there.

Pren waited for two months before he heard of a boat heading that way. The captain had room and was willing to take them. He loved stopping at Sena. It was his greatest ambition to sleep with each of the nine priestesses and he spent many pleasant hours planning how he'd do this, but in the years he'd travelled to Sena he'd not yet managed to get them so separated that they were unable to call up a storm.

Each time he thought he was close to accomplishing the huge feat of getting just one priestess alone with him, having the others distracted by his sailors, something had gone wrong and the inevitable storm began to blow. He never grew tired of trying though, and eagerly took the strange trio on his latest mission.

As he considered Pren with his scarred face, Xavista the ancient Greek, and Filethas an eighteen-year old beauty, a goddess herself, the captain happily contemplated his forthcoming attempt.

He had no more success on this trip than any other and was forced to leave the island the very day they arrived, leaving his passengers behind in the midst of a mighty storm. The priestesses welcomed Filethas warmly.

Although not a priestess herself she was an intelligent young girl and a virgin, which stood in her favour. With the increasing number of youngsters joining them on the island they were in desperate need of help. They needed someone to look after the very small girls until they reached the age of eight, when the priestesses would take over tutoring them.

Filethas gratefully accepted this new role and by the time a visiting ship with room for Pren and Xavista was ready to sail, she had already won over the hearts of the little girls in her care as well as the Priestesses of Gallizena.

Filethas stood on the beach and waved happily to her brother as he boarded, leaving Pren with mixed feelings. He'd always loved Filethas but had taken her presence for granted, now suddenly he faced his future without her radiance, and he felt immensely sad.

The familiar people in his life were dwindling rapidly and if he was unable to find Lovernios, he'd be left with only the strange old man standing beside him, his tutor and friend, the ancient Greek Xavista.

With so many Druids living in the north, it was becoming difficult to find forests and groves that could hide and support them, and food became scarce. During one of his visits to Britain, Obetach realised that they had no choice but to spread out and move southwards once again. For those living on the island of Mona their constant concern was the safety and well being of the priests in Britain, which prompted Obetach to make frequent trips across the sea to visit and encourage them.

Gamenta and Lovernios were delighted to see Obetach and spent time with him while he rested before returning to Mona. As soon as he left, they prepared to move to Vernemeton, a familiar place to the group that Gamenta was still teaching, and so it was with great excitement but also some trepidation that they left the Black Lake. A new home with a fresh source of food would be most welcome.

The past few months of scrounging for each meal had become tiresome and the priests could feel themselves losing strength. Gamenta was looking thinner than ever, as he always made sure that Alana had sufficient before eating himself. However, even the thought of food couldn't dispel their fear of being closer to the Romans and the constant threat to their lives.

As had become the custom they travelled by night and the march was a slow one. The moon was seldom seen through the heavy clouds and the stars were not visible to guide them. It took them twice as long to reach the safety of the deeply forested area than they'd anticipated. To get to Vernemeton from the south, the Roman Legions would follow the straight line of their new Fosse Way due northeast through the city of Ratae.

Fourteen miles beyond Ratae the Fosse Way changed direction slightly as it went over a hill. Vernemeton lay on the western slope of the hill. The Druids moving from the north approached Vernemeton from the opposite direction, but nevertheless took care to stay well clear of the busy Roman highway.

If they'd been travelling by day they would have arrived at Vernemeton sooner and would not have missed Pren, who'd travelled up the Fosse Way and stopped at Vernemeton first in search of his brother. It was many weeks later, after Pren and Xavista met some priests north of the Maeresea, the river meaning 'Boundary', in the land of the Brigantes that they learned that Lovernios had moved south to Vernemeton.

A month after they'd settled in their new home the priests became aware of someone searching the forests, looking for them. Gamenta was quite sure it was other priests when he first saw signs of them, as the Romans generally marched in, in full force without attempting to hide their presence, wiping out everyone they found. The trail Gamenta had seen was of one or two people moving slowly and carefully, systematically searching the area.

After a few days of watching the signs, Lovernios recognised a piece of cloth carefully pinned to a thorn tree, where it would be found.

"Pren! It is Pren!" he cried out, "I know that cloth, it was woven by our mother."

He jumped and shouted for joy, yelling at the top of his voice, careless of rousing any soldiers but wanting Pren to hear. It was only a short while before Pren appeared, as stealthily as a lion, and scared Lovernios from behind.

The reunion was an emotional one. It had been many years since they'd last seen each other and they marvelled at how they'd both become men. For Pren the resemblance between Lovernios and Vitaicus was startling.

For Lovernios the memory of Trasand's beautiful face came to the fore as he looked at his stepbrother. Despite his scarred face and missing eye, he was a good-looking man. He'd grown well and although still smaller and less muscular than Lovernios he was no longer the skinny and slight figure that Lovernios remembered.

Pren waited until they'd moved back into the glade where the rest of the priests and priestesses were before he introduced Xavista. All work and learning stopped and Gamenta welcomed them both warmly. A fire was lit and freshly caught fish cooked for the guests. A few priestesses went off in search of mushrooms and roots to add to the pot.

The priests sat round and listened intently as Gamenta and Lovernios questioned the Greek. They'd never been in the company of so learned a man who was not himself a priest, and they were fascinated by his ability to write.

When Pren shyly added that he too could read and write and could speak Greek and Latin, Lovernios was stunned. They spent the next few hours talking, eating and enjoying each other with the rest of the group, before Lovernios and Pren moved off together to discuss more personal issues.

Realising that Pren's presence here with his tutor was not a good omen, Lovernios was reluctant to ask about home but waited for Pren to tell him. They ventured far from the others before Pren motioned for Lovernios to sit.

He started hesitantly at first, but once the first awful words were out, "father is dead!" the rest of the dreadful story flowed like the sea at spring tide. Lovernios listened without question, until fully spent, Pren fell back against the tree stump where they were sitting, no detail left untold.

"You did well, my brother." Lovernios finally said. "You did all that I would have done, and I thank you."

Pren looked at Lovernios and saw the earnestness with which he spoke and he knew that Lovernios meant what he said. They embraced and after a while Lovernios allowed himself to weep.

Although a man now, and a priest, he was a Celt at heart, an emotional race of people, and he held nothing back. All the hurts and heartaches of the years, the hardships of being away from his family, the regret of not being with them as they dwindled and died, all these emotions assailed him and he yelled out at the gods that had surely abandoned him and his family, and deserted his father in his greatest hour of need.

He yelled so loudly and mourned so bitterly that his laments were heard at the fireside where the Druids waited, praying softly as they understood some awful thing had been told to Lovernios.

Eventually Gamenta and Maeve went and comforted him, and brought him back to the warmth of the fire where they gave him a draught to drink, and mercifully he slept.

The following day when he woke, Pren was there keeping vigil beside him. As soon as he saw that Lovernios was awake, Pren presented him with one of the wooden cauldrons, the one with the fox and the eagle, and he showed Lovernios the cloak that he'd covered him with the night before as he lay sleeping. The gifts immediately cheered Lovernios, especially when he saw that Pren kept for himself a cloak and cauldron.

Gamenta allowed Lovernios to spend the next few days with Pren excusing him from lessons and the two walked through the forest talking and catching up on the years.

Xavista took the time to recover from the hard months of non-stop journeying and seldom left the fireside. The priestesses spoiled him. They fed him and washed and groomed him. They rubbed his feet and neck and sang to him and he felt that he'd left this earth and gone to heaven, a place the priestesses didn't believe in, but one he knew to be very real during those days.

Gamenta pondered the new situation and knowing in his heart what must be done, he woke Lovernios before daylight. "We must go at once to Obetach," he announced, "we've only just had a visitation from the senior Druids, they'll not come again for weeks. We can't wait for them, and I think it would be best to tell Obetach in person of this latest tragedy and get his guidance on the question of Pren."

Lovernios was delighted with the news until he heard that Maeve wouldn't be going. They'd sworn never to be separated again and Lovernios felt it an ill omen to break that vow, but Gamenta was adamant.

"Alana will stay here and tutor in my place, and Maeve will assist her. We may be gone a long while and the remainder of the novices mustn't be made to suffer. There's much still to be learnt before your next degree, they must continue with their studies. I'll teach you what I can on the way, and we'll take with us only enough priests that we'll be safe to travel."

"Please may Pren come?" Lovernios asked hopefully. After some consideration Gamenta agreed.

"Yes, he, Mardial and Kierona can accompany us and we'll take a small party of Bards and Vates. We leave at once."

Chapter 27

AD 53
Winter

Lovernios stopped to rest Slydau and dismounted to gaze at the glorious scenery. He'd been trotting ahead of the rest of the Druids who'd fallen quite far behind. He was on the very edge of the mountain, winding up a narrow pathway that had been made by travellers over the centuries.

Lovernios craned his head and looked up at the distance they still had to travel, then moving closer to the edge of the path, he looked into the valley to see how far they'd already come. The rest of the party had almost reached him and he decided they were about halfway up the pass, but the steepest part had already been climbed.

He sat on his haunches and waited. The sights and sounds of birds and other little creatures were music to his ears. He sighed with pleasure and then astonishment as he thought he heard his sigh echoed back. He listened attentively and realised that what he'd heard was actually a whimper. Standing up again he peered down the steep mountainside. He could see nothing unusual but heard the whimper again, rising faintly from below.

He moved a little way along the path and then he saw her. More than halfway down the cliff lying on a natural shelf but tangled in a thorn bush, was the inert form of a young girl. He stood dumbfounded, not sure what to do next, when with relief he heard his fellow priests approaching. He called and they hurried to where he stood.

After he'd pointed out the girl a lengthy debate ensued with the consensus being to leave her be. Probably already close to death, and possibly pushed over the mountainside by hungry gods wanting her to join them in the Otherworld, the Druids felt she should be left well alone, besides which, apart from interfering in affairs in which they had no business they would delay their own progress and were reluctant to do so.

The journey had already been quite long enough and the party was weary and ready to reach their destination, and it would be extremely difficult to reach her, they argued.

Lovernios countered each argument until eventually he said he'd rescue her on his own and risk the wrath of the gods. He told the priests to go on without him.

Seeing his determination Gamenta relented and with this the rest of the party had no choice but to remain too. Reluctantly they retraced their steps down the mountainside, leaving their horses and supplies in the care of the Bards. Gamenta pointed out a clearing in the valley, a rendezvous point with Lovernios who'd attempt to get the girl's body free and carry her there.

Lovernios began his descent quickly but his first few steps sent loose stones and rocks skipping down towards the ledge where the girl lay. Realising that he was in danger of hurting her further he angled his descent away from her. He slipped and fell a number of times, catching onto long grasses and shrubs, cutting his hands and ripping his clothing. Pulling at his cloak impatiently, he ripped it further as he made his way slowly down the treacherous mountainside, until he felt he must be level with the shelf.

He stopped to catch his breath and brush himself down. His hands stung as blood oozed out of his palms and his knees were scraped. He realised that by aiming his descent slightly to the left of the girl, he'd ended up a lot further away than he'd expected and had to work his way back along the steep incline, taking care not to slip even lower.

This new effort left him a few feet short of the ledge and he had to hoist himself up and across to reach it. The muscles in his legs ached and his head throbbed from the tension and exertion and he thought briefly that the Druids had been right, maybe he should have just left her. Gathering up his last reserves he pulled himself up and lay panting next to the still body, gasping for breath in the icy winter air.

A low moan brought him back to the present and he got to his knees, careful to keep away from the edge of the narrow shelf, below which was a sheer drop. He couldn't believe that having clambered down so far, it was still such a long way to the valley below. It made him feel giddy to look down so he turned and tended to the girl instead.

He felt her forehead, which was hot to the touch. 'Good,' he thought, 'she hasn't been here long enough to freeze.'

He leaned over her with his ear close to her mouth. Her breath was shallow but constant. Moving his hand over her left breast he was relieved when he felt the slow but steady thump, thump, thump and he smiled to himself. She was obviously strong and healthy.

He began a cursory examination of her injuries all the while gently disentangling her from the thorn bush, which had left her white skin ripped and scratched in numerous places. Her arms seemed intact, he felt her left leg and again detected no serious injury, but just the slight pressure of his hand on her right shin caused the unconscious girl to whimper again.

He lifted her robe and was aghast at the sight. Her leg was badly broken, the bone not only bent at an extreme angle, it jutted through the skin just below her knee. His stomach pulled into a tight knot and his hands began to shake as he continued his examination.

As he lifted her head slightly off the rock his hand came away covered in blood. There was a large laceration at the back of her head and her hair was matted into the bloody dent.

Shouts from below seemed to come from miles away and it took a while for him to realise that it was his companions calling to him.

"She's alive," he called back, "but badly injured. You'll need to prepare a litter to carry her if we hope to get her anywhere."

The Druids shook their heads impatiently. Why not just leave her there, it was getting late and would soon be dark. Another long discussion ensued with some of the priests wishing to go on and leave them both to their fate, while the others felt they should stay together and assist Lovernios. Much to Pren's relief, they again agreed to help.

Lovernios knew he had to stop the bleeding from the girl's head. Taking his already ripped cloak in his hands, he tore the cleanest part into a long strip and wrapped it tightly around the wound. Standing on tiptoe he managed to reach two branches of a young birch and cleaned them of leaves and small side branches, not wanting to waste too much time, but knowing that the pressure of any sharp point against the girl's already painful leg would be agony even in her unconscious state. Satisfied that he had the smoothest possible splints he ripped at his cloak once again, tearing strips of cloth to keep the branches in place.

Now he faced the worst task, he had to straighten her leg and somehow push the bone back in and away from the surface of her skin before he could use his crude splints. Taking a deep breath he took hold of it firmly in both hands and pulled. She screamed. He pulled again and she continued to scream until she slumped into an even deeper state of unconsciousness.

Lovernios was sweating and fought back tears but eventually he was satisfied that he had the bone properly positioned. Gingerly he ripped at the girl's robe, tearing off a sizable piece, leaving her long legs exposed. He balled the cloth into a wad and placed it over the torn skin before carefully placing his splints in position, and tied them in place. Deeply unconscious the girl moaned softly at this new pain. At last he was satisfied and stood up and looked around.

The only way down was to the right for a few hundred feet and then he could begin the descent. He lifted his patient and positioned her leg so that he could see where he was going without overbalancing, while causing her the least possible discomfort, before he began the long, slow trip to the valley. His arms ached, his back was breaking and the splints were digging into his thighs. He was light headed and dizzy and sure he'd never cope, but he was committed, he had no choice but to keep going.

This time the loose rocks fell freely, bounding down the hillside, sending small creatures scuttling and causing birds to fly up squawking in indignation. Eventually he could go no further and he lowered his charge to the ground. He flopped down next to her panting, unable to get his breath, charged with emotion and exhaustion.

The cold air made the task worse, and his chest burned. He cupped his hands over his mouth and warmed the air, breathing in and out slowly, until he felt in control again. He was close to the bottom of the hill and could hear the priests somewhere below. He called and the comforting voice of Mardial answered. He felt a new surge of energy at the sound and picked the girl up once more.

The pain of the jarring had kept her deeply unconscious but now she began to surface and when he bent to lift her, her eyes fluttered open momentarily. They were piercingly green, he noticed, startling against her dark red hair and pale freckled complexion. As they closed again she murmured something he couldn't hear and as he lifted her she cried out, although she no longer had the energy to scream.

Once at the floor of the valley eager hands took the girl from Lovernios, who was close to collapsing himself.

The Druids had already found a small spring of water and they stripped the makeshift bandaging from her head and legs and bathed her injuries in the cold healing waters, chanting to the gods as they did so.

Gamenta took sphagnum moss from his leather pouch, and placed it over the wound at the back of her head. It was bleeding again but at least it was clean blood, and the sphagnum would staunch it.

Following the initiative of Lovernios, Mardial tore his robe in strips, and tied the sphagnum tightly around her head. As Gamenta began to work on her broken leg, Lovernios sat crossed legged and cupped the unconscious girl's head in his lap and gently mopped her forehead, which was hotter now than ever.

Ducildan felt herself floating steadily down a long tunnel. At times she had the sensation of great speed and then she felt as though she was hardly moving at all. She tried to reach out and touch the sides of the tunnel, but her arms wouldn't move. She wondered briefly how she was travelling and thought she must be flying, but she was aware of liquid, perhaps water, all round her, although it felt thick and sticky like blood.

She thought she might be swimming but knew her legs weren't moving, so perhaps she was just being carried by some tide, but it was all irrelevant. Suddenly the tunnel grew dark and she was afraid. She must have caught her leg against something in the dark, for the pain in it was excruciating. She heard herself scream and the tunnel lightened immediately.

As soon as she stopped screaming it became dark again, but she didn't have control over her voice. Slowly she became aware that she was on her way to the Otherworld, to peace and happiness and eternal life. She knew she should be happy already but decided she didn't want to go there yet. She wanted to see her mother and her sister, to at least say goodbye and implore them to come with her on her journey. She whimpered but she wasn't sure if it was out of sadness or pain. The light cleared again and she could see further down the tunnel. There was a cave ahead and she knew that in the cave would be a lake, the final entrance to the Otherworld.

Suddenly she felt the tunnel become steeper, she was moving downhill rapidly, and she could hear strange sounds, like that of thunder rolling. She felt the sensation of slipping and sliding but was too tired and in too much pain to work it all out. She allowed herself to be taken along with the flow, and with that the tunnel became very dark indeed. Time seemed suspended and she was aware that the pain had dimmed and all motion stopped, but she knew she hadn't reached the cave. It felt good to be suspended in this place, although she was curious about where she was and forced her eyes to open.

Through thin slits she looked briefly into the face of a god and wondered which one he was. She tried to ask him but her voice wasn't obeying her. She heard herself make a strange sound that made no sense at all. And then the pain wracked her body again and her voice screamed out loud of its own accord and everything went dark once more.

She became aware of intense heat and felt that her body was on fire. She was certain she'd reached the cave and lay next to a fire that was burning brightly in the corner. Strange, it wasn't an inviting fire and the heat of it didn't warm her, it seemed rather to consume her. She heard herself whimpering and wished she could move away.

She knew her journey was almost over, the lake lay just beyond the fire, and the gods awaited her there. She hoped that the god she'd seen earlier would be there too. She tried to open her eyes again but they wouldn't obey. She lay perfectly still, no longer feeling suspended, not sensing motion, considering what would happen next.

Cold water touched her burning forehead, her arms and legs, and she was sure she must have passed through the fire and entered the lake. She felt herself being moved again and was aware of hands pulling at her. Then she heard voices, pleasant voices, singing and chanting and she knew they were hovering over her. The voices were responsible for the cold water, they were pulling at her, binding her.

She could feel pressure at first on her head, then her leg. They were making her feel better – were they the gods? Was she there yet, was she supposed to feel happy? As her body cooled down she realised she was no longer near the fire, perhaps no longer in the cave as she was getting cold, but she was sure she hadn't been through the lake yet.

Slowly a thought began to form, maybe she wasn't dead, perhaps she'd cheated the gods and not made it to the Otherworld after all. Maybe these voices had saved her. Saved her? A strange thought as she wasn't afraid of dying, but then she remembered that she'd wanted to see her mother and sister again. Could they be taking her to say goodbye before she made the journey? Was it possible that she had a little more time in this life? The thought made her smile.

They carried her on a litter through the valley, following a path that led to a nearby settlement. The sun was close to setting as they approached the hamlet and Lovernios listened to a wolf howling in the distance as they plodded wearily on. His body no longer ached, it was numbed through from exhaustion and cold. Only the slight smile on the face of the girl lying on the litter below him kept him going, one ordered step in front of the other.

A young boy came running out of the first mud hut they approached, eager to greet his visitors, so seldom were strangers seen in their valley. He ran up to the Druids, lowered his eyes in respect and greeted them quickly, before turning his attention to the litter. He gasped and clapped his hand over his mouth. The colour drained from his face and he ran screeching incoherently back into his home.

His parents came out instantly and they too greeted the Druids respectfully, but briefly, before peering down at the litter. Their reaction was much the same as their son's had been.

"What is it?" demanded Gamenta,"why do you react so?"

"Don't know who you have on the litter?" the woman asked bluntly.

"No. We found her lying wounded on the side of the mountain. Lovernios here risked his life to climb down and rescue her. We've been held up half a day from our journey because of her, but she's alive and safe and now that we've found you to take charge of her, we can be on our way."

"We can't take charge of her," the man responded, "you need to take her back immediately, or there'll be repercussions throughout the region."

"Take her back where?" asked Lovernios, "and why will there be repercussions, surely she's just a local girl, a slave even. Perhaps you were right Gamenta, we should have saved ourselves the trouble, which is greater than anticipated, and left her to the gods."

"Don't say that, please!" whispered the woman, "the gods and her mother, the queen, will take vengeance on you and us alike."

"The queen! You surely don't mean Queen Boudica?"

"Yes," answered the man, "she is Ducildan, the eldest daughter of Queen Boudica and heir to the throne. You should take her before the last of daylight is done."

Stunned at this news the priests looked at each other questioningly. Having taken the lead all day, Lovernios asked where Queen Boudica resided. The young boy quickly volunteered to lead them there, promising that they'd arrive before the sky was fully dark, but pointing in the opposite direction to the journey the Druids were taking. Gamenta sighed. Would they ever reach the coast and leave for Mona. Seeing the priests' hesitation, Lovernios began issuing orders. Gamenta was pleased to see his protégé take charge and hear the wisdom of his words.

"Kierona, return to the mountain with Pren and the rest of the party and journey on to the coast. We'll meet with you there within eight nights, when we'll continue on to Mona. Gamenta, Mardial and I will return the queen's daughter to her. We'll stay there to make sure that she's well before continuing on our way. If we tarry longer than eight nights, then know that all is not well and return to Vernemeton. We'll meet with you there at the turn of the new month and make our journey to Mona after the Festival of Imbolc."

Queen Boudica was as intimidating as they'd feared she would be. She was a huge woman and her large frame towered over them all. Her hair was a wild mass of bright red that hung to her knees and shimmered in the light of the torch that her slave held in front of her.

She wore an enormous golden torc, which Lovernios judged would weigh more than he could comfortably carry round his own neck. Her tunic was multicoloured and vibrant, and was covered by a loose mantle of red, fastened just below her torc with a brooch of gold, encrusted with diamonds and pearls. She held in her right hand in a most menacing manner, a long spear, sharpened and ready for use.

When she spoke, her voice was harsh and terrifying. Her mission was to strike fear into all who crossed her path, and she did so admirably. The priests, powerful men with all the gods at their disposal, were visibly shaken.

"For what purpose have the gods sent priests to me?" She bellowed.

Lovernios was the first to recover from shock at the sight and sound of her, and stepped forward. The queen bowed slightly out of respect for the holy man, but continued to hold her spear ready and to intimidate with her piercing stare.

"We've come to return your daughter to you," he said. "We found her on our travels, fallen from the mountainside and injured."

The queen looked at him suspiciously, then beyond him to the litter where Ducildan lay groaning.

"Well bring her in, bring her in, what are you waiting for?" She turned and waddled off, her great body moving with surprising speed as she issued instructions to slaves and servants on her way.

Once they'd carried Ducildan to her chamber the priests were dismissed and sent to the dining hall where they were served an enormous meal. Before they'd finished eating, a smaller version of Queen Boudica entered. She was Luanadeld, she told them, Ducildan's younger sister.

She looked very much the same as Ducildan with similar piercing green eyes and long, wild red hair. The girls were the image of their mother, only smaller, and all three women gave the impression of fearlessness, and an almost savage brutality. The priests were fascinated by them.

Used as they were to the subdued personalities of the priestesses they'd lived with for so many years, the outspoken and forthright manner of these women unnerved them, yet Lovernios found himself so drawn to Ducildan that he had no desire to leave.

Queen Boudica was an incredibly strong ruler, while her husband, King Prasutagus, was king in name only, more concerned with increasing his extreme wealth than ruling his people. It was Boudica's personality that carried her and she raised her daughters to be as strong as she. Her rule wasn't one of compromise, and her subjects, the people of Iceni, feared but respected her and obeyed her without question.

Ducildan's recovery was swift. Although she wouldn't be able to walk for many months without aid, her head wound healed and her fever left her. Lovernios spent three days in her company, using her ill health as an excuse. He tended to her as though she were a fragile bird with a broken wing, however even she knew that his fascination with her had nothing at all to do with her injuries.

Still, she allowed him to minister to her, and took great pleasure in his strong hands working over her. She studied his face intently from every angle as she talked to him of all sorts of things, deliberately attempting to shock him, and each time Ducildan fell silent, Lovernios asked her to speak.

He wanted to learn as much as possible about her and continually compared her outrageous character to that of Maeve's, so opposite in every way. There was no doubt in his mind that Ducildan wouldn't follow him or any other man to the Otherworld, she'd use him and then discard him.

He was amazed at how hard she was, a true warrior, with her stirring beauty her only feminine trait and even that was so different to the soft beauty of Maeve.

Ducildan was grateful that Lovernios had saved her life, but she said so only once, and very perfunctorily. They'd been talking of horses when she suddenly asked whether the priests had found hers.

Lovernios was startled. He hadn't even thought to look for one, assuming that she'd been out walking. He stuttered and stumbled over an apology, explaining that he'd only been interested in saving her.

She looked away, her face reddening with anger. Her horse was her single most prized possession. She'd send slaves to look for him immediately.

As soon as she summoned her servant she looked across at Lovernios and said sulkily, "I suppose you did at least save my life."

The queen was no more effusive in her thanks than Ducildan. It seemed it was expected of the priests to find and save missing or injured people! As Gamenta and his party left on the fourth morning, Boudica, who'd not seen them since the first day, came out to them. They were already mounted up and thanking the grooms when she walked towards them, commanding attention like any military leader.

The grooms fled while the servants stood still and awaited her instructions. She ignored them but looked up at the priests with her huge frame making the horses appear small. Lovernios felt himself cringe in the presence of this powerful woman.

"Thank you for bringing Ducildan home. Go safely on your journey," and she turned and left As the priests made their way up the winding pathway that led out of the royal property, Luanadeld appeared through the bushes They'd seen little of her during their stay, but she did seem to be less intimidating than her mother or sister.

"I wished to bid farewell to you," she started, "and to thank you for saving Ducildan. I know you didn't need to, and, well, they think nothing of it, but I thank you for them."

And with that she disappeared back into the bushes.

Lovernios' mind was in a whirl as they continued on their way. Ducildan had barely said goodbye. It was as if the novelty of the priests had worn off by the third day.

She'd grown tired of Lovernios and his constant attention, his face no longer pleased her, and she was angry that the slaves hadn't found her horse. She was angry that the priests hadn't brought him back with her, and angry that she couldn't walk, and her fiery red-haired temper showed.

Lovernios decided that their mission was over there was no point in staying to watch Ducildan take her displeasure out on everyone.

When Lovernios went in to her day room to tell her they were leaving, Ducildan barely looked at him.

"Oh," she said, "farewell then," and she continued her discussion with Luanadeld who looked away in embarrassment.

As he thought of the two girls so similar in looks and stature but so different in their ways, Lovernios recognised some of Maeve in Luanadeld yet found himself so drawn to Ducildan that guilt began to overcome him. Nothing he could do, no amount of praying, chanting or talking to the other priests the following days could take his mind off the bewitching creature, and he secretly hoped that he'd meet with her again one day.

Chapter 28

When they finally arrived on Mona they found Obetach in some kind of trance, muttering repeatedly the number thirty.

"Obetach, Obetach, it is I, Lovernios."

The Druid looked up and saw Lovernios standing before him, as if the gods had just transported him from across the seas. He'd spent many hours chanting and dancing, seeking their will, and all of a sudden they'd answered him.

For days he'd seen the number thirty in everything he did, wherever he went, always a thirty, and he longed for Lovernios, longed for Vitaicus, so he could tell them what it was that the gods had revealed. And now Lovernios was here, standing in front of him. Obetach shook himself, fully out of his trance.

"Is it really you?" he asked in a shaky voice.

He looked round and saw not only Lovernios but also Gamenta and Mardial, and off to the side Kierona standing with, could it possibly be, yes, yes it was Pren. Obetach stepped forward and his legs buckled as Lovernios caught hold of him. They embraced fondly and although full of questions, Obetach greeted the others in turn before taking them to where he was living and making them comfortable.

Lovernios allowed Pren to relate the most recent tragic events to the shocked priest. For a long time he said nothing, then sadly shook his head.

"Lovernios, when you were born, the gods showed me the number thirty but they didn't reveal its significance until this day, this auspicious day, made so sad for me with your news."

They waited while the priest mused over the good and bad luck that had befallen his day.

"It nearly drove the king mad," he continued and they were confused. "He ran around for months looking for this mystical thirty." Obetach laughed mirthlessly.

"He kept a vigil beside your bed every time you turned thirty hours, days, months. He counted chariots, horses, warriors, even bees." Obetach lapsed into silence as he remembered all those years ago, those early frantic days of the life of this fine young man who sat before him, and now that he had the answer, his king was not here to receive it, but perhaps in the Otherworld he already knew and was waiting to receive his son.

"It's years Lovernios, they require you to be the Supreme Sacrifice when you've reached thirty years, then the sacrifice will be so great it will save the land."

He sat back exhausted from his grief and the effort of many days of divination and having uttered the words, the burden of twenty-three years was lifted from his shoulders.

The trip to Mona almost killed Gamenta, and he never fully recovered from it. He became ill on the way over and it seemed the cold waters seeped into his bones. While on the island he was ill with fever and coughing, but rallied sufficiently to travel back, although the senior Druids questioned the wisdom of this.

Knowing how his health had been over the past few years, they debated keeping him on the island with the other infirm priests, but Gamenta argued that he still had much to do and many novices to teach. Eventually they relented and the return trip was planned.

The weather was good and the crossing swift, but even so Gamenta began to shiver and shake and by the time they disembarked he was unconscious and burning with fever. It took many months for him to recover and he realised he'd never be fit enough to teach again. Alana took over his students and Gamenta spent his time as advisor, staying in the grove where they lived, exchanging his vast knowledge with that of Xavista.

The Supreme Druid Pantra and his advisors had agreed that with changing circumstances across the land, Xavista and Pren could remain with the priests but they were to live on the fringes of the grove, not so close that they'd learn the secret ways of the gods, but close enough that they would always be at hand and able to give assistance if needed.

Both men learnt an enormous amount from the other and Gamenta secretly learned to read and write, something that delighted him, although he could never tell the other priests, not even Lovernios, only Pren knew.

Chapter 29

AD 54

Autumn

From the day Claudius was pronounced Emperor, he'd worked incessantly at earning the title he coveted the most, "Extender of the Empire" and added twenty-seven new provinces to his Empire, as he continued to conquer the world. In his Province of Britannia he fostered good relations with as many of the previous chiefs and kings as possible.

One of his most notable conquests was Cartimandua. He'd installed her as Queen of the Brigantes in return for her role in conquering Caratacus. Her loyalty to Claudius and Rome was unquestioned, unlike the loyalty of his own wife and household.

Britain was developing rapidly and becoming more romanised each year, with only the remote agricultural regions remaining unchanged. The one single area where there was still resistance to Roman ways was the adoption of a money economy. The tribesman continued to barter and trade rather than put their trust in coins.

Roman capital was pouring into Britain, and although urbanization was relatively slow, cities were growing, and more roads were being built. The first major road had been the Fosse Way, along which was Aquae Sulis, Durocornovium, Ratae, Venta Belgarum and Verulamium the fastest developing Roman Municipium.

As the Celts became accustomed to the constant presence of the Romans and the progress being made in the country, they accepted the paying of tributes and taxes to the Empire, and did so with little complaint, provided they weren't treated unjustly.

They were happy to be ruled by others but not to be treated as slaves. However the Romans were unjust, and there were pockets of unrest. Although the Empire controlled virtually all of Britain from east to west, there remained the kingdom of the Regni under King

Cogidubnus who was never the less loyal to Rome, and the Iceni under King Prasutagus and his wife, Queen Boudica, who fiercely withstood the rule of Rome.

Claudius' wife, Agrippina, was almost certain that her son Nero would become Emperor rather than Claudius' own son Britannicus, but even so she wasn't entirely satisfied. Narcissus, her husband's Secretary-general, was urging Claudius to designate Britannicus rather than Nero as his successor, and Agrippina was afraid Claudius might have second thoughts.

She desperately wanted to rule his vast and powerful Empire, but was concerned that Claudius would live many years and that by the time Nero became Emperor, he would no longer need her. Her desire was to be a woman Emperor, and she could do this through her weak and young son. If Claudius died now, Nero would need her advice.

Seeing no other solution she employed the services of a notorious poisoner named Locusta, who wasted no time in planting poison into a dish of mushrooms that she fed to her husband.

Emperor Tiberius Claudius Drusus Caesar died in agony the following morning, September 13.

At the time of his death his legions were at the border of Wales and were advancing to attack the last vestiges of Druidism on the island of Mona.

At the age of sixteen, Nero Claudius Caesar was proclaimed Emperor of Rome and shortly after taking office he appointed Suetonius Paulinus as Governor of the Province of Britannia.

Suetonius brought about a new and thorough approach to the settlement of Britain and the campaign against the Druids. The Roman grip on the Celts tightened. Land near Colchester was taken for retired legionaries to settle on, and the carrying of arms by Celts was banned.

Nero spent his imperial revenues and looked around his Empire for further funds. He knew that Britain had great wealth and had not in his opinion contributed enough in tributes and taxes due to the stubbornness of the Silures and Ordovices, who refused to give in to the Empire.

Nero realised that he had to destroy their warriors and their supply lines along with their spiritual base on Mona.

Suetonius had just concluded a brilliantly successful campaign against the Moors in Mauritania when Nero appointed him as Governor and he tackled his new mission of fully conquering Britain with single mindedness.

He had his eye on the wealth that remained untouched in Wales and on Mona, and set his attention on getting it.

Chapter 30

AD 56
Summer

With so many novices still in their Vate years under Alana, she asked permission of Gamenta to take them to Salisbury Plain, where they could better learn about the moon and the stars.

Gamenta readily agreed and put Lovernios, Mardial and Kierona in charge of their own group of novice priests, while Maeve, Couvena and Rynath looked after a small group of priestesses, under the supervision of Alana. Gamenta was too ill to travel and remained behind in the care of Pren and Xavista.

Lovernios loved teaching and looked forward to the trip with great enthusiasm. As he and Maeve talked about it the afternoon before they left, they thought back to their first trip there, and realised that their love for each other, just beginning to grow then, had become a powerful force and swore once again never to be parted.

When Maeve first heard that Lovernios would be leaving to go to the gods when he turned thirty, she promised to go with him. Now as they sat together quietly waiting for nightfall she promised once again to join him on his journey to the Otherworld.

When the Druids returned from Salisbury many months later, Gamenta was deathly ill. Pren was so relieved to see Lovernios that he babbled incoherently until Lovernios made him be quiet and take a deep breath. Xavista put his arm around the shoulder of the distraught young man.

"Gamenta has been seriously ill while you were away and we thought we'd lost him on a number of occasions. Pren has administered every medicine and powerful incantation that he knows, and I have even appealed to my own gods, but to no avail. He is slowly slipping away from us," he finished sadly.

Alana and Lovernios rushed to the side of Gamenta. The smell of death was about him and they knew he was close to joining the gods.

They did all they could for him, with every priest and priestess fasting and praying. They lit fires and danced and chanted until Lovernios thought his back would break and his legs snap in two. They fed him every conceivable potion and waved plants and herbs over his fever-ridden body, but he continued to slip away. He was seldom conscious and when he was, he was incoherent.

On the fourth day, when their spirits were failing, Gamenta opened his eyes and spoke for the first time.

"Lovernios," he croaked. Lovernios was at his side instantly.

"I'll see you shortly."

After a brief pause he whispered one more word, the number 'thirty' and then he was gone to the Otherworld to be with his gods, to join all those who had gone before him.

Obetach was sent for but Lovernios knew he wouldn't arrive for weeks and it was left to him and Alana to make decisions and arrangements. It would be unsafe to have a large funeral pyre for Gamenta and so they chose to send him to the gods at the bottom of the lake, given to them as a sacrifice.

Lovernios led the sombre procession with his magnificent white horse, Slydau, drawing the chariot that carried the body of his beloved priest.

As he walked beside the chariot, chanting softly to Esus, begging him to fetch Gamenta and carry him into the Otherworld, Lovernios looked down at the familiar face, so grey now and solemn, not the ruddy complexion and smiling freckled face that he was used to.

Gamenta's hair, normally spiky and unruly, was neatly combed and plastered to his head with a thick coating of lime, its bright red colour no longer visible. His mouth, which used to move incessantly with large front teeth protruding, was still forever.

Lovernios felt numbed to death. He'd endured so much of it in his own family, and faced his own death soon too, and so this became just another ritual to be endured and he tried to do so without feeling.

He thought of Obetach and wished he were here. Obetach had suffered much ill health in his early years as a priest and yet had rallied and was now remarkably well in his sixty-eighth year, while Gamenta who was so young, was struck down and taken, surely by the gods themselves.

As they continued to march towards the lake, Lovernios thought of all the people that Gamenta would soon be joining. Vitaicus, the father he missed so much but who at least had Flauston with him. Hilfuth, the mother he never knew and Trasand, who really was his mother. Her precious children, his siblings Kwethin, Mellund and Tylad.

He wondered if the twins, grotesque and deformed as they were, would also have reached the Otherworld, or if they'd forever remain in the ground near the river. Pren had only recently told him the full details of the deformity and death of the twins, and he shuddered at the thought.

Lovernios knew he'd see them all soon, but what then of Pren and Filethas. He would never see Filethas again in this world, so far away on the island of Sena, but what of Pren? Where would he go when Lovernios went to join Gamenta and the others? These thoughts tormented him and in the place of sadness he felt confusion.

It was a relief to reach the lake. Lovernios was tired, cold and dispirited and he wanted this ceremony over and done with as quickly as possible. There would be no feast, as cattle were scarce, and no fire for fear of detection, just subdued singing and dancing until the Druids felt certain that the gods had accepted their offering.

Lovernios, Mardial, Kierona and Pren lifted the body of Gamenta from the carriage and carried him to the water's edge. The priestesses waited there with a white cloak to wrap around the priest. They laid his body on top of the cloak and danced in circles around it. Only Alana remained motionless as the others chanted and prayed. She sat beside her lost love and sobbed. She desperately wanted to join him on his journey, but had already been warned by the other priests that she couldn't, she was too valuable here as there were already far too few senior Druids left.

She contemplated life without Gamenta, and begged the gods to take her of their own accord so that she needn't remain on this earth without the most precious person she'd ever known. She was barely aware that the chanting had come to an end a few hours later.

At Lovernios' signal the body was lifted above their heads and they stepped into the water, wading out as far as they could. When only their heads remained above the surface, they lowered the body into the water and waited for it to sink, calling on the gods of the lake to accept their offering, giving thanks to Teutates for allowing them to bring Gamenta to him.

Afterwards, they sat on the bank in their wet robes, while the priestesses fetched dry ones, and Lovernios finally allowed himself to weep at the loss of his mentor and friend, Gamenta the Priest.

Agrippina's high hopes that having her son reign as Emperor would gain her fame and position began to fade as the true leaders behind the new ruler emerged. They were the philosopher, Seneca and the Praetorian, Burrus, and Nero relied almost entirely on them, seldom turning to his mother for advice. With time Nero proved to be more interested in sensual pleasures than in the affairs of Rome, which gave the two men further influence and power.

Young Nero loved literature, music, the arts and women. Although married to his late uncle Claudius' daughter, Octavia, he took for himself a concubine by the name of Acte. However even she wasn't enough to keep the Emperor happy and he turned his attention to the Sun God, Apollo, whom he was attracted to in a most unhealthy manner. He worshipped the god to the point of falling in love with him.

Octavia was most unsympathetic to her husband's strange quirks and whims and desperately wanted to divorce him. Nero too favoured a divorce, but his mother refused to give her consent and a furious argument developed between them.

Seeing that her plan to rule through her weak and miserable god loving son had failed, she threatened to restore Claudius' son, Britannicus to the throne and turned her attention to championing his cause in the senate.

Nero was furious and commissioned Locusta to poison Britannicus in the same way his father had been poisoned. Once Britannicus was dead however, Nero became terrified of other possible rivals in the royal household, and even feared his own mother.

He was encouraged by Seneca and Burrus to get rid of anyone who stood in his way and prevented him ruling as he wished, and so Agrippina was accused of treason and was removed from the palace, her limited influence over Nero over, and with that move the Roman world was effectively ruled by Seneca and Burrus.

It was many months after the death of Gamenta that Obetach finally arrived to take over the tutoring of the pupils and to officiate at the ceremony that would take place when they graduated with their penultimate degree.

Obetach brought with him two other senior priests to assist and they planned to return to Mona shortly afterwards, taking with them the few eight year olds who'd been brought to Gamenta for the start of their twenty years of training.

When Lovernios was inducted eighteen years earlier, thousands of children were sent to the Druids to be tutored every year. This year only forty-seven had been brought to the few places in the country where Druids were in hiding and attempting to teach.

Since Suetonius had been appointed Governor life in Britain had become unbearable for the Celts and more dangerous than ever for the Druids and so their final two years of training would take place in Tara.

Chapter 31

AD 56
Autumn

The ceremony to bestow their degree on the novices was smaller and simpler than any previous one. Obetach and his assistants attempted to make it as meaningful as possible, without the use of fires or loud chanting.

As the arch Druid present, Obetach wore his highest ceremonial outfit. On his head was a garland of oak leaves, freshly picked and woven by the youngest priestesses, surrounded by a tiara of gold studded with adder stones. He wore a white surplice fastened on the shoulder by a magnificent golden brooch.

At the end of the ceremony the novices handed their green gowns to Obetach and they were each given a new one. This final gown was white to signify their purity as they embarked on the final stage of their learning. Obetach addressed his graduates with pride.

"You've worked hard in the most difficult time in our land and your seniors are proud of you. As you go forward into your final two years of study remember always the Bards of old, Plennydd, who represents Light, Alawn who represents Harmony and Gwron who represents Energy. May their spirits go with you as you continue on your spiritual journey. May Light, Harmony and Energy be your constant companions."

When the ceremony was over, Obetach said they'd be leaving for Tara just as soon as the weather permitted, travelling through Mona on the way. During the months that he'd been back in Britain, Obetach had seen the extent of the spread of Roman rule and influence, and he was deeply afraid. With the building of the Fosse Way, Watling Road and other major highways, many of the Druid's sacred forests had been destroyed.

As new cities emerged and kings and tribal chiefs made treaties, the lives of the priests were at risk, even from the Celts. Only a few hundred druids were left alive of the many thousands who used to live in Britain and they had no choice but to flee, regroup and train up more priests in the safety of Tara. One day they'd return in strength to call on the gods to set the people free from the tyranny of Rome.

It was with heavy hearts that the Druids gathered up their few possessions for the final time and made the long and now dangerous journey to the coast. For some of the younger priests it was their first trip to Mona and they were filled with awe from the moment they first set foot on the holy island.

Encouraged by the senior Druids living there, they remained for a few months to rest, continuing their studies while enjoying the relative peace and safety of the sacred haven, until Obetach announced four months later that it was time to leave.

They left the island, now the country's Druidic stronghold, with great reluctance, not imagining what was to take place once they'd gone, but looking forward to the day when they would return as fully fledged priests to join their brothers and sisters in this most sacred of all sacred places.

The journey to Tara was one of great expectation. Few of the priests had been there before, and those who had were questioned incessantly about the little known place until they were exhausted.

For the first time in many of their lives the following eighteen months brought about peace and security, something previously unknown. They were able to settle in one place and concentrate on their studies.

For Lovernios and Maeve it was a wonderful time spent together, learning and discovering still more about the gods that ruled them and their world.

Lovernios often thought of Ducildan and Luanadeld and the daunting Queen Boudica, but his love for Maeve outweighed his fanciful fascination with the red haired women. His bond with Maeve was as indestructible as his bond with Pren. Although Pren was not permitted to live in the grove with the priests, he and Xavista set up a comfortable abode on the outskirts of the forest and they saw Lovernios daily.

Pren continued to be taught by Xavista while the Druids were busy with their studies, but whenever Obetach allowed they spent time with the priests, dancing and chanting round large fires, a luxury they'd not enjoyed in recent years when they were hiding from the Romans.

The months flew by and just before their final degree news finally arrived of Britain. Roman rule was harsh as ever and their people were suffering without the guidance and prayers of the priests. The Druids were desperate to get back but waited for the gods to grant them permission.

Obetach and the senior Druids spent weeks in prayer, but the gods were silent. Autumn came and a long awaited night finally arrived. After twenty harsh years of studying Lovernios and his fellow priests and priestesses were fully fledged Druids, but the ceremony to celebrate the occasion which should have been the happiest and most auspicious day of their lives was in fact a dark and depressing one.

It matched equally the dark and depressing time in which they lived and waited, but still there was no word from the gods.

Part Three

Chapter 1

AD 59
Autumn

With time, and despite Agrippina's removal from the palace and her lack of control over her son, Nero grew to hate and fear her, a hatred spurred on by Seneca and Burrus. He feared her ambition to rule, and was convinced that his mother planned to have him poisoned.

He decided to act first and so he and his consorts arranged to have her drowned. Unfortunately for Nero she was rescued by a fishing boat. When Nero heard, he asked Anicetus, the Prefect of the Fleet at Misenum, to assassinate her. As Prefect, he had no trouble in ordering his sailors to do the deed for him.

And so at last the end came for the incredibly wicked woman at the indirect hand of her own son, Emperor Nero, on the 22nd day of the month of March, a month that had become sinister and inauspicious in Rome with many a murder taking place during that particular period each year.

On seeing the body of his dead mother, Nero's only remark was, "I never knew she was so good looking."

Freed at last from the overbearing and powerful woman, Nero divorced his wife Octavia, and married his newest love, Poppaea Sabina who had also been instrumental in persuading Nero to get rid of his mother so they could marry.

Still in Tara, at the sacred grove of Taltiu, Lovernios and a few of the other priests and priestesses felt totally helpless. After twenty years of training, they were desperate to be of some use to their people. The wanted to serve in a royal household and to officiate at ceremonies in the way they'd been taught and they found the months of waiting frustrating, despite the enormous patience they'd learned over the years.

They were relieved when the Festival of Samain drew near and they were able to prepare for the feast, the first major ceremony they'd officiate in as Druids and also the first festival held in years in which they could light fires and celebrate without fear.

Samain, which literally meant the end of the warm season, was one of the two annual fire festivals celebrated at the start of winter when darkness, cold and hunger would be upon them. Winter was a season of potential danger and uncertainty, with the possibility of crop failure and starvation. It was the time when the veil between the reality of this world and the Otherworld was most easily penetrated, the only festival that celebrated all the gods of the Otherworld.

The druids travelled to the sacred grove of Tlachtga for the celebration. During this Samain Festival, when Britain faced such danger and uncertainty, they threw themselves fully into prayer and supplication, lighting huge fires and dancing day and night for three days, until exhausted they knew they could do no more for their people. Britain lay in the hands of all the gods, but also in the hands of the Romans.

When news reached Tara of the death of King Prasutagus shortly after Samain, Lovernios was saddened beyond words. Although he'd not met the king he felt the loss of his own father once again and understood how the king's family must be feeling and felt sympathy for Queen Boudica and her daughters whom he still thought of often.

He'd watch Maeve and see Luanadeld and then compare the two to the fiery Ducildan, and his fascination with the princess grew despite the short time spent with her so long ago.

As he sat contemplating, Lovernios had no idea how momentous the death of King Prasutagus would be, for him, for the Druids or for Britain. To him it was simply another sad event in a long line of sad events.

At his death King Prasutagus left half his enormous estate to his daughters and the remainder to Rome in the hope that this great wealth would satisfy Nero's greed and that his family would be left in peace.

Prasutagus had already made a treaty with Rome and the Iceni had finally become a client state, sacrificing their independence for the promise of protection. As a client king, Prasutagus couldn't appoint his successor, but assumed that his wife, Queen Boudica would be allowed to continue to rule.

Rome had different ideas, and the Iceni along with the royal family were treated as a conquered kingdom. Nero refused to allow Boudica to inherit, or to rule her kingdom.

All financial grants which had been made to the Iceni years before by Claudius, were recalled by Nero's philosopher and henchman Seneca. Nobles were expelled from their homes, their estates were confiscated and taxation and conscription were enforced. Before absorbing the Iceni into the Roman Province, the king's legacy was divided between the soldiers and other Roman officials.

Boudica protested at the heavy taxes they were expected to pay and at the treatment she and her people were receiving. Decianus Catus, the Imperial Procurator in Britain, had been pursing Nero's new financial policies with diligence. Catus was attempting to obtain the whole of Prasutagus estate and absorb it into the Roman Empire.

In answer to Boudica's protests at the vicious mismanagement and expropriation by the Romans of their lands and of the dreadful and unnecessary abuse of her family, Decianus confiscated most of the property which the king had given to her daughters.

Troops marched on Boudica's residence where they confiscated her personal possessions. Her servants attacked the troops and they retaliated with vengeance. The queen was dragged from her house and flogged like a common criminal. Her daughters were brutally raped.

When the Supreme Druid Pantra heard this news and rumours that the Roman soldiers were readying themselves to come across the Menai Strait to Mona where they planned to destroy the entire Druidical order, he called for warriors to protect them. Men and women hardened in battle came to the island, anxious to set eyes on their common enemy and fight them off to save the priests.

When news arrived in Tara of the flogging of Boudica and the rape of her daughters, the indignation was such that Obetach ordered a time of fasting and prayer. The gods finally wakened from their long sleep. Before midnight on the third night, Obetach announced that it was time for the Druids to return home.

Lovernios had been devastated when he heard the further dreadful fate that had befallen Ducildan and Luanadeld and he was anxious to see them both. He'd only mentioned them briefly to

Maeve and he pondered the problem of telling her that he wished to visit them.

Now that they were no longer students, the priests were free to travel at will, and as permission had been granted to return home, once there Lovernios was free to go where he wished.

He discussed his dilemma with Pren and in his wisdom his brother cautioned him not to say anything until they were actually over the sea and in Britain, then to see what the gods had in store for them. Relieved that he needn't say or do anything yet, Lovernios and the other Druids prepared to leave the peaceful place that had been home for the past two years.

At the same time the Iceni were suffering under the hands of the Romans, the Trinovantes were suffering insults too. They'd been given the responsibility of maintaining and running the Temple of Claudius, temple of the Deified Emperor, which was designed to promote loyalty from the Celts towards Rome and its Emperors.

This burden had fallen on the nobles of the Trinovantes and they were unhappy with the task and the great cost involved.The temple had been built at Camulodunum and it became the focus of hatred of the people towards Rome. Besides this, Roman colonists were settling in Britain and with the encouragement of serving solders, seized the lands of the Celts and treated them with utter contempt.

Aristocrats and commoners were facing financial ruin. As word spread that all grants made previously to the people by Claudius were being recalled, along with all more recent loans made by Seneca, the entire land faced financial crises.

Queen Boudica was not prepared to stand for any further abuse to herself, her family or her people. She called on her warriors and they responded. With her own tribe, the Iceni and her closest neighbours, the Trinovantes, she rose in rebellion.

Obetach and his priests travelled the short distance from where they were living to the coast, where they waited for the weather to permit them to cross to Mona before journeying home. No news had reached them since they'd heard of the atrocities done to Boudica and they were most concerned. Despite the poor weather conditions, merchants often ventured across the sea, but none came and the priests set up camp just above the beach and waited with trepidation.

Chapter 2

AD 60

Spring

Suetonius Paulinus was still occupied with his ongoing campaign in the mountainous area of northern Wales when Boudica and the Iceni rebelled.

The Roman Legions were struggling to get through the mountains and into the land of the Silures and the Ordovices, who'd been preventing them from gaining access to the gold, lead and copper deposits in the area.

This was primarily the wealth of the Druids, and the Ordovices and Silures protected it with fervour. In his pursuit of the elusive Druids, Suetonius moved into the treacherous area and after a lengthy battle in which the Celtic warriors stood their ground and fought furiously, he was finally closing in on them and on the Druids on the island of Mona.

Suetonius took his troops around the edge of the Snowdon Massif in preparation for moving his forces to the island, where he planned to complete what Caesar had begun and wipe out the Druids entirely. It was while he was there that he received the news of Boudica's rebellion.

His Second Legion was tied down by attacks from the Silures, and Suetonius felt certain these had been planned to coincide with the uprising of the Iceni. He faced a serious problem as his forces were both widely dispersed and vastly outnumbered.

He decided to continue with his present mission and push on towards the Menai Strait between mainland Wales and the island of Mona. He had with him two legions, some auxiliaries and a small battle fleet and they crossed the sea with ease. When they arrived on Mona, the Romans were surprised to find themselves faced by an armed mass of warriors and Druids who stood on the beach shrieking curses at the soldiers.

Men and women, commoner and priest, all massed together, and the sight of them was so strange and unnerving to the Roman troops that they stood rooted to the spot and watched in terror.

The Druids lifted their hands to the skies and called down the most dreadful curses on Rome and the terrified soldiers. They were paralysed at the sight of such an unfamiliar enemy.

The Roman generals came to their senses first, and realising they faced impending disaster they raised their standards and led the way, marching forward, calling for the troops to follow. At the sight of their brave leaders the soldiers followed and the might of the Roman army took over once again as their military training and discipline came to the fore. They swiftly wiped out all resistance.

Every warrior who'd been sent to the island to protect the Druids was butchered. Every priest and priestess was annihilated. Not satisfied with murdering the Druids, the soldiers set out to destroy their sacred groves. They axed them and then set them alight using the flames of the priest's own brands.

It was ironic that Suetonius had once accused Caesar of destroying all the temples in Gaul, as he now became responsible for doing the same to the temples of the decimated priests of Britain. The once holy and sacred island of Mona was devastated.

The soldiers returned to the mainland where they waited for further orders, writing letters as they rested, bragging of their bravery and triumph. Back in Londinium the news of the victory on Mona reached the small garrison stationed there and Caius Porteus Maximus wrote to his parents telling of their wonderful success.

"Two days ago, dear parents, we exterminated the last of the Druids, and a strange business it was, I can tell you. They and their followers had gathered on a small island called Mona, off the extreme west coast of Britannia, past the territory of the Degeangli tribe we have been fighting recently. The Governor was determined to crush them, and so we prepared to cross the narrow straits with the whole of the Fourteenth Legion and most of the Twentieth Legion too. They were burning fires all along the shoreline opposite, and what with the fires, and the shrieks they made, and the surf pounding, our troops hesitated for a moment. But not for long! The infantry crossed in boats and those of us who were mounted swam across on our horses; when we got over it was not so bad. They fought well, but in the end they had to surrender and our own losses were not heavy."

The soldiers discussed the Celtic women for many nights after the battle. It was the women they'd really feared, fighting half naked in brightly painted colours, fully armed and vicious. With their long hair streaming in the wind, they shook their knives and spears, and danced and gesticulated as though possessed.

They gave high piercing war cries with a terrible unearthly sound, which unnerved the Roman soldiers more than they were prepared to admit. These women were so unlike those of Rome, and the soldiers were not sure whether to admire or despise them.

When the rain that had been falling for days stopped long enough for Obetach and his Druids to climb into their rickety boats and leave Tara, their spirits were high, and they spent their last day on the beach dancing and thanking the gods for the splendid weather which would allow them to sail the following morning.

Their trip across the Irish Sea was uneventful, but as they neared Mona, their buoyant mood changed swiftly as they at first smelled and then saw the smoke of many fires. Dismayed, they fell silent as their boats rowed slowly towards the island. When they landed in the late afternoon, they stood on a beach blackened by soot, huddled together in fear, and waited until all the crafts arrived.

Silently they began the ten-mile march across the breadth of the island and with each mile their despair grew as they passed through one devastated sacred grove after another.

At first they assumed fire had overtaken the island, but as they progressed they began to see that the groves had been axed before being set to flame.

Walking beside Obetach, Lovernios whispered to the emotional old priest, "Perhaps the priests did this rather than leave the island to the Romans?"

"Nay, Lovernios, this isn't the work of the priests. I've seen the very same devastation of sacred groves in Gaul. This is the work of Roman soldiers. I fear what we'll find once we reach the residence of the Supreme Druid."

His worst fears were confirmed as their march continued. With the ground blackened and still smouldering in places, there was nowhere to stop and rest and they wandered through the night, crisscrossing the island. They arrived at their destination at dawn.

Smoke tendrils curled up through the dew and swirled round their feet, and through the smoky haze they saw the Supreme Druid's residence razed to the ground, he and his priests and priestesses dead. Their holy sanctuary had not only been devastated it had been sacrilegiously decimated. The few remaining Druids of Britain wept.

Chapter 3

AD 60

Autumn

While the Roman Legions rested and revelled in their victory, tens of thousands of Celts were moving on Camulodunum. Porteus Maximus, who was still waiting in Londinium for word from Suetonius, was in a state.

He was receiving regular reports of the rebellion and of the thousands of Celts marching southwards towards Camulodunum, after which they'd surely head for Londinium. For some reasons Suetonius didn't react to his reports or pleas for assistance.

Camulodunum was the first Roman Provincial Centre, their first Colonia, the highest rank for a provincial settlement. It contained a forum, a temple, law courts and other administrative offices around its walled centre. Farms that were confiscated from the Celts were given to retired legionnaires as it was the custom of the Romans to grant land to soldiers in whichever province they'd served.

Camulodunum was now a typical Roman colony. It was wealthy, complacent and undefended but for one small garrison of soldiers under the leadership of Porteus, who waited in Londinium for support.

Boudica's army was a large horde of incensed warriors, and they moved against the town and caught the Roman legion off guard. Porteus sent further messages west to Suetonius, desperately requesting help.

Suetonius finally reacted and despatched his Twentieth and Twenty Fourth Legions, but he'd delayed too long. They left as soon as Suetonius received the final desperate plea from Porteus and planned to meet other legions on the way to Verulamium, but they had far to travel. Realising it would probably be too late to save Camulodunum,

Suetonius intended to try and save Londinium. Three hundred cavalry moved down the new Roman highway, Watling Street, heading towards Londinium. It was a cold dark and damp autumn, the weather matching the cold and dark mood of the people.

Marching towards Londinium from the northeast under Commander Petilius Cerialis were two thousand Legionaries. Before they reached Londinium they met Boudica and her army, which now numbered tens of thousands of warriors. Boudica completely massacred the legions and only Cerialis and his cavalry escaped alive.

This devastating news reached Suetonius just as he left Mona on the second day after his victory there. He finally reached Veralamium five days later. Verulamium was still a small settlement and he went there expecting to meet the garrison of his Twentieth Legion. He planned to march with them to Londinium but he was shocked to find the garrison wasn't there.

The commander at Glevum had ignored Suetonius' order to meet with him. Suetonius was a brave soldier and a great general and he was undaunted, if temporarily thrown. He made the decision to march on with his small cavalry force.

Suetonius left Verulamium at nightfall, telling the people there to flee for their lives, as he and his men rode out on their way towards Londinium. Londinium was not a Colonia like Camulodunum, but a large and sprawling city with warehouses along the river, beside the houses of the traders.

The Romans had built a makeshift forum and many storehouses for their military equipment. Most of these buildings were of wood. Porteus knew in his heart that Londinium couldn't be defended. He had a handful of troops but no Second Legion. He and his soldiers waited while constant, devastating reports arrived.

He learned with shock of the Emperor's Temple being burned at Camulodunum, the bust of the Emperor broken, its head thrown into the river Alde. He heard how the entire colony was torched and every Roman or pro-Roman inhabitant slaughtered.

When Suetonius finally reached the undefended city of Londinium some time later, he was amazed to find it was untouched. Boudica hadn't been there with her horde. It was with great relief that Porteus greeted Suetonius and his cavalry. If Boudica had decided not to attack Londinium after she'd destroyed Camulodunum, as he'd anticipated she would, the question he had to ask himself was, "why?" He and Porteus pondered long and hard.

As it was, Boudica had turned north instead, planning to meet up with the Ninth Legion, who were hurrying south. Her plans weren't those of a military genius, but they were effective. She'd prepared a clever and devastating ambush for the Ninth Legion.

When news reached Suetonius from an unknown battlefield north of where he waited, it was the most unbelievable and numbing of his career. His Ninth Legion had been decimated. Boudica was encouraged by her great success, and her warriors were inflamed in true Celtic fashion. A good fight brought out the best in them.

They headed for Londinium knowing it was only protected by Suetonius with his small band of cavalry along with Porteus and his handful of troops.

As news of her victory in Camulodunum spread, so more Celts joined her, and her horde grew as they marched on Londinium. By the time they arrived they numbered seventy thousand. Men, women and children, each and every one an incensed warrior intent on destroying the might of Rome.

Although distraught at the loss of his Ninth Legion, Suetonius reacted with the calmness of a seasoned campaigner. He knew that his small force, ill equipped as they were, would be unlikely to beat the massive horde of rebellious Britons. He knew too that the city of Londinium was indefensible.

He had only one hope of defeating Boudica, but for this he needed the infantry of his Fourteenth and Twentieth Legions who were already on their way down Watling Street. He faced two choices, wait for them, and they would surely arrive too late, or go and meet them and draw Boudica away from Londinium.

Once he had his full force together he could face her for a final showdown. The longer he could delay this proposed battle the greater his chances were of winning it but only if Boudica played into his hands, and also, only if he abandoned Londinium, the second city of the new Roman Province and a viable and thriving trading centre. It was one of the toughest decisions he'd ever had to make.

Suetonius chose to leave Londinium and he knew in his heart that it was an enormous risk, but he went ahead, trusting purely in his military instincts. When he and his troops moved out of the city, they left behind them frightened and outraged citizens who knew they were being abandoned, sheep for slaughter.

With his small force in which he included those who could ride in his cavalry, he went rapidly up Watling Street, praying that he'd soon meet with his legions marching towards him. He knew he faced the risk of Boudica pursuing him and his cavalry, and if she did, she would destroy them. But Boudica did as he hoped and chose to attack Londinium.

Suetonius guessed correctly that after the battle with the Ninth Legion her seething mass of warriors would be spurred on and head for the city that embodied the Roman Empire, where Romans were using the wealth of the British people. She guessed that her army wouldn't wait any longer to get their hands on this rich plunder. Even if she'd wished to she couldn't hold them back.

By sacrificing Londinium, Suetonius achieved his aim, he bought the time he needed to meet his legions, regroup his forces, and then pick a battlefield that would suit his disciplined army and the manner in which they'd been taught to fight. Suetonius never guessed at the great cost of his decision, far greater than he'd ever imagined.

With the rage of Boudica to fuel them, her army ignored Suetonius and his fleeing cavalry and continued towards defenceless Londinium. They attacked with such force and brutal savagery that Suetonius was stunned. They raced through the city, killing without question and then set alight what remained.

The destruction was so complete, so thorough that layers of ash and charcoal lie there still, a sombre reminder of the determination of Boudica to avenge her country and her family, and to wipe out all things Roman.

That night Suetonius and his men watched the flames of Londinium as it burned. Before dawn he received word that Boudica and her warriors were heading his way. Suetonius was nervous, but continued on with his cavalry in the hope of finding more troops to bolster his numbers. That night they again looked on a red sky, this time the flames they saw were of Verulamium as it burned.

Once Londinium had been destroyed Boudica's army marched on, far from satiated, and attacked Verulamium twenty miles to the north of Londinium. Suetonius had truly believed that after they'd looted Londinium Boudica's warriors would be satisfied and would drift back to their homes, secure in their belief that they'd won.

He was sadly mistaken. Although he'd bought the time he needed to face the mighty Queen and Warrior on his terms, it was at a far higher price than he ever imagined he, or the people, would pay.

The Empire's three newest cities had been completely destroyed, and thousands of people had been killed, Romans, Celts and foreign merchants, none were spared by Boudica and her army. So incensed were they that they mutilated the Romans, and the woman in particular were killed in a dreadful fashion.

Boudica, both Queen and Priestess, allowed her warriors to sacrifice them to the bloodthirsty Goddess Andraste, to appease her for the injustices done to the people of Britain. Boudica was present during these sacrifices, calling on Andraste and all the gods to help her destroy the Romans and protect the few remaining priests and priestesses still alive and in hiding in Ireland and Britain.

Before leaving the devastation of Mona, Lovernios and the priests once again implored the gods to hear them. In a short and simple ceremony, Lovernios removed his torc, his last remaining possession of value, and offered it to the gods who lived at the bottom of the blackened and ash coated waters of the Lake of Llyn Cerrig Bach, the Lake of Little Stones.

The golden torc shimmered momentarily in the sunlight against a background of black, before it slowly sank to the depths, there to lie as a symbolic sacrifice to the gods who seemed not to be there at all.

Obetach and his dispirited Druids left Mona and sailed across the dangerous Menai Strait, now ruled by Roman soldiers, and headed for home where once again they were forced to march by night and hide by day. They made their way slowly towards the Black Lake hoping to find other Druids along the way, but it seemed there were none.

The handful of priests and priestesses with Obetach appeared to be the only Druids remaining from the many thousands that once lived in Britain.

Chapter 4

The Fourteenth and Twentieth Legions finally met up with Suetonius. They were force marched over the two hundred miles in record time, carrying heavy equipment, but the troops were battle hardened and suffered little. Recently victorious their mood was buoyant and they were outraged at every word of Boudica and her rebellion.

With his two legions and his cavalry united, Suetonius prepared for battle. His troops were ready and eager to fight. Their day of revenge, their day against Boudica had arrived.

Although Suetonius wasn't inclined to panic, he knew if he were beaten in this all important and final fight against Boudica the Province of Britannia would be left with only one legion intact, and that legion was still occupied in keeping the Silures in check.

He couldn't allow Rome's hold over its new Province to be weakened to that degree lest it become ungovernable, leaving the way clear for other tribes to rise up in rebellion. He was keenly aware that failure would place the country out of Roman reach. It was now or never, he had no choice but to succeed, and that thought strengthened him.

The final battle came sooner than anticipated, just two days later, and it turned a once tranquil place into one of the most dreadful battlegrounds even the Roman soldiers had ever seen. During his hours of deliberation, Suetonius chose the battlefield with his usual military brilliance.

The centre of the ground was reached through a long, narrow gorge, its sides protected by sloping ground, with a steep approach for Boudica and her warriors to bring their chariots through. At the top of the slope on either side were dense woods, with the Anker

River, the 'Winding River', on the left. The Romans waited in the wooded hillsides to the right of the proposed battleground. Not only was it an excellent position for the Romans, the defenders, it was chosen too for its closeness to one of the greatest sacred sites of the Druids, the sanctuary of Vernemeton, the Great Grove.

Suetonius knew he was choosing a battle field that would incite Boudica and her warriors further, forcing her into retaliation not only for herself, her family and her people, but for the Druids as well, whose sacred groves were about to be desecrated.

As he waited for Boudica to arrive, Suetonius arranged his troops so that her army would have to move up the slope towards its narrowest point before they could reach the Roman soldiers. This would be where they would meet her.

She came early in the morning with her army of men, women and children, some on foot, others in war chariots and wagons. They carried with them a motley collection of spears, clubs, swords and flaming torches and they howled in indignation and sheer rage as they approached.

Once they were in position and ready to advance through the cleverly chosen pathway, Boudica moved among her warriors in her chariot. She screamed instructions and encouragement to them while both tribes, the Iceni and the Trinovantes, roared back their praise and approval.

With her huge army of warriors and chariots in place she'd inadvertently sealed off the fourth side of the battleground. There was no escape for the Romans, or for Boudica's warriors.

Queen Boudica raised her huge arms and an unearthly silence descended over the battlefield. In her hand she held a raven that would cry out only if she gained victory. In her chariot was a sacred hare, which a slave handed to her.

She lifted the frightened creature for her warriors to see, and then released it between the drawn armies. The hare ran in terror along the front line of Boudica's army towards the Roman soldiers. This was the mark of a priestess seeking augury, and the warriors watched in anticipation as Boudica prophesised victory.

The Romans watched in silence. They knew they were outnumbered being only some ten thousand, but it was not until they witnessed the sight of Boudica's army which had increased to eighty thousand incensed warriors that they realised just how hugely outnumbered they really were.

They'd been confident in their ability before Boudica arrived, laughing over tales of their enemy attacking them with pitch forks and farming implements, bringing women and children to do battle with seasoned Roman soldiers, but now, seeing how they responded to the enigmatic Boudica, they realised that no matter how the army facing them appeared they were fierce and unafraid, and would fight to the death.

Suetonius turned to face his ranks of disciplined soldiers, and he too raised his hands in encouragement. He reminded them of their many victories throughout the world and their years of military training, superior equipment and shields for protection.

Finally he reminded them of his own brilliant military judgement and told them they would prevail against the untrained and unprotected rabble that faced them. By the time he'd finished addressing his soldiers, their fear had left them and they were ready.

As soon as the sacred hare was out of sight, having fled up the slope towards the woods, Boudica began to incite her army again and the moment her back was turned and her warriors had their eyes set on her, Suetonius gave the word and his soldiers advanced.

Boudica gave the battle cry and her warriors charged, but the first lines came crashing up against the protective Roman shields, while the javelins of the soldiers rained down on them. They fell to the ground in their hundreds, and as they fell so the soldiers walked over them cutting down still more as they went.

As each wave of brave warriors moved forward to meet the enemy so the Romans held their shields firm and slaughtered them. Despite the enormous number of warriors still facing them, they sensed the battle was turning their way and they became vicious and unstoppable.

Suetonius gave the order for the cavalry to charge and his legions advanced at a run. Boudica watched in horror as her undisciplined army floundered, falling over their own dead, unable to move back for the thousands of warriors behind them.

Without room to fight they began running about in confusion, trying to get up the sloping flanks, attempting to retreat, some even endeavouring to make headway against the soldiers, but as they ran the Roman cavalry cut them down.

The charioteers tried in vain to bring their wagons into the fight, but they were unable to ride in the narrow area and fell over, crashing in a huge tangled mass of broken wood and spinning wheels. Horses screamed in pain and terror but the piteous sound was unheard in the dreadful roar of battle.

Suetonius watched the horror impatiently and turning to his general, Julius Agricola, ordered him to slaughter those who were trapped beneath the chariots. He wasn't going to take any prisoners.

As the morning wore on and the battle progressed it became entirely one-sided and swift, and before midday it was over. Eighty thousand brave Celts perished while only a few hundred Roman soldiers lost their lives. With eighty thousand once able-bodied men, women and children out of a total population of two million dead, the loss was unbelievably numbing, the overall effect of the slaughter profound.

The country was devastated economically through the destruction of its three most important cities and economic centres. It was devastated agriculturally as farmers turned warrior and were slaughtered, their farms left untended, their crops unplanted, and it was devastated emotionally as the people gave up their fight and gave themselves over to the might of Rome.

Not even Emperor Claudius could have guessed at how profound the slaughter of Boudica's army would be.

Seeing her brave warriors cut down in the most brutal manner, witnessing the enormous loss that lay before her and realising the full implication of the defeat for herself and her country, Boudica considered her options.

Her husband was dead, her kingdom had been seized and she and her family had been flogged, raped and treated as outlaws. Her victories in view of the devastation in front of her were hollow and meaningless. She fled the disastrous battlefield taking her daughters with her.

She made for the woods, beside the desecrated groves of Vernemeton, and there along with her daughters the once mighty Boudica, Queen, Priestess and Warrior committed suicide.

Chapter 5

Pren and Xavista were able to travel more freely than the Druids and they undertook the task of fetching and carrying news to the priests in hiding.

Just a few weeks after the greatest revolt ever raised against the Romans, Pren and his old companion returned to the Black Lake with the tragic news that Boudica had failed. Her army had been slain, the mighty and proud Iceni and their brave neighbours the Trinovantes no longer existed.

The news that Boudica and her daughters were dead left Lovernios and the Druids numbed, and they sat in stunned silence in the grove in which they were hiding.

Lovernios left the others and made his way to the lake, stumbling as he went, tears flowing freely down his handsome face. He was as devastated as the sanctuary of Mona. He couldn't bear any more heartache.

He sat by the cold water and remembered the vibrantly beautiful young women and their enormous and powerful mother and he wept at their piteous death. Death at their own hands without priests to see them on their way into the Otherworld. Now their souls would forever wander around this tormented and black country.

They were too late. He and the other Druids had returned too late to help the only person brave or strong enough to stand up against the might of Rome. They'd failed her, they'd failed the country and they'd failed its people.

Suetonius and his legions travelled back to the cities of Verulamium and Londinium, where they found no building left standing. They stood amongst the charred debris in silence. Although victorious, there seemed little reason to celebrate, the cost had simply been too high.

As they wandered through the streets and saw their own dead, and the cruel manner in which they'd been killed, they became incensed and went on the rampage, killing and confiscating up and down the country, and the remaining Celts were cowed into submission.

The new Roman Province of Britannia, once a prosperous and viable land was left poorer and more desperate than ever before.

Late in the winter a new procurator arrived to replace Decianus Catus, who'd fled to Gaul in fear of his life. He was Julius Classicus and he immediately moved into the legionaries' camp at Camulodunum, which was in the process of being rebuilt. There he began his own reign of terror.

Britain lay at the mercy of Rome's remaining legions and they weren't going to allow an uprising again as they regrouped and reinforced their ranks. Suetonius was still furious over the loss of his Ninth Legion and his slaughter of Boudica's army didn't make up for it. He took his anger out on the surviving Celts, ruling them mercilessly. Every known rebel and fugitive was hunted down and killed.

He began rebuilding the three cities that had been destroyed and he kept them under his iron-fisted control. He built legionary fortresses and camps in all the territories he occupied and linked them together with typical arrow straight Roman roads.

Once the building of the great legionary Fortress of Deva was complete, it served as a marker of the line of Roman advance across Britannia. Rome's hold over the Celts was consolidated and pushed ever further northwards and westwards and they reigned supreme over a devastated country that faced famine from neglected fields.

In the east the gold route was finally lost, wrested from the Celts, and with it went the wealth of the decimated Iceni. This was surely Britain's darkest hour, the people having suffered a great triple loss. The loss of their priests and the sanctuary of Mona.

The loss of the spring harvest, as no crops were planted and the loss of eighty thousand brave warriors who'd been annihilated by the Romans. There was surely no end to the cruel rule of the Empire.

The sacred and as yet undefiled land of Ireland was all that remained, but what would stop the Romans invading it, if the curses of the Druids on Mona and the fearless warriors of Boudica hadn't stopped them.

Surely only the gods could stay them; but it seemed that their gods had deserted them, they'd slept through the turmoil and destruction of Britain, her people and her priests.

Chapter 6

AD 61

Spring

Lovernios and the few remaining Druids wandered around, remaining hidden until early spring, and time for the Festival of Beltain. With Mona destroyed the marshy and unsafe area around the Black Lake was the only suitable hiding place left.

It was the one place the Romans dared not take their troops during their continued reign of terror as they swept across the land hunting out priest and Celt alike. The Black Lake was unfrequented by man and ignored by the soldiers. It lay in a narrow triangle of land between the Brigantes to the north, and the new Roman military frontier established by Suetonius.

The priests knew they couldn't risk moving south for fear of being seen, and should they attempt to move north into the land of the Brigantes they would face the same fate as Caratacus. They had little choice but to go to the place that had long been home for them, the marshes of the Black Lake.

The night of the Festival of Beltain finally arrived, the feast of the mighty Sun God Belenos. Beltain was usually celebrated with massive fires built on hilltops, where all the people could see the flames. Beltain fires were marked by a sense of urgency and power and at each feast there would be two built to ward off evil, illness and other misfortune.

Livestock was driven between these fires for the purpose of purification, protection and fertility. Each year special offerings of animal and humans were made to placate the gods, as death and sacrifice, life and fruition, were central to the festival.

It was the peak of the blossom season when animals bore their young and crops gave forth their harvest, if the gods were pleased. If the gods were displeased there would be no young, and no harvests, a time of potential danger and great uncertainty.

This year there was no feast as there were no crops and the country faced starvation. There was no livestock either as the Romans confiscated what little remained in the land. No festivals were being planned among the weary and dispirited Celts and the Druids had never greeted Beltain as sombrely as in this dark year.

Lovernios thought much on these things through the long days while they waited for the first day of the new month the Romans called May. He thought too of his own part in the festival. He'd reached his thirtieth year and it was time for him to leave this world and go to the gods.

He considered how his father had reacted to the news of the god's requirements on the tragic, yet blessed day of his birth. Vitaicus had eventually accepted his son's fate with stoic bravery and pride, and trusted implicitly in the word of Obetach and the gods.

Lovernios thought of the prophecy made at his birth thirty years ago and contemplated his impending death with mixed feelings. On one hand he felt awe and pride at being the Chosen One – the Supreme Sacrifice, chosen above all others to save the land and its people. He looked forward with excitement to the Otherworld, as death held no fear for him, but his overriding emotion was one of perplexity.

What of Maeve? His chest tightened at the very thought of her. How could he go into the Otherworld without her, would she really dare to follow him? How could he love her so? Why were his emotions over her so tangled and confusing?

He was a Prince and a Druid, he'd studied twenty long years to be who he was. He should be at peace with the world and the gods, so why then did he feel so bereft at the thought of leaving this place, this priestess.

As the Chosen One he was given the highest honour of all time, yet he would gladly exchange it to be able to spend a few more years with Maeve. The sweet smell of her body, the soft feel of her skin, the silkiness of her long wavy hair, the comforting sound of her voice, all these things and many more drove his mind round in circles, tormenting him.

His stomach churned when he was near her, his loins reacted

violently at her touch, his throat became parched at the feel of her lips, and now he had to leave it all. His eyes pricked with hot tears and he became angry and impatient with himself, as these thoughts assailed him, one long cold night after the other, but now, finally, it was time. The festival was about to take place.

The Druids waited for the moon to rise over the marshes in the glade where they hid. The priestesses had spent the day gathering ingredients for the sacred bannock the priests would bake that evening.

Maeve gathered Heather leaves from the heath land and then spotted some mistletoe and was delighted with the auspicious find. Without a priest present, without a white cloth or golden sickle, without bulls for an offering, she climbed the Hawthorne tree and gathered the precious mistletoe, begging the gods to forgive her for the manner in which she did so. She stood aside as the ingredients were placed into a large earthen bowl and mixed together later that afternoon.

The bannock was made from barley, and a mixture of rye and wheat and the priestesses added a small portion of sphagnum moss into the mixture as part of the ritual. As the last item was added, Maeve slipped in the Heather leaves. The bannock was an unleavened bread or cake, which was cooked very quickly on a griddle over a hot flame. It would be left on the flat griddle for a few minutes only, before a small portion was scorched and branded with a hot stake that had been placed in the burning coals. As the priestesses prepared Lovernios' last drink, Maeve dropped in some of the mistletoe, offering up a final prayer.

As soon as it was dark Obetach ordered two small fires to be lit, one to ward off evil and sickness, the other to bake the bannock that the priestesses were preparing, the bread that would symbolically signal the choice of priest for the Supreme Sacrifice. This Beltain there would be no large fire for fear of being sighted by the Romans.

Once the dough was mixed and placed on the griddle, the priestesses were dismissed. They were to go back into the forest and hide and pray until it was all over.

They left with heavy hearts, and without being given the opportunity of saying farewell to Lovernios.

Maeve explained to Obetach that she wished to follow Lovernios into the Otherworld, to join him in the sacrifice. She told the priest of the pact they'd made, but Obetach refused her permission to join Lovernios.

"We need every single priest and priestess so that we can train up novices and rebuild our Order. You're too valuable, you can't leave this world yet, not until the gods decree."

He turned and left Maeve in tears, knowing full well that once he'd spoken, she dare not disobey.

Maeve peered through the bushes at the dancing flames of the fires. The leaves of the birch trees rustled in the slight breeze and in her isolated spot, the darkness and chill added to her sense of foreboding. The patches of boggy ground were flecked with green moss that made the area unsuitable for the Roman soldiers.

From her hiding place she was well concealed, but the branches of the trees in front of her obstructed her view. Careless of the mud and moss she went down on her stomach and inched her way slowly, silently closer to the holy sacrificial death of her love.

She shivered, not from the cold but from the thought of what was about to take place. Her beloved Lovernios knelt on the ground in front of the fire, surrounded by the priests. The ritual of the last meal was already over. The bannock had been passed around with each of the priests breaking off a small piece and waiting until they all had one. They waited in silence until it was Lovernios' turn.

When the bannock reached him, only the burnt piece remained, yet none of the other priests had looked as they'd broken off their own portion. Lovernios glanced at the piece facing him with its mark like that of a blackened thumbprint. He broke it off and began to eat it, solemnly confirming his selection as the sacrificial offering – the selection made by the gods thirty years ago at his traumatic birth.

Midnight approached and Maeve felt ill. A noise behind startled her and she clamped her hand over her mouth lest she cry out in fear. It was Pren. He'd been searching for her since the priestesses had been told to leave the area. He too wasn't allowed to be part of the ceremony being played out in front of them.

He lay beside Maeve in the cold bog and watched with morbid fascination as the life of his brother was taken from him, and each minute seemed an eternity. Maeve held her breath as Obetach stood, and Pren shuddered beside her. She reached out and took his hand in hers.

Obetach raised his right arm, the signal for the final phase of the ceremony to begin. Calmly, peacefully, Lovernios turned to face him.

"May the gods keep you, and use you until we join you. May our sacrifice appease them," he intoned, and the priests joined him and repeated the words three times.

"May the crops grow, the rains fall, the nation prosper. May the Romans be defeated and driven out of our land, and may Ireland ever be safe." Lovernios was nodding his head and praying softly.

"May Mona be rebuilt and the Druids rise up again to rule this land. May the gods be appeased after these dreadful dark years. Bless you, Lovernios the Chosen One. We offer you as the Supreme Sacrifice. Journey safely into the Otherworld."

Lovernios acknowledged their blessing with raised hands, and blessed the priests in return, then turned his head from Obetach and at last, at peace, he bowed his head in submission. Mardial came from behind him, and with an axe struck Lovernios cleanly on the back of the head.

Maeve gasped at the force and power with which the first blow was delivered to the crown of his head. It was the power of a thunderbolt, delivered with such strength to appease Taranis the Thunder God. The vertebrae in his neck snapped instantly. The might of the blow caused his teeth to grind together with such force that his molars broke off at the crowns. She held her hand over her mouth tighter still to stop herself from screaming.

As his body fell forward, the priests watched its convulsions with practised eyes and with every movement divined the future. Mardial raised the axe again and a second blow followed swiftly, almost on top of the site of the first, the blade of the axe causing a deep wound in his skull and fracturing it. His body barely convulsed this time, it was almost lifeless now.

With a third blow using the flat side of the axe to the base of his skull, Lovernios slumped forward further still and lay without moving, in a foetal position. Pren squeezed her hand.

As they watched his still form the priests declared that the first year following this sacrifice would continue to be tumultuous as the Celts fought to stave off the power of the Romans. The second year would be quieter as the Druids regained their stronghold and the gods worked in their favour to bring about fresh crops. By the third year, the Romans would be vanquished and the land would be theirs once again.

The first of three deaths in a ritual where three featured strongly was over. Although already dead, only one god had been appeased.

Two priests came forward and lifted Lovernios' lifeless body and seated him on a stool, while Mardial arranged a garrotte around his neck. He did this in a gentle and respectful manner despite the violent nature of the death Lovernios had already suffered. The garrotte had been specially prepared using the gut of a fox. It had three knots tied in it to represent the three gods for whom this ritual sacrifice was being performed.

When he was ready, Mardial pulled the cord and the force with which he did so made a mockery of his earlier gentleness. A second priest rotated a stick placed within the tightly bound garrotte. The power of it was so great that it would have killed Lovernios swiftly and cleanly had he not already been dead. His air passage was closed tightly and instantly by the massive constriction. Lovernios' neck snapped and as Mardial let go of the rope, his head slumped to the right, settling tightly against his shoulder in a position that resembled that of a child sleeping peacefully.

The garrotte dug deeply into his skin, leaving three ligatures from each of the knots, one at the front, and one on either side of his neck.

As soon as Mardial finished, Kierona stabbed Lovernios swiftly and with great precision into his jugular using a knife sharp enough to have severed his head from his body had he wished to. A large cauldron was placed directly under the flow of blood, then a second and a third.

"So much blood," Maeve whimpered as Pren who was shaking violently, placed his arm round her. They lay huddled together watching the macabre scene before them in shocked silence. The blood, the very life of her love was pouring from his limp body in a gushing stream.

"Will it never end?" Pren whispered. Finally after what seemed an eternity the deep red flood stopped, Esus, the Lord and Master had been placated.

Twice dead already the ritual was not yet complete. Two gods had been appeased, but there was one left, Teutates. Maeve wept silently as she watched the scene before her.

The lifeless body of her beloved was taken from the stool and placed in the chariot that she and the priestesses had garlanded with flowers earlier that day. It was drawn by Lovernios' magnificent white horse Slydau, and next to Slydau was Mardial's horse, Avon, meaning 'River', for the horse had been in the water when Mardial chose him all those years previously when they'd been to see the Goddess Epona.

With the Vates chanting to the great Goddess Anu and to Teutates who awaited them at a small tributary leading into the lake, the procession moved forward, led by Obetach, with Mardial and Kierona following, leading the horses.

They travelled just over a mile along a rough track through the thick and eerie woods of the sacred hill, moving slowly and solemnly towards Lovernios' final resting place. Pren and Maeve followed hand in hand, also in silence. Once they reached the river they found a new hiding place where they could watch the remainder of the sacrificial offering. Mardial and Kierona lifted Lovernios out of the chariot.

They held him high straining under the great weight of his muscle-hardened body and carried him towards the river where they placed him with great reverence, face down in four feet of cold, dark and dirty water, where Teutates, the God of the People, waited to carry him into the Otherworld, into the eternal care of all the gods.

Although he was already dead, Maeve recoiled at this fresh horror of symbolic drowning, as Obetach called upon Teutates to accept him. The thought that his earthly body would lie in that awful water for the rest of eternity, even though she believed he'd rise again in the Otherworld, was more than she could bear. She crept away swiftly, careless of the noise she made, unable to bear the nightmare any longer, leaving Pren to his own grief.

Obetach and his priests stayed the remainder of the night beside their sacrifice and sang and chanted under the moonlight, imploring the gods to rise up in anger against the Romans. In awe of this solemn occasion, the culmination of thirty years of waiting, they kept up their pleading throughout the night, watching the passing of the moon, until physically, emotionally and spiritually exhausted, they slipped back into hiding, under the cover of darkness.

With the sunrise of the new day, a fresh surge of hope began to rise within them, and as the buds of spring and the promise of another season lay before them, so the promise of the fulfilment of a prophecy lay before them too, and they no longer feared the bleak future.

Instead they looked forward to the gradual change that would be brought about by this Supreme Sacrifice, this priest, this king, born to live at the will of the gods, given this highest of honours, to be the catalyst that would ultimately end the night of terror and destroy the might of Rome.

The End

Disclaimer

This book is designed to provide condensed information. It is not intended to reprint all the information that is otherwise available, but instead to complement, amplify and supplement other texts. You are urged to read all the available material, learn as much as possible and tailor the information to your individual needs.

Every effort has been made to make this book as complete and as accurate as possible. However, there may be mistakes, both typographical and in content. Therefore, this text should be used only as a general guide and not as the ultimate source of information.

The purpose of this book is to educate. The author shall have neither liability nor responsibility to any person or entity with respect to any loss or damage caused, or alleged to have been caused, directly or indirectly, by the information contained in this book

E & OE accepted.

Note

The Romans never did invade Ireland, so perhaps Lovernios' death did indeed placate the gods, protect the holy sanctuary, and save Britain from the iron fisted might of Rome.

The few remaining Druids in Britain retreated into the mountains of Scotland, Ireland and Wales and stayed there until Christianity came.

For two thousand years the body of *Lovernios* lay where it was placed, in the exact position it had landed, with its broken neck forcing the head to rest upon the shoulder. Over the years as the water tables changed, the area dried up and a peat bog formed, preserving the body in the most miraculous way.

The land was farmed for peat and it was during a peat cutting operation that the sharp blades of a harvester sliced the body of Lovernios roughly in half at his torso, but still it lay in its grave until eventually on 1st August 1984 it was discovered on *Lindow Moss* near Manchester. Archaeologists and scientists were ecstatic at the find.

He was taken to the *Harwell Research Laboratory* where radiocarbon dating and other scientific testing found him to be two thousand years old.

Named the *Lindow Man*, work began immediately to determine as much as possible about his past. The fascinating details as researched and recorded by Anne Ross and Don Robins in their book entitled, *"The Life and Death of a Druid Prince,"* showed that he went to his death with full acceptance. His face wasn't distorted by fear or rage. X-rays revealed that his right ribs had been broken at some stage in his life, while his neck vertebrae were broken at the time of his death.

He had sustained three massive blows to the back of his head, by a blunt instrument like an axe. Two blows were on top of each other, while one on the crown appeared to have been done with the flattened edge of the axe. His head rested into his right shoulder. His molar teeth had been ground together and sheared off by the force of the blows.

He'd been garrotted with fox gut, and the garrotte had three knots tied into it. These knots had caused three ligatures on his neck, one on the front and one on either side. He'd been stabbed in the jugular with an extremely sharp instrument and was bled, before being placed face down in four feet of water in the vicinity of the *Black Lake*. X-rays proved him to be about thirty years of age, and in his prime.

He showed no battle wounds or scars, such as would have been evident had he been a farmer or a warrior. His hands were un-calloused and his nails manicured. There were signs of mild and early arthritis in his spine and osteoarthritis in his leg, but he showed no other signs of ailment or injury. He was a muscular and well-built man of 5'6" and of the 'O' Blood group, which would place him as an insular Celt.

The contents of his stomach showed his last, small meal, eaten immediately prior to his death, to have been a bannock of barley, wheat and rye, with traces of sphagnum moss, and both charred and un-charred leaves of Heather. His last drink had contained small traces of Mistletoe pollen. A tiny portion of the meal had been scorched.

He had an armband of fox fur around his upper left arm.

Bibliography

The Life and Death of a Druid Prince
Authors: Anne Ross and Don Robins
Summit Books NY, Rider, an imprint of Century Books, UK, 1989

The Celtic Realms (New Ed)
Author: Myles Dillon , Nora Chadwick
Paperback / Published 01 Jan 2001
Publisher: Phoenix Press

Sarum (Reissue)
Author: Edward Rutherfurd
Paperback (A format) / Published 04 Jun 1992
Publisher: Arrow

A History of the British Isles
Author: Jeremy Black
Paperback
Publisher: Palgrave-Macmillan C/O Vhps Holtzbrinck Publishing

The Kingfisher Book of Mythology
Author: David Bellingham
Editor: David Bellingham
Hardback
Publisher: Larousse Kingfisher Chambers C/O Houghton Mifflin Co Attn Trade Customer Service

The Druid Source Book
Author: John Matthews
Paperback / Published 21 Aug 1997
Publisher: Cassell Illustrated

The Druid Source Book
Author: John Matthews
Hardback / Published 01 Jan 2000
Publisher: Caxton Editions

The History of England
Author: Thomas Babington Macaulay
Editor: Hugh Trevor-Roper
Paperback (B format) / Published 01 Jan 1979
Publisher: Penguin Books

A History of England (4th Ed)
Author: Stuart E Prall, David Harris Willson,
Paperback / Published 20 Dec 1990
Publisher: Thomson Learning

Illustrated History of England (New Ed)
Author: G M Trevelyan
Hardback / Published 03 Dec 1973
Publisher: Longman

A New History of England
Author: Jeremy Black
Paperback / Published 20 Apr 2000
Publisher: Sutton Publishing

History in Evidence : Prehistoric Britain
Author: Barry M. Marsden
Paperback / Published 1996
Publisher: Hodder Wayland

Clans and Chiefs
Author: Ian Grimble
Paperback / Published May 2000
Publisher: Birlinn Limited

The Atlas of Ancient Worlds (1st American Ed)
Author: Anne Millard
Hardback
Publisher: Dorling Kindersley

About the Author

Heather knew that she wanted to be a writer when she was 13 years old and wrote her first short story during a school writing assignment, but it was only when her children were in their mid-teens that she had the time to write her first novel, Lovernios. After a year of research and planning, she spent a further year writing the novel, which is now available on Amazon.

There followed a number of other adult novels, one of which is ***Pure Gold.*** This book is the biography, written as a novel, and is about a friend who she admired greatly for her courage and commitment during a life of adversity.

Heather has also written for children and has four published novels in schools in South Africa. These are English Language reading books and are aimed at the age range 11 – 16 year olds.

After her eldest son was diagnosed with cancer, Heather and her family set up the ***Bainbridge Believe Project,*** a fund raising foundation aimed at raising funds for children with cancer through an organisation called CHOC. Much of her spare time is spent in fundraising, specifically through cycling.

When she isn't reading or writing, Heather, a retired runner, now enjoys cycling, playing golf and watching almost all sport on television.

Heather is a committed Christian, the mother of 3 adult children and 2 step-children and she lives in Edenvale, South Africa with her husband.

Contact Heather:
heather.hearn@gmail.com

Thank you for reading my book. If you enjoyed it, please take a moment to leave a review.

More Titles by the Author

PURE GOLD

PURE GOLD takes you on a journey of endurance and sacrifice. There will not be many today who have the commitment and the focus needed to make such a trip where at times all seemed lost – but the faithfulness of God prevailed throughout this riviting story of dedicated love and servanthood. PURE GOLD will motivate you to re-examine your own life and priorities.

PURE GOLD is the biography – written as a novel – about a friend who I admired greatly for her courage and commitment during a life of adversity. It tells the story of a life filled with the grace of God, a life willing to be obedient to God, no matter what the cost.

How many of us have asked the question *"Why me, Lord?"* You may well find yourself asking that same question after reading this story filled with compassion, hurt, anxiety, uncertainty, fear, turmoil and triumph. The question is, would you be willing to listen and to obey the voice of God or would you be one of those who would prefer the easy road? You need to read PURE GOLD to find that answer within yourself.

heather.hearn@gmail.com

51277739R00231

Made in the USA
Lexington, KY
18 April 2016